Your
Chinese
Horoscope
2017

Neil Somerville

What the Year of the Rooster holds in store for you

Your
Chinese
Horoscope
2017

Thorsons

ISBN: 978-0-00-818764-4

Printed and bound in the United States of America
by RR Donnelley

2 4 6 8 10 9 7 5 3 1

About the Author

Neil Somerville is one of the leading writers in the West on Chinese horoscopes. He has been interested in Eastern forms of divination for many years and believes that much can be learned from the ancient wisdom of the East. His annual book on Chinese horoscopes has built up an international following and he is also the author of *What's Your Chinese Love Sign?* (Thorsons, 2000; HarperElement, 2013), *Chinese Success Signs* (Thorsons, 2001) and *The Answers* (Element, 2004).

Neil Somerville was born in the year of the Water Snake. His wife was born under the sign of the Monkey, his son is an Ox and daughter a Horse.

TO ROS, RICHARD AND EMILY

As we march into a new year,
we each have our hopes, our ambitions and our dreams.

Sometimes fate and circumstance will assist us,
sometimes we will struggle and despair,
but march we must.

For it is those who keep going,
and who keep their aspirations alive,
who stand the greatest chance of securing what they want.

March determinedly,
and your determination will, in some way, be rewarded.

Neil Somerville

Contents

Acknowledgements

In writing *Your Chinese Horoscope 2017* I am grateful for the assistance and invaluable support that those around me have given.

I would also like to acknowledge Theodora Lau's *The Handbook of Chinese Horoscopes* (Harper & Row, 1979; Arrow, 1981), which was particularly useful to me in my research.

In addition to Ms Lau's work, I commend the following books to those who wish to find out more about Chinese horoscopes: Kristyna Arcarti, *Chinese Horoscopes for Beginners* (Headway, 1995); Catherine Aubier, *Chinese Zodiac Signs* (Arrow, 1984), series of 12 books; E. A. Crawford and Teresa Kennedy, *Chinese Elemental Astrology* (Piatkus Books, 1992); Paula Delsol, *Chinese Horoscopes* (Pan, 1973); Barry Fantoni, *Barry Fantoni's Chinese Horoscopes* (Warner, 1994); Bridget Giles and the Diagram Group, *Chinese Astrology* (HarperCollins*Publishers*, 1996); Kwok Man-Ho, *Complete Chinese Horoscopes* (Sunburst Books, 1995); Lori Reid, *The Complete Book of Chinese Horoscopes* (Element Books, 1997); Paul Rigby and Harvey Bean, *Chinese Astrologics* (Publications Division, South China Morning Post Ltd, 1981); Ruth Q. Sun, *The Asian Animal Zodiac* (Charles E. Tuttle Company, Inc., 1996); Derek Walters, *Ming Shu* (Pagoda Books, 1987) and *The Chinese Astrology Workbook* (The Aquarian Press, 1988); Suzanne White, *The New Astrology* (Pan, 1987), *The New Chinese Astrology* (Pan, 1994) and *Chinese Astrology Plain and Simple* (Eden Grove Editions, 1998).

In addition, I would like to record my thanks to all at HarperCollins who have helped with the editing, production and promotion of *Your Chinese Horoscope* over the years, as well as to thank my current editor, Carolyn Thorne, for her input and my copy editor, Lizzie Henry, for her wonderful work over so many years.

Introduction

The origins of Chinese horoscopes have been lost in the mists of time. It is known, however, that oriental astrologers practised their art many thousands of years ago and even today Chinese astrology continues to fascinate and intrigue.

In Chinese astrology there are 12 signs named after 12 different animals. No one quite knows how the signs acquired their names, but there is one legend that offers an explanation. According to this legend, one Chinese New Year the Buddha invited all the animals in his kingdom to come before him. Unfortunately, for reasons best known to the animals, only 12 turned up. The first to arrive was the Rat, followed by the Ox, Tiger, Rabbit, Dragon, Snake, Horse, Goat, Monkey, Rooster, Dog and finally Pig. In gratitude, the Buddha decided to name a year after each of the animals and that those born during that year would inherit some of the personality of that animal. Therefore those born in the year of the Ox would be hardworking, resolute and stubborn, just like the Ox, while those born in the year of the Dog would be loyal and faithful, just like the Dog. While it is not possible that everyone born in a particular year can have all the characteristics of the sign, it is incredible what similarities do occur, and this is partly where the fascination of Chinese horoscopes lies.

In addition to the 12 signs of the Chinese zodiac there are five elements and these have a strengthening or moderating influence upon the signs. Details about the effects of the elements are given in each of the chapters on the signs.

To find out which sign you were born under, refer to the tables on the following pages. As the Chinese year is based on the lunar year and does not start until late January or early February, it is particularly important for anyone born in those two months to check carefully the dates of the Chinese year in which they were born.

Also included, in the appendix, are two charts showing the compatibility between the signs for personal and business relationships and details about the signs ruling the different hours of the day. From this it is possible to locate your ascendant and, as in Western astrology, this has a significant influence on your personality.

In writing this book I have taken the unusual step of combining the intriguing nature of Chinese horoscopes with the Western desire to know what the future holds, and have based my interpretations upon various factors relating to each of the signs. Over the years in which *Your Chinese Horoscope* has been published I have been pleased that so many have found the sections on the forthcoming year of interest and hope that the horoscope has been constructive and useful. Remember, though, that at all times you are master of your own destiny. I sincerely hope that *Your Chinese Horoscope 2017* will prove interesting and helpful for the year ahead.

This edition also marks the thirtieth year of publication and a personal milestone for me. I would like to take this opportunity to thank all who have bought this and other books in the series. Indeed, some, I know, have read *Your Chinese Horoscope* for many years. I am grateful to you all for your support and interest. However, with deep regret I have decided that this will be the last annual book in the series. Instead, I will turn my attention to a new volume and hope to share with you and many others special insights on Chinese horoscopes, including ways of making the best of your sign and a horoscope for each and every year. I hope such a volume, entitled *Your Chinese Horoscope for Each and Every Year*, will be of value and lasting interest.

But for the moment, the Year of the Rooster is one rewarding effort and commitment and I hope it rewards you well.

The Chinese Years

Horse	11 February	1918	to	31 January	1919
Goat	1 February	1919	to	19 February	1920
Monkey	20 February	1920	to	7 February	1921
Rooster	8 February	1921	to	27 January	1922
Dog	28 January	1922	to	15 February	1923
Pig	16 February	1923	to	4 February	1924
Rat	5 February	1924	to	23 January	1925
Ox	24 January	1925	to	12 February	1926
Tiger	13 February	1926	to	1 February	1927
Rabbit	2 February	1927	to	22 January	1928
Dragon	23 January	1928	to	9 February	1929
Snake	10 February	1929	to	29 January	1930
Horse	30 January	1930	to	16 February	1931
Goat	17 February	1931	to	5 February	1932
Monkey	6 February	1932	to	25 January	1933
Rooster	26 January	1933	to	13 February	1934
Dog	14 February	1934	to	3 February	1935
Pig	4 February	1935	to	23 January	1936
Rat	24 January	1936	to	10 February	1937
Ox	11 February	1937	to	30 January	1938
Tiger	31 January	1938	to	18 February	1939
Rabbit	19 February	1939	to	7 February	1940
Dragon	8 February	1940	to	26 January	1941
Snake	27 January	1941	to	14 February	1942
Horse	15 February	1942	to	4 February	1943
Goat	5 February	1943	to	24 January	1944
Monkey	25 January	1944	to	12 February	1945
Rooster	13 February	1945	to	1 February	1946

Dog	2 February	1946	to	21 January	1947
Pig	22 January	1947	to	9 February	1948
Rat	10 February	1948	to	28 January	1949
Ox	29 January	1949	to	16 February	1950
Tiger	17 February	1950	to	5 February	1951
Rabbit	6 February	1951	to	26 January	1952
Dragon	27 January	1952	to	13 February	1953
Snake	14 February	1953	to	2 February	1954
Horse	3 February	1954	to	23 January	1955
Goat	24 January	1955	to	11 February	1956
Monkey	12 February	1956	to	30 January	1957
Rooster	31 January	1957	to	17 February	1958
Dog	18 February	1958	to	7 February	1959
Pig	8 February	1959	to	27 January	1960
Rat	28 January	1960	to	14 February	1961
Ox	15 February	1961	to	4 February	1962
Tiger	5 February	1962	to	24 January	1963
Rabbit	25 January	1963	to	12 February	1964
Dragon	13 February	1964	to	1 February	1965
Snake	2 February	1965	to	20 January	1966
Horse	21 January	1966	to	8 February	1967
Goat	9 February	1967	to	29 January	1968
Monkey	30 January	1968	to	16 February	1969
Rooster	17 February	1969	to	5 February	1970
Dog	6 February	1970	to	26 January	1971
Pig	27 January	1971	to	14 February	1972
Rat	15 February	1972	to	2 February	1973
Ox	3 February	1973	to	22 January	1974
Tiger	23 January	1974	to	10 February	1975
Rabbit	11 February	1975	to	30 January	1976
Dragon	31 January	1976	to	17 February	1977
Snake	18 February	1977	to	6 February	1978
Horse	7 February	1978	to	27 January	1979
Goat	28 January	1979	to	15 February	1980
Monkey	16 February	1980	to	4 February	1981

Rooster	5 February	1981	to	24 January	1982
Dog	25 January	1982	to	12 February	1983
Pig	13 February	1983	to	1 February	1984
Rat	2 February	1984	to	19 February	1985
Ox	20 February	1985	to	8 February	1986
Tiger	9 February	1986	to	28 January	1987
Rabbit	29 January	1987	to	16 February	1988
Dragon	17 February	1988	to	5 February	1989
Snake	6 February	1989	to	26 January	1990
Horse	27 January	1990	to	14 February	1991
Goat	15 February	1991	to	3 February	1992
Monkey	4 February	1992	to	22 January	1993
Rooster	23 January	1993	to	9 February	1994
Dog	10 February	1994	to	30 January	1995
Pig	31 January	1995	to	18 February	1996
Rat	19 February	1996	to	6 February	1997
Ox	7 February	1997	to	27 January	1998
Tiger	28 January	1998	to	15 February	1999
Rabbit	16 February	1999	to	4 February	2000
Dragon	5 February	2000	to	23 January	2001
Snake	24 January	2001	to	11 February	2002
Horse	12 February	2002	to	31 January	2003
Goat	1 February	2003	to	21 January	2004
Monkey	22 January	2004	to	8 February	2005
Rooster	9 February	2005	to	28 January	2006
Dog	29 January	2006	to	17 February	2007
Pig	18 February	2007	to	6 February	2008
Rat	7 February	2008	to	25 January	2009
Ox	26 January	2009	to	13 February	2010
Tiger	14 February	2010	to	2 February	2011
Rabbit	3 February	2011	to	22 January	2012
Dragon	23 January	2012	to	9 February	2013
Snake	10 February	2013	to	30 January	2014
Horse	31 January	2014	to	18 February	2015
Goat	19 February	2015	to	7 February	2016

| Monkey | 8 February | 2016 | to | 27 January | 2017 |
| Rooster | 28 January | 2017 | to | 15 February | 2018 |

Note

The names of the signs in the Chinese zodiac occasionally differ, although the characteristics of the signs remain the same. In some books the Ox is referred to as the Buffalo or Bull, the Rabbit as the Hare or Cat, the Goat as the Sheep and the Pig as the Boar.

For the sake of convenience, the male gender is used throughout this book. Unless otherwise stated, the characteristics of the signs apply to both sexes.

Welcome to the
Year of the Rooster

With his shrill cock-a-doodle-do, proud strutting and distinctive plumage, the Rooster is an impressive bird. He commands attention and, with his beady eyes, is always alert and summing up situations. And his vigilant nature will be seen in his own year.

The Year of the Rooster promises much, but above all it calls for effort and hard work. Those who slack could feel the effects of the Rooster's beak! Roosters have high standards and over the year important progress will be made.

On the international stage there could be much posturing and flexing of military muscle. As a result there could be periods of tension in some areas, especially where there is a power vacuum or a strong surge of nationalism, but a lot of the posturing of the Rooster year is just for show and in many instances agreements will be brokered and tensions eased.

A further feature of the year will be the increasing voice of some minorities. Long-standing resentment can surface and in some instances sweep away established orders. Some of the year will be unsettling and its effects – including on some national borders – far-reaching.

Early in 2017 the newly elected American president will take office and be quick to exert their authority. Not only will they be keen to start on their own legislative programme but also eager to make their mark on American foreign policy. International developments early on in the Rooster year could lead to swift responses and set the tenor of the new administration. In addition, the Rooster year will see much dialogue between world leaders, with key issues being addressed, especially ones relating to global security, environmental concerns and trade. Some landmark treaties will be signed and their effect can be considerable.

Within many nation states there will also be much internal dialogue and many decisions concerning policies and future directions. Rooster years can see much soul-searching and this process can be hastened by several prominent leaders standing aside.

With the world stage seeing times of uncertainty, the financial markets will be jittery and speculators will need to be on their guard. This is no year for 'easy money' or 'get rich quick' strategies. Instead, hard work will be the order of the day, although important growth will be seen during the year. With the Rooster priding himself on his appearance, the fashion industry could be especially buoyant, with new styles coming to the fore. Tourism and the fitness industry are also set to fare well. In addition, the internet will continue to influence the lives of many, as well as shape commerce. Interestingly, it was the last Rooster year, 2005, that saw the launch of YouTube, the channel that has given a platform and voice to so many. Further technological advances will be made this year and they are set to become very influential.

Rooster years can also be marked by some splendid achievements, which are often the culmination of many years of effort and planning. It was in previous Rooster years that man first stepped onto the moon and Concorde made its first supersonic flight. Other historic advances can be expected this year, with new discoveries in space likely to be particularly exciting.

Rooster years also favour spectacle and the British royal family will play its part. Previous Rooster years have seen the splendours of Queen Victoria's Diamond Jubilee, the pageantry surrounding the Investiture of Prince Charles as Prince of Wales and, in 1981, his marriage to Lady Diana Spencer, an event which had an estimated worldwide audience of 1,000 million viewers and listeners, or almost a quarter of the world's population. This Rooster year will again witness some historic and regal events.

The turbulent weather patterns seen in previous years unfortunately show no signs of abating. It was in the last Rooster year that one of the deadliest hurricanes ever seen, Katrina, wreaked havoc in the United States, causing an estimated US$108 billion worth of damage. While it is hoped that this year will be free from such disasters, there could be several major catastrophes, including some man-made ones.

For the individual, the Rooster year brings some good opportunities but it does require application. This is no time to be half-hearted or trust to luck. It is effort and willingness to strive hard that will bring results. And these will be all the more deserved. As the Chinese proverb reminds us, 'Diligence leads to riches,' and diligence can produce some good rewards this year.

The Rooster has often been said to possess the five Chinese virtues: his crown, which resembles a cap of authority, symbolizes his authority (propriety) and literary prowess (wisdom); his spur represents the military and therefore his courage in standing up for himself (righteousness); his tendency to share food shows his benevolence; and his early morning crowing is a sign of reliability and trustworthiness (fidelity). The Rooster is all this and more. He is a fine bird and a resolute one. And his influence on his own year can be considerable. It may not always be an easy year, but it will be dynamic and eventful. It is a time for effort, hard work and making things happen.

Give this year your best and I hope your efforts reward you well.

Your
Chinese
Horoscope
2017

5 February 1924 to 23 January 1925 — *Wood Rat*

24 January 1936 to 10 February 1937 — *Fire Rat*

10 February 1948 to 28 January 1949 — *Earth Rat*

28 January 1960 to 14 February 1961 — *Metal Rat*

15 February 1972 to 2 February 1973 — *Water Rat*

2 February 1984 to 19 February 1985 — *Wood Rat*

19 February 1996 to 6 February 1997 — *Fire Rat*

7 February 2008 to 25 January 2009 — *Earth Rat*

The Rat

The Personality of the Rat

To see,
and to see what others do not see.
That is true vision.

The Rat is born under the sign of charm. He is intelligent, popular and loves attending parties and large social gatherings. He is able to establish friendships with remarkable ease and people generally feel relaxed in his company. He is a very social creature and is genuinely interested in the welfare and activities of others. He has a good understanding of human nature and his advice and opinions are often sought.

The Rat is a hard and diligent worker. He is also very imaginative and is never short of ideas. However, he does sometimes lack the confidence to promote his ideas and this can often prevent him from securing the recognition he deserves.

The Rat is very observant and many Rats have made excellent writers and journalists. The Rat also excels at personnel and PR work and any job that brings him into contact with people and the media. His skills are particularly appreciated in times of crisis, for the Rat has an incredibly strong sense of self-preservation. When it comes to finding a way out of an awkward situation, he is certain to be the one who comes up with a solution.

The Rat loves to be where there is a lot of action, but should he ever find himself in a very bureaucratic or restrictive environment he can become a stickler for discipline and routine. He is also something of an opportunist and is constantly on the lookout for ways in which he can improve his wealth and lifestyle. He rarely lets an opportunity go by and can become involved in so many plans and schemes that he sometimes squanders his energies and achieves very little as a result. He is also rather gullible and can be taken in by those less scrupulous than himself.

Another characteristic of the Rat is his attitude towards money. He is very thrifty and to some he may appear a little mean. The reason for this is purely that he likes to keep his money within his family. He can be most generous to his partner, his children and close friends and relatives. He can also be generous to himself, for he often finds it impossible to deprive himself of any luxury or object he fancies. He is very acquisitive and can be a notorious hoarder. He also hates waste and is rarely prepared to throw anything away. He can be rather greedy and will rarely refuse an invitation to a free meal or a complimentary ticket to a lavish function.

The Rat is a good conversationalist, although he can occasionally be a little indiscreet. He can be highly critical of others – for an honest and unbiased opinion, the Rat is a superb critic – and will sometimes use confidential information to his own advantage. However, as he has such a bright and irresistible nature, most people are prepared to forgive him his slight indiscretions.

Throughout his long and eventful life the Rat will make many friends and will find that he is especially well suited to those born under his own sign and those of the Ox, Dragon and Monkey. He can also get on well with those born under the signs of the Tiger, Snake, Rooster, Dog and Pig, but the rather sensitive Rabbit and Goat will find him a little too critical and blunt for their liking. The Horse and Rat will also find it difficult to get on with each other – the Rat craves security and will find the Horse's changeable moods and rather independent nature a little unsettling.

The Rat is very family orientated and will do anything to please his nearest and dearest. He is exceptionally loyal to his parents and can himself be a very caring and loving parent. He will take an interest in all his children's activities and see that they want for nothing. He usually has a large family.

The female Rat has a kindly, outgoing nature and involves herself in a multitude of different activities. She has a wide circle of friends, enjoys entertaining and is an attentive hostess. She is also conscientious about the upkeep of her home and has good taste in home furnishings. She is most supportive to the other members of her family and, due to her resourceful, friendly and persevering nature, can do well in practically any career she chooses.

Although the Rat is essentially outgoing, he is also a very private individual. He tends to keep his feelings to himself and while he is not averse to learning what other people are doing, he resents anyone prying too closely into his own affairs. He also does not like solitude and if he is alone for any length of time he can easily get depressed.

The Rat is undoubtedly very talented, but he does sometimes fail to capitalize on his many abilities. He has a tendency to become involved in too many schemes and chase after too many opportunities at once. If he can slow down and concentrate on one thing at a time, he can become very successful. If not, success and wealth can elude him. But, with his tremendous ability to charm, he will rarely, if ever, be without friends.

The Five Different Types of Rat

In addition to the 12 signs of the Chinese zodiac there are five elements and these have a strengthening or moderating influence on the signs. The effects of the elements on the Rat are described below, together with the years in which they were exercising their influence. Therefore Rats born in 1960 are Metal Rats, Rats born in 1972 are Water Rats, and so on.

Metal Rat: 1960

This Rat has excellent taste and certainly knows how to appreciate the finer things in life. His home is comfortable and nicely decorated and he likes to entertain and mix in fashionable circles. He has considerable financial acumen and invests his money well. On the surface he appears cheerful and confident, but deep down he can be troubled by worries that are quite often of his own making. He is exceptionally loyal to his family and friends.

Water Rat: 1972

The Water Rat is intelligent and very astute. He is a deep thinker and can express his thoughts clearly and persuasively. He is always eager to learn and is talented in many different areas. He is usually very popular, but his fear of loneliness can sometimes lead him into mixing with the wrong sort of company. He is a particularly skilful writer, but can get sidetracked very easily and should try to concentrate on just one thing at a time.

Wood Rat: 1924, 1984

The Wood Rat has a friendly, outgoing personality and is popular with his colleagues and friends. He has a quick, agile brain and likes to turn his hand to anything he thinks may be useful. His one fear is insecurity, but given his intelligence and capabilities, this fear is usually unfounded. He has a good sense of humour, enjoys travel and, due to his highly imaginative nature, can be a gifted writer or artist.

Fire Rat: 1936, 1996

The Fire Rat is rarely still and seems to have a never-ending supply of energy and enthusiasm. He loves being involved in some form of action, be it travel, following up new ideas or campaigning for a cause in which he fervently believes. He is an original thinker and hates being bound by petty restrictions or the dictates of others. He can be forthright in his views but can sometimes get carried away in the excitement of the moment and commit himself to various undertakings without thinking through all the implications. Yet he has a resilient nature and with the right support can go far in life.

Earth Rat: 1948, 2008

This Rat is astute and very level-headed. He rarely takes unnecessary chances and while he is constantly trying to improve his financial status, he is prepared to proceed slowly and leave nothing to chance. He is probably not as adventurous as the other types of Rat and prefers to remain in familiar territory rather than rush headlong into something he knows little about. He is talented, conscientious and caring towards his loved ones, but at the same time can be self-conscious and worry a little too much about the image he is trying to project.

Prospects for the Rat in 2017

The Rat is resourceful and sets about his activities with great energy. And his efforts in the Monkey year (8 February 2016–27 January 2017) will have enabled him to do a great deal and enjoy some pleasing results. However, in the remaining months he will need to focus and use his time well. With an increased number of commitments, he could find some weeks especially busy, and the better organized he is, the more he will be able to benefit.

At work, many Rats will take on additional duties or a new role. While this will often be pleasing, these Rats should concentrate on their objectives and avoid being sidetracked. It is through focus that the best results will be achieved. The end of the year will bring pressures, but could see potentially significant developments.

The Rat should be disciplined in his spending at this time. His outgoings are set to increase, but by thinking through his purchases, he can make some good decisions and find some bargains.

The Rat always attaches great importance to his relations with others and the closing months of the year will see a flurry of activity, including opportunities to go out. Many Rats will also enjoy surprise occasions and treats and welcome the kindness shown by their loved ones. In some instances, if the Rat talks over his concerns or hopes with those around him, he could find their advice well worth heeding.

The Year of the Rooster starts on 28 January and will be an eventful one for the Rat. There will be several highs and lows to the year, but thanks to the Rat's skills and resourcefulness, far more of these will be highs.

A key factor for the Rat is to listen to his inner voice. Proceeding with something he has misgivings about could lead to problems and regrets later on. At times the Rat will have to be firm and prepared to state his case. This need for openness extends to virtually all aspects of his life, and indeed, almost all aspects will see a considerable amount happen over the year.

For the unattached Rat, there will be good romantic possibilities, although it will be a case of proceeding steadily and allowing a relationship to strengthen over time rather than rushing into a commitment. Some Rats will find true love this year, while others will find that some romances are not meant to be. For these Rats, there will be lessons to learn and chances to move on. A lot will happen for a reason this year and will work out to the Rat's ultimate advantage. March, June, August and December could be key months for meeting others, making personal decisions or enjoying some good personal news.

For Rats with a partner, this can be a busy year, and here again, openness will be to the Rat's advantage. If he has ideas for home improvements, including purchases, he should let these be known. Similarly, if there are activities, holiday destinations or new interests that appeal to him, if he talks these through with his loved ones, he will often be encouraged to take his ideas further.

Ambitious projects will go ahead in many a Rat home and in some instances plans which have been considered for some time will now be undertaken. Disruption and inconvenience will inevitably occur and effort be required, but the results will be worthwhile. Some Rats will also decide to move. For these Rats, the Rooster year will also see times of intense activity, but by the year's end, a lot will have been accomplished and many Rats will appreciate the benefits (and opportunities) their actions have brought.

The Rooster year will also be eventful work-wise, with almost all Rats feeling the effects of change. Over the year many will face increasing demands as new responsibilities are given and pressures increase. In some cases, a flurry of activity will make some weeks frenetic and the Rat may feel overwhelmed. However, the challenges that arise will give the Rat the chance to demonstrate his judgement and underline his strengths. The reputation of many Rats can be considerably enhanced over the year and when further opportunities arise, they will be in a strong position to benefit. April, May, September and October could be busy and significant months for work developments.

For Rats seeking work or hoping to move to something different, the Rooster year can have surprises in store. These Rats may make many applications to no avail and then suddenly their luck changes and within a short space of time their prospects (and immediate future) are transformed. And once these Rats are given an opportunity, they will revel in the chance to prove themselves. Rooster years acknowledge the Rat's skills and he can be a major beneficiary of the year's transformative trends.

In view of the work decisions the Rat will have to take, it is, however, important that he does what he feels is right. Once again he is advised to listen to his inner voice. If he has uncertainties or questions, he also needs to seek advice from those who are qualified to assist. Ill-considered decisions could cause problems later. Rats, take note.

This need for care also applies to money matters. Over the year the Rat will have expensive plans to carry through and will face additional outgoings, including repair bills and transport costs. He should budget carefully and also be attentive to paperwork and thorough when taking on new commitments.

Synergy can be an important factor in 2017 and in addition to the help the Rat receives from others, he will have many chances to assist those around him. Once again his help can make an appreciable difference, and his ability to empathize and suggest practical ways forward will be valued.

With his busy lifestyle, he should, if possible, aim to take a holiday at some time during the year. Driving himself relentlessly could take its toll and it is important he allows himself the chance to unwind. Talking over possible holiday destinations or ways of enjoying quality time with his loved ones can give rise to some interesting suggestions as well as set certain plans in motion.

The Rat should also make sure his personal interests are not neglected this year. With the Rooster year bringing new possibilities, if he is attracted by a particular activity or thinks of a way of developing an existing interest, he should take it further. This is a year to follow up what appeals to him.

Rats who are sedentary for much of the day should also consider incorporating some exercise into their routine. By seeking professional advice on the best way to proceed, they can be introduced to new activities and, for those who join fitness classes, enjoy social benefits too. In 2017 the Rat should aim to pay some attention to his well-being, and if he has any medical concerns, get them checked out.

By the end of the Rooster year, many Rats will be astonished by all they have been able to do. This will be an active and encouraging year, but to fully benefit, the Rat will need to be disciplined, act on his ideas and embrace emerging opportunities. Domestically and socially, this will be a rewarding year, with plans advanced and some potentially signifi-cant new relationships and friendships made. Work-wise, while the demands may be considerable, there will be scope for the Rat to use his strengths to advantage and often prepare the way for future progress. Overall, an active and rewarding year.

The Metal Rat

There is a Chinese proverb which reminds us, 'Diligence is the mother of good fortune,' and this is a year when the Metal Rat's diligence can reward him well. This is a time for building on his present position, pursuing his key aims and being alert to new developments. He does, though, need to act in accordance with his true feelings and avoid risk and rush.

His personal and family life are particularly well aspected and cele-brations are likely to be in store, possibly a wedding or the birth of a grandchild. In addition, news concerning another person could delight the Metal Rat and he could be in a position to offer wise advice. Metal Rats who have more senior relations could give help that is more mean-ingful than they realize, and while occasional generational friction may occur, the Metal Rat will play a valued role in the lives of many of those around him. There will be several family activities to look forward to throughout the year, and March, June and September could be particu-larly active.

The Metal Rat himself will also benefit from the help of family members. By sharing his hopes and any matters on his mind, he will find decisions can be made easier and assistance given. This is a time for openness and sharing.

The Metal Rat takes pride in his home and during the year he will be keen to make improvements, perhaps altering the décor or layout of certain rooms. A lot can be accomplished, but the Metal Rat should spread practical undertakings out rather than commit himself to too many at any one time.

It is also important that he allows himself a break over the year and, where possible, a holiday with his loved ones. Time away in a carefully chosen destination can do everyone good. May, late summer and the end of the year could all see interesting travel possibilities.

In view of his commitments, the Metal Rat will be selective in his socializing this year, but by taking up invitations and going to events that appeal to him he will enjoy the mix of occasions he is able to attend. For the concert-goer and sporting enthusiast, the year can contain some particular highlights.

For the unattached Metal Rat, romance, too, may add sparkle to the year, with an existing friendship becoming more significant or someone new entering the Metal Rat's life. For Metal Rats who are feeling lonely or that something has been missing from their life of late, the Rooster year can mark a considerable upturn. However, in the early stages of a romance it would be better to enjoy the moment and let the relationship develop in its own way rather than rush into a commitment. March, June, August and December could see the most social activity as well as be good for meeting others.

The Rooster year can also lead to some important decisions work-wise. Many Metal Rats will see considerable change in their place of work as long-standing colleagues leave and new working practices are implemented. In view of the volatility, many Metal Rats will think care-fully about their present position, take advantage of newly created open-ings (including promotion) or decide the time is right to look elsewhere. Here again the Metal Rat should act in accordance with what *he* feels is right. Whatever he chooses to do, however, he will rise to the challenges and opportunities the year brings and enjoy the chance to develop his skills in new ways.

For Metal Rats seeking work, the Rooster year can also bring encour-aging developments. Although some of these Metal Rats may have felt despondent recently, they could discover or be alerted to an ideal vacancy almost by chance and it may seem as if it was meant to be. The positions some secure may be different from their previous roles, but they will give these Metal Rats the chance to prove themselves in another capacity. Work-wise, the transitory nature of the Rooster year can bring uncertain moments, but the skills and fortitude of many Metal Rats will shine through. Late March to early June, September and October could see encouraging developments, although such is the nature of the year that opportunities could arise at almost any time.

The income of many Metal Rats will increase this year, but the Metal Rat will still need to manage his outgoings well. Expensive plans need to be budgeted for and risks avoided. Should the Metal Rat be uncharacteristically lax, problems could ensue. This is a year for fiscal care.

With an often demanding lifestyle, the Metal Rat also needs to preserve some time to relax and unwind. If lacking regular exercise, he should seek advice on which activities it would be appropriate for him to do. Some attention to his lifestyle can make a noticeable difference this year and if he is feeling below par at any time or has any health concerns, he should get these checked out.

Overall, the Rooster year will be a busy and often special one for the Metal Rat. In his personal and family life there will be some good news to enjoy, and the more that can be carried out together, the better. The Metal Rat's work and personal interests can also develop in encouraging ways and there will be the opportunity for him to add to his expertise. Throughout the year he will need to follow his instincts and proceed carefully, but if he acts in ways that feel right for him, he can enjoy an active and personally rewarding year.

Tip for the Year

Value your relations with those who are important to you. Also, preserve some time for yourself and your interests. Aim for a good lifestyle balance and enjoy what this year will bring.

The Water Rat

The element of water brings out a sign's communicative skills and the Water Rat is a highly effective communicator. Not only does he listen well, but he is able to voice his ideas clearly and often persuasively. And his talents can help make this a successful year. However, while a lot can go well, he does need to manage his time carefully. During parts of the year the pressure will be considerable, and to get the best results, he will need to focus on what is important.

In his work, changes are afoot. Although many Water Rats will be established in a certain type of work, there will be the chance for them to extend their role and considerably change their duties. This may arise through staff movements and promotion opportunities or through the Water Rat himself seeking a new challenge. In either case, his reputation and experience will stand him in good stead. Some weeks could prove demanding, but the Water Rat will have the chance to demonstrate his skills and move ahead. In addition, his ability to forge good working relations with those around him will be to his advantage and this can be a successful time, especially for those whose work involves conveying ideas and information.

For Water Rats seeking work the Rooster year can have surprising developments in store and some of them will secure a position which is very different from what they have done before. Again the learning curve can be considerable, but the year will give many Water Rats new purpose and incentive. April, May and September to early November could see particularly encouraging developments.

Many Water Rats will enjoy a modest rise in income over the year and some will also receive funds from another source. However, with plans and purchases, together with increased commitments, the Water Rat will find this a costly year. Throughout, he needs to monitor his spending and check the terms of any agreement he enters into. This is no time for risks or assumptions.

With his busy lifestyle and often increasing pressures, he should, however, try to make provision for a holiday this year. A change of scene can do him considerable good. Some Water Rats may be able to link a holiday to an interest or event and so make their time away more mean-ingful. Short breaks may appeal too. During this frequently demanding year, the Water Rat should enjoy some of the rewards he works so hard for.

It is also important he does not allow personal interests to fall away. These can help him unwind and often bring other benefits too. Creative activities could bring him particular enjoyment this year, including photography, a source of increasing pleasure for many.

The Water Rat should also pay some attention to his own well-being, including his diet and general level of exercise. If he feels either is defi-cient, or has any health concerns, he should seek advice.

His domestic life will see considerable activity and once again his ability to communicate and emphathize will be valued. However, a particular matter could be of concern this year and while the Water Rat will be keen to assist, he should not feel he has to carry the burden alone. If necessary, he should seek professional advice or call on someone who has first-hand experience. Rooster years can bring moments of concern, but the problems will be surmountable and often short-lived.

Over the year many Water Rats will take pleasure in home and garden projects, but they will need to allow sufficient time and avoid haste. Domestically, March, June and September could be gratifying months and could bring pleasing news.

Socially, the Water Rat will find himself in demand as well as be tempted by particular events. While he may sometimes feel he already has enough to do, he should aim to go out when he can. Meeting his friends can be of particular benefit, as input from people he trusts can assist in several matters this year. For the unattached, the Rooster year is not without romantic possibilities, although any new romance should be allowed to develop over time rather than be rushed. March, June, August and December could see the most social activity.

Overall, a lot is set to happen this year and much will be demanded of the Water Rat. However, by making the most of his ideas and oppor-tunities, he can make important progress. At work, this is a time for furthering his knowledge and taking on new challenges, while in his personal interests, his creativity can bring him particular pleasure.

Domestically, there will be much to do and family members to assist, and the Water Rat's thoughtfulness will be appreciated. Rewarding family moments, personal and professional successes and (sometimes travel-related) surprises can all be highlights of the Rooster year.

Tip for the Year
Keep your lifestyle in balance so that you can better appreciate what is around you and enjoy the rewards you work so hard for. Give time to yourself and your loved ones and savour your well-deserved successes.

The Wood Rat

The Wood Rat has a keen and alert nature and is particularly adept at evaluating situations. In this Rooster year his talents will serve him well. This can be a constructive year for him, although to make the most of it he will need to show flexibility and seize opportunities.

In his work the aspects are especially encouraging. Recent changes are set to continue, with some unanticipated developments helping the Wood Rat's prospects. Some Wood Rats will find senior colleagues encouraging them to familiarize themselves with other aspects of their work so they can take on greater responsibilities. Others may be offered the chance to work on a particular project or cover for absent staff or, if in a large organization, see tempting opportunities in another department. By taking advantage of what is on offer, many will not only considerably widen their skills but also advance their career. What the Wood Rat succeeds in doing this year should not be underestimated.

For Wood Rats who are unfulfilled in their present role and would welcome a change, as well as those seeking work, the Rooster year can also bring encouraging developments. To benefit fully, these Wood Rats should talk to employment advisers and other contacts as well as widen their search. By chance many could discover a type of work that proves ideal. Openings could arise at almost any time, but April, May, September and October could be important months.

Progress made at work will bring an increase in income, but the Wood Rat will need to manage his financial situation carefully, including checking the terms of any new agreement he enters into. If he has any doubts or misgivings, he should get these addressed before proceeding. This is a year for vigilance.

The element of wood adds to a sign's practical qualities and over the year the Wood Rat will be keen to undertake several practical projects. Some improvements to his home can be immensely satisfying. In addition, he will enjoy seeing how some ideas related to his interests develop. Sometimes sharing thoughts with others will give his projects a useful fillip and joining a local group or enrolling on a course could give him a new incentive. His days may be full and free time limited, but developing his skills and interests can be of great value to him.

Throughout the year he should also give some thought to his level of exercise and the quality of his diet. If he neglects his own well-being, he could feel below par or be susceptible to minor ailments. Wood Rats, take note.

More positively, the Rooster year can present some interesting travel opportunities, sometimes at short notice. Whenever possible, the Wood Rat should take advantage of them. A break and the chance to visit new areas and attractions can benefit him in several ways. May, September and the end of the year could be particularly busy travel-wise.

The Rooster year will also see a lot happen in the Wood Rat's personal life. Some Wood Rats may decide to marry, see an addition to their family or mark another personal milestone. What happens over the year can energize the Wood Rat and result in him doing and succeeding in much more.

For any Wood Rat who is alone or has had some personal sadness to bear, the Rooster year can bring a considerable brightening in their situation. By going out and perhaps joining a social or interest group, these Wood Rats can form new friendships and sometimes find romance too. Roosters years reward action. March, June, August, early September and December could be busy and gratifying months, both personally and for socializing.

Domestically, the Wood Rat will enjoy sharing plans with his loved ones and can accomplish a great deal, although important projects and sizeable transactions should not be rushed, and ideally should be spread out throughout the year.

In general, the Year of the Rooster will be a busy and constructive one for the Wood Rat. It will suit his practical nature and give him the chance to build on his strengths. Work-wise, what he learns can be highly significant for his onward development and the way his personal interests develop can also be satisfying. In money matters he will need to exercise care and he should not be neglectful of his well-being this year. However, he will be encouraged by the support of his loved ones and friends and the year will bring some personal highlights, some good news and some great times to share.

Tip for the Year
Pursue your goals but be prepared to adapt. There are many routes to the top and by making the most of this year you can enhance your prospects considerably. Rooster years can have long-term significance.

The Fire Rat

The Rooster year offers great possibilities for the Fire Rat, and with determination and a willingness to make the most of it, he can not only help his present situation but also gain skills and experience he can build on in the future. The benefits can be considerable *and* far-reaching.

On a personal level, the year is rich in possibility, with affairs of the heart likely to be special. For unattached Fire Rats there will be excellent chances to meet others and, if experiencing a change in circumstances, to build up a new social circle. Someone met now could soon become very special. However, while the aspects are promising, the Fire Rat should be careful not to rush. If he allows time for each person to get to know the other better, the relationship can often be built on a stronger foundation. Quite a few Fire Rats will find true love this year, and those whose romances flounder can soon see someone else entering their life. The Rooster year is capable of surprising developments and the Fire Rat will be learning a lot about himself, others and the mysteries and glorious wonders of love. Late February, March, June, August and December could be significant months both personally and socially.

With his enquiring nature, the Fire Rat has diverse interests and over the year will derive considerable pleasure from sharing these with his friends. In addition, whether attending parties, concerts or sporting events or visiting attractions, he will enjoy the variety and the fun times the year offers. On a social level, this promises to be a busy time, and any Fire Rats who start the year despondent will find that by going out more and giving themselves the chance to meet others, they can greatly improve their situation. Shy and retiring Fire Rats, take careful note and involve yourself more. Your efforts *will* make a noticeable difference.

For Fire Rats with a partner, the Rooster year can again be special. There will be plans to work towards, and even though finances may sometimes be stretched, with the Fire Rat's resourcefulness, a great deal can still be accomplished. Family and friends can be supportive, and luck too can play a part, especially in advancing key plans.

For the many Fire Rats in education this will be a busy year. There will sometimes be difficult concepts to master and the Fire Rat will need to remain focused. What he learns now will be an important platform to build on in the future and some Fire Rats will now make career choices or be alerted to subject areas that suit their strengths. This year can open up options which have long-term significance.

In view of the importance of the present time, the Fire Rat should avail himself of the support available to him. If he is worried over aspects of his studying or has another problem, he should talk to those with the knowledge to assist. This is not a time to keep anxieties to himself.

Fire Rats in work can make important headway. Many will be offered training and additional responsibilities, while some will decide on change and/or seek better remuneration elsewhere. This is no year to stand still. Good progress can be made and prospects enhanced. April, May, September and October could see encouraging developments.

Fire Rats seeking work will find that researching vacancies, finding out about the duties involved and stressing their (relevant) interests and experience may well lead to the offer of a position. Determined effort and the Fire Rat's enthusiasm can be an effective combination.

All Fire Rats will, however, need to be careful in money matters. Rush, risk or carelessness could lead to possible losses. Good financial management is required and if in doubt about any matter, the Fire Rat would do well to seek clarification.

However, while resources may be limited, if possible the Fire Rat should take advantage of any travel opportunities that come his way. Visits to new areas and attractions can be highly enjoyable.

Although the Fire Rat keeps himself active, he should also pay some attention to his well-being. Pushing himself without adequate rest or ignoring the quality of his diet could leave him lacking his usual energy or susceptible to minor ailments. Fire Rats, take note and look after yourselves.

Overall, this promises to be a full year for the Fire Rat. At times the pressures will be considerable, particularly when he has decisions to take. However, by rising to the challenges (and seeking assistance if need be), he can prove himself in many ways. His gains this year will require effort but be considerable. His personal life can also be a source of much happiness. Some Fire Rats may, though, have moments of heartache but, as the Fire Rat will discover, the Rooster year is rich in experience and he will take a great deal from it.

Tip for the Year
This is a year of opportunity – seize those opportunities and look to learn. Within you are the riches of your tomorrow.

The Earth Rat

This Rooster year can be a rewarding one for the Earth Rat, with many activities proceeding well, although, as with all years, there could also be problems to address. However, by proceeding in his usual careful way and seeking advice when necessary, the Earth Rat will generally be content with how his plans develop.

As always, family life will be central to many Earth Rats and they will follow the progress of close relations with fond interest. With some relatives embarking on career change or entering new stages of their education, the support the Earth Rat will give will be particularly appreciated. Those who are grandparents or great-grandparents will also value spending time with younger family members and enjoying the special bonds they often share.

The Earth Rat will do much to help family members, but it is also important that he himself asks for assistance if he has any anxieties or requires help with certain undertakings (including technical matters). Keeping nagging worries to himself could compound problems and help *is* available if required.

The Earth Rat also needs to take good care of himself this year. If he has something potentially hazardous or strenuous to do, he should follow the guidelines and/or seek assistance. This is no year for taking risks or compromising his safety. Similarly, if he has any medical concerns he should get these checked out.

Many Earth Rats will also give some thought to their lifestyle over the year, perhaps improving their diet or incorporating some additional exercise into their routine. By seeking advice and, where exercise is involved, maybe joining a class or group, they will soon be able to appreciate the benefits. Actions taken in the Rooster year can often have unexpected but beneficial consequences.

This also applies to the Earth Rat's personal interests. With his extensive knowledge in certain areas, he will often enjoy contact with other enthusiasts and the chance to share thoughts. Creative interests could be particularly inspiring and some could bring monetary reward.

In addition to the family get-togethers that take place over the year, the Earth Rat will enjoy the year's social opportunities. If he is involved in local groups he will often enjoy participating over the year and if there are other local activities and events that appeal to him, he should consider going. By taking advantage of what is available to him, he will often greatly enjoy himself. March, June, August and December could be active months socially.

Travel, too, can bring considerable pleasure this year, and by planning ahead, the Earth Rat can look forward to seeing some inspiring sights. Once he acts on his ideas and makes enquiries, some lucky chances or the helpfulness of others can lead to potentially exciting outcomes. Some of his trips can have an element of surprise, too. It may be that he sees attractions he did not expect to see or takes up a last-minute offer. May, July and September could have particularly tempting opportunities.

However, the Earth Rat cannot afford to be lax in financial matters this year. He prides himself on his thoroughness, but where major outlay is involved, he needs to check the details and implications. If he has doubts, he should seek expert opinion. As the saying goes, 'It is better to be safe than sorry.' He should also attend to important correspondence carefully. Delays or an inadequate response could be to his disadvantage. Earth Rats, take note.

Overall, the Rooster year will be a full and satisfying one for the Earth Rat. As he will find, once he takes action, he will often be encouraged by others and benefit from timely developments. Travel, local events and contact with friends will also add much to his year, although to benefit fully he does need to be active and take up opportunities. He will take considerable pride in family developments and do much to assist his loved ones. Money matters require careful attention, and when problems or concerns arise, it is important the Earth Rat draws on the support available to him. If he acts upon his ideas, however, he can make this a personally satisfying year.

Tip for the Year

Spend time on your personal interests. Also, take advantage of events and recreational facilities in your area, including those that can help well-being and fitness levels. These can bring a beneficial element to your lifestyle and year.

Famous Rats

Ben Affleck, Ursula Andress, Louis Armstrong, Lauren Bacall, Dame Shirley Bassey, Kathy Bates, Irving Berlin, Kenneth Branagh, Marlon Brando, Charlotte Brontë, Jackson Browne, George H. W. Bush, Glen Campbell, Jimmy Carter, Jeremy Clarkson, Aaron Copland, Cameron Diaz, David Duchovny, Duffy, T. S. Eliot, Eminem, Colin Firth, Pope Francis I, Clark Gable, Neil Gaiman, Hugh Grant, Lewis Hamilton, Thomas Hardy, Prince Harry, Charlton Heston, Buddy Holly, Mick Hucknall, Henrik Ibsen, Jeremy Irons, Samuel L. Jackson, LeBron James, Jean-Michel Jarre, Scarlett Johansson, Gene Kelly, Jude Law, Gary Lineker, Lord Andrew Lloyd Webber, Ian McEwan, Katie Melua, Claude Monet, Julianne Moore, Olly Murs, Richard Nixon, Ozzy Osbourne, Brad Paisley, Sean Penn, Katy Perry, Philippe I, King of the Belgians, Sir Terry Pratchett, Ian Rankin, Burt Reynolds, Rossini, William Shakespeare, James Taylor, Leo Tolstoy, Spencer Tracy, the Prince of Wales, George Washington, the Duke of York, Emile Zola.

24 January 1925 to 12 February 1926 — *Wood Ox*

11 February 1937 to 30 January 1938 — *Fire Ox*

29 January 1949 to 16 February 1950 — *Earth Ox*

15 February 1961 to 4 February 1962 — *Metal Ox*

3 February 1973 to 22 January 1974 — *Water Ox*

20 February 1985 to 8 February 1986 — *Wood Ox*

7 February 1997 to 27 January 1998 — *Fire Ox*

26 January 2009 to 13 February 2010 — *Earth Ox*

The Ox

The Personality of the Ox

The more considered the way,
the more considerable the journey.

The Ox is born under the signs of equilibrium and tenacity. He is a hard and conscientious worker and sets about everything he does in a resolute, methodical and determined manner. He has considerable leadership qualities and is often admired for his tough and uncompromising nature. He knows what he wants to achieve in life and, as far as possible, will not be deflected from his ultimate objective.

The Ox takes his responsibilities and duties very seriously. He is decisive and quick to take advantage of any opportunity that comes his way. He is also sincere and places a great deal of trust in his friends and colleagues. He is, nevertheless, something of a loner. He is a quiet and private individual and often keeps his thoughts to himself. He also cherishes his independence and prefers to set about things in his own way rather than be bound by the dictates of others or influenced by outside pressures.

The Ox tends to have a calm and tranquil nature, but if something angers him or he feels that someone has let him down, he can have a fearsome temper. He can also be stubborn and obstinate and this can lead him into conflict with others. Usually he will succeed in getting his own way, but should things go against him he is a poor loser and will take any defeat or setback extremely badly.

The Ox is often a deep thinker and rather studious. He is not particularly renowned for his sense of humour and does not take kindly to new gimmicks or anything too innovative. He is too solid and traditional for that and prefers to stick to the more conventional norm.

His home is very important to him and in some respects he treats it as a private sanctuary. His family tends to be closely knit and the Ox will make sure that each member does their fair share around the house. He tends to be a hoarder, but he is always well organized and neat. He also places great importance on punctuality and there is nothing that infuriates him more than to be kept waiting, particularly if it is due to someone's inefficiency. The Ox can be a hard taskmaster!

Once settled in a job or house, the Ox will quite happily remain there for many years. He does not like change and he is also not particularly keen on travel. He does, however, enjoy gardening and other outdoor pursuits and he will often spend much of his spare time out of doors. He is usually an excellent gardener and whenever possible will make sure he has a large area of ground to maintain. He usually prefers to live in the country rather than the town.

Due to his dedicated and dependable nature, the Ox will usually do well in his chosen career, providing he is given enough freedom to act on his own initiative. He invariably does well in politics, agriculture and careers which need specialized training. He is also very gifted artistically and many Oxen have enjoyed considerable success as musicians or composers.

The Ox is not as outgoing as some and it often takes him a long time to establish friendships and feel relaxed in another person's company. His courtships are likely to be long, but once he is settled, he will remain devoted and loyal to his partner. He is particularly well suited to those born under the signs of the Rat, Rabbit, Snake and Rooster. He can also establish a good relationship with the Monkey, Dog, Pig and another Ox, but he will find that he has little in common with the whimsical and sensitive Goat. He will also find it difficult to get on with the Horse, Dragon and Tiger – the Ox prefers a quiet and peaceful existence and those born under these three signs tend to be a little too lively and impulsive for his liking.

The female Ox has a kind and caring nature and her home and family are very much her pride and joy. She always tries to do her best for her partner and can be a most conscientious and loving parent. She is an excellent organizer and a very determined person who will often succeed in getting what she wants in life. She usually has a deep interest in the arts and is often a talented artist or musician.

The Ox is a very down-to-earth character. He is sincere, loyal and unpretentious. He can, however, be rather reserved and to some he may appear distant and aloof. He has a quiet nature, but underneath he is very strong-willed and ambitious. He has the courage of his convictions and is often prepared to stand up for what he believes to be right, regardless of the consequences. He inspires confidence and trust and throughout his life he will rarely be short of people who are ready to support him.

The Five Different Types of Ox

In addition to the 12 signs of the Chinese zodiac there are five elements and these have a strengthening or moderating influence on the signs. The effects of the elements on the Ox are described below, together with the years in which they were exercising their influence. Therefore Oxen born in 1961 are Metal Oxen, Oxen born in 1973 are Water Oxen, and so on.

Metal Ox: 1961

This Ox is confident and very strong-willed. He can be blunt and forth-right in his views and is not afraid of speaking his mind. He sets about his objectives with dogged determination, but he can become so involved in his various activities that he can be oblivious to the thoughts and feelings of those around him, and this can sometimes be to his detri-ment. He is honest and dependable and will never promise more than he can deliver. He has a good appreciation of the arts and usually a small circle of very good and loyal friends.

Water Ox: 1973

This Ox has a sharp and penetrating mind. He is a good organizer and sets about his work in a methodical manner. He is not as narrow-minded as some of the other types of Ox and is more willing to involve others in his plans and aspirations. He usually has very high moral standards and is often attracted to careers in public service. He is a good judge of character and has such a friendly and persuasive manner that he usually experiences little difficulty in securing his objectives. He is popular and has an excellent way with children.

Wood Ox: 1925, 1985

The Wood Ox conducts himself with an air of dignity and authority and will often take a leading role in any enterprise in which he becomes involved. He is very self-confident and is direct in his dealings with others. He does, however, have a quick temper and has no hesitation in speaking his mind. He has tremendous drive and willpower and an extremely good memory. He is particularly loyal and devoted to the members of his family and has a most caring nature.

Fire Ox: 1937, 1997

The Fire Ox has a powerful and assertive personality and is a hard and conscientious worker. He holds strong views and has very little patience when things do not go his way. He can also get carried away in the excitement of the moment and does not always take into account the views of those around him. He nevertheless has many leadership qualities and will often reach positions of power, eminence and wealth. He usually has a small group of loyal and close friends and is very devoted to his family.

Earth Ox: 1949, 2009

This Ox sets about everything he does in a sensible and level-headed manner. He is ambitious but also realistic in his aims and is often prepared to work long hours to secure his objectives. He is shrewd in financial and business matters and is a very good judge of character. He has a quiet nature and is greatly admired for his sincerity and integrity. He is also very loyal to his family and friends and his views are often sought.

Prospects for the Ox in 2017

The Year of the Monkey (8 February 2016–27 January 2017) is invariably fast paced and some of its developments will have worried the Ox, who likes to proceed in a measured fashion. However, despite the pressures, for the most part he will have fared well.

There will be little let-up in activity in the closing months of the Monkey year. At work, the Ox could face a growing workload with challenging objectives to meet as well as other matters to deal with. These can be exacting times, but the Ox is tenacious and can add to his reputation. September and November can be important months, including for promotion or possible new openings.

There will also be an increasing number of social occasions towards the end of the year, including the chance to meet some people the Ox has not seen for a while. In addition, a friend could impart some surprising news. By taking up his invitations, the Ox can enjoy many convivial times.

He will also be keen to make some specific purchases, and by taking the time to consider his options, will be pleased with what he acquires.

Domestically, there will be several ideas he is keen to implement and it is important he talks these through with those around him. Discussion can lead to a lot happening and shared activities result in satisfying outcomes. December will be a particularly full month in many an Ox household, with travel possibilities and impromptu family occasions.

The Year of the Rooster starts on 28 January and will be an encouraging one for the Ox. Like the Ox, the Rooster favours planning and consistency, and the Ox will find the Rooster year gives him the chance to put his strengths to more effective use. However, while many aspects are positive, the Rooster year also has its more cautionary elements, and in particular the Ox should be wary of taking people and situations at face value. Without care, there is a risk he could be misled. Extra alertness would be wise this year.

Another important feature of the year is that the Ox will often feel the time is right for change and will act on plans he has been considering for some time. These could include taking on fresh challenges at work, taking up a new interest or moving house. Once the Ox has an idea in mind, he likes to see it through, and the Rooster year is very much one for action.

At work many Oxen will have been giving some thought to their situation, especially in the light of recent developments. For those who are dissatisfied or consider themselves in a rut, this is a year to take action. Some may be tempted by a complete career change, but whatever the Ox decides to do, by keeping alert for openings and seeking advice, he could find a position that better suits his skills as well as offers potential for future growth. Oxen do not embark on change lightly, but work-wise this year favours progress.

For Oxen who decide to remain with their existing employer, again the Rooster year can bring significant opportunities. New initiatives could need staffing or staff movements open up positions with greater responsibility. Here many of the Oxen's proven skills will enable them to take their career to a new level. The Ox is quietly ambitious and the Rooster year will reward his commitment.

The prospects are also encouraging for Oxen currently seeking work. By widening the scope of their search, quite a few could secure a position which provides a fresh challenge. Although there will be much to learn, the Rooster year can re-energize the career of many Oxen. April, June, September and October could see interesting possibilities, although whenever the Ox sees an opening that appeals to him, he should pursue it.

However, while the aspects are encouraging, the Ox still needs to exercise care. During the year an issue with a colleague could concern him, and if he senses a possible difficulty, he needs to be wary and discreet and remain focused on what he has to do. Similarly, if he has doubts over any matter, he should check the situation himself. By remaining vigilant he can steer himself round many of the obstacles and niggling matters that may arise this year.

This need for care also applies to financial matters. When making major transactions or entering into agreements, the Ox needs to check the costs and implications and seek professional advice if necessary. If he lends to another person, again he needs to be careful. Verbal agreements in particular may give rise to later difficulty. Oxen, take note and remain vigilant.

More positively, the Ox's personal interests can develop in encouraging ways this year. Some Oxen will take up new interests and welcome the challenge this brings, while for those who would like to meet others, a local interest group might prove ideal. In addition, some will be keen to make lifestyle changes, perhaps starting an exercise discipline, improving their diet or allowing more time for recreation. This may not only help their lifestyle balance but also do them a lot of personal good.

The Rooster year can also give rise to some pleasing social occasions. May, June, August and September could be lively months, and Oxen who keep themselves to themselves will find it worth making the effort to go out more. Again, by broadening their lifestyle, they can enjoy good times and other benefits.

Oxen who are enjoying romance or who find love this year will, in true Ox fashion, like to take this steadily. For some, a relationship started now can become a permanent one. The Rooster year does have long-term significance.

The Ox's home life is also set to enjoy positive developments. A small number of Oxen will move and enjoy settling into their new area. However, almost all Oxen will enjoy carrying out home improvements, with the Ox's practical nature once again coming to the fore. Redecorating, rearranging rooms and replacing equipment will be on the agenda of many an Ox, although, despite early planning, timescales may need to be kept elastic and some projects may prove more extensive (and costly) than anticipated.

The Ox will also delight in arranging some family occasions this year. July and September could be marked by some pleasing times, with the Ox often the driving force behind trips out and a possible holiday. Quality time with his loved ones will be an important part of his year.

Overall, the Year of the Rooster will be a full and satisfying one for the Ox. It is a time for carrying out plans and the Ox should look to develop his ideas both professionally and personally. Some attention to his lifestyle can be of benefit and he does need to remain his thorough self, especially with finances, and tread carefully during times of uncertainty. However, he can look forward to a variety of pleasing social occasions and a busy and satisfying domestic life. Generally, the Rooster year will suit him well, and with commitment, he can make good progress.

The Metal Ox

The Metal Ox possesses great resolve and likes to proceed in a measured manner. Never one to rush decisions, he is careful and an astute planner. And his approach can reward him well this year. He can look forward to making good headway and seeing many of his plans come to fruition.

His work in particular can benefit from positive developments. Some Metal Oxen will see ideas they have nurtured or projects they have been working on gaining momentum and their skills coming into their own. Impressive results can be secured this year and many Metal Oxen will feel more energized than they have for some time. As a result of current developments, many will have the chance to take on greater responsibilities and further their career. This is a year when the Metal Ox can make his strengths *really* count.

There will, though, be some Metal Oxen who will feel they have accomplished all they can in their present capacity and who would welcome a fresh challenge. For these Metal Oxen, as well as those seeking work, the Rooster year can see encouraging developments. By making enquiries and talking to others, many could be alerted to new openings, including a different but attractive position. It will take time, but the Metal Ox's tenacity will often enable him to secure the chance to prove himself in new ways. April, June and September to mid-November could be significant months.

Although the Metal Ox enjoys positive relations with many of his colleagues, there could, though, be a possible rivalry, difference of opinion or personality clash this year. Should this arise, the Metal Ox should not let it distract him from what needs to be done. If he can directly address and defuse the issue, so much the better. Throughout the Rooster year, he does need to be alert to possible difficulties and keep them in perspective.

Another area which requires care is finance. When making large purchases or entering into agreements, the Metal Ox needs to check the terms and implications and be wary of accepting all that he is told at face value. Without care, he could be misled. Similarly, if he lends to another person, it needs to be handled properly. This need for care also applies to financial paperwork. This is no year for risk.

In view of his busy lifestyle, the Metal Ox may give some consideration to his well-being this year. Setting some time aside for himself and perhaps starting an appropriate exercise discipline will be of benefit.

Many Metal Oxen will also be keen to build on certain interests, perhaps making more of their ideas, developing their skills or attending gatherings. Both professionally and recreationally, the year offers considerable scope.

Where possible, the Metal Ox should also take advantage of any chances to travel. While he is a keen planner, some trips could be arranged at short notice.

The Metal Ox likes to keep his social circle relatively small, and in it will be some friends he has known for many decades. During the year a close friend could face a problem and the help the Metal Ox is able to give may be of more consequence than he may realize. He, too, will welcome the support friends will offer and the chance to seek their opinion on ideas he is considering.

For Metal Oxen who would welcome more company and/or romance, the Rooster year has good possibilities. However, to benefit, these Metal Oxen should aim to go out more, including joining classes or activity groups in their area. As many will find, once positive action is taken, encouraging developments can quickly follow on. May, June, August and September will see particularly good social opportunities.

The Metal Ox's domestic life will also see much activity. Existing arrangements may need to be altered and adjustments made, perhaps as another family member moves out of the household or work routines change. As ever, the Metal Ox will be keen to do his best for all concerned. Shared times will also be an important part of the year and can be to the benefit of all. July and September could be active and pleasing months domestically and could bring travel opportunities as well.

In general, the Year of the Rooster will be a constructive one for the Metal Ox and will allow him to make more of his strengths. Both his work prospects and personal interests are favourably aspected and by setting about his objectives in his usual determined way, he can enjoy some deserved success. He will need to be careful in financial matters and alert to potential differences of opinion, particularly with a colleague. However he is by nature careful and throughout the year he will take pleasure in much that this interesting year makes possible.

Tip for the Year
Use your knowledge and experience well. They count for a great deal. Build on them and put yourself forward. That way, important opportunities can open up for you.

The Water Ox

A hallmark of the Ox's character is his determination and this is very evident in the Water Ox. When he sets his mind to a specific purpose, he works tirelessly to achieve his aim. Over the years, he will have enjoyed many fine achievements and in the Rooster year he will continue to make progress as well as reap some often substantial rewards, particularly from recent efforts.

In his work, the aspects are particularly favourable. Having proved himself in different capacities and shown himself to be dependable, the Water Ox may well be encouraged to extend his duties and be excellently placed when promotion opportunities arise. This is very much a year to build on his achievements *and advance*.

The majority of Water Oxen will make important strides with their present employer, but for those who are seeking a move, the year can bring significant opportunities. By talking to their contacts (which can be important) and keeping alert for openings, these Water Oxen can secure a position which takes their career to a new level.

Those seeking work should also actively make enquiries and be quick to follow up opportunities. Although the job-seeking process is rarely easy, by having faith in themselves, many will find an opening which gives them a new challenge and sense of purpose. April, June and September to mid-November could be important months for work developments.

However, while the Water Ox can do his prospects a lot of good, he could find office politics or the attitude of a colleague troubling. Care and discretion are advised. Also, the Water Ox should not let himself be distracted from his objectives. All years have their challenging aspects and this one will be no exception. Water Oxen, take note.

Finance also requires care. During the year many Water Oxen will have additional accommodation costs as well as take on new commitments. In all cases, the Water Ox needs to check his obligations and question anything that is unclear. Money matters cannot be left to chance this year. Important paperwork also requires close attention. The Water Ox may find it helpful to keep a set of accounts so he can keep better track of his position.

While the pressures on the Water Ox's budget can be considerable, if possible he should make allowance for a possible holiday. Even if not travelling too far, he will find that a change of scene can do him a lot of good and offer some interesting new experiences.

It is also important that he does not let his interests and recreational pursuits fall away. These can not only be an outlet for certain talents but also bring balance to his lifestyle, including giving him the chance of additional exercise or social contact.

The Water Ox will be selective in his socializing this year, but he should not deny himself the chance to enjoy occasions that appeal to him. In addition he will appreciate meeting up with his friends and sharing news as well as support. For Water Oxen who are feeling lonely and/or have had a recent personal upset, pursuing their interests can often lead to meeting someone new and potentially significant. May, June and August to early October could see the most social activity.

The Water Ox's home life will be busy, and with commitments, changing work patterns and close relations facing keynote decisions, the pressures may be considerable. Being conscientious, the Water Ox will be keen to see everything goes well. His disciplined approach will help and he may well take pride in several family achievements over the year as well as offer valuable guidance (including to more senior relations). Shared family activities can be especially gratifying. July and September will be active months in many a Water Ox household, and for a few there could be prospects of a move. These can be busy and sometimes exciting times.

The Year of the Rooster is one of great opportunity for the Water Ox. With his skills, resolve and experience, he can secure an important new role and use his strengths to advantage. Care is needed in financial matters, and with many demands on his time, he needs to focus on priorities and make sure his lifestyle stays in balance. Recreational pursuits and quality time with those who are special to him can help. Overall, an active and rewarding year.

Tip for the Year

Make more of your strengths, for that is where your greatest successes are likely to come from, especially work-wise. Seize any chances to widen your experience. Also, devote time to your loved ones and to enjoying the pleasures this fulfilling year will bring.

The Wood Ox

In recent years the Wood Ox may have felt buffeted by events which were not always under his control. Certain hopes may have felt elusive and circumstances frustrating. However, in the Rooster year, a lot will move in his favour and his previous efforts and patience will be rewarded. Almost all areas of his life can enjoy positive developments.

Over the year quite a few Wood Oxen will be giving some thought to their accommodation. The hopes of many of those wanting to get on the property ladder and/or move elsewhere will now be realized and those who remain where they are will also be likely to make noticeable improvements to their home.

However, while a lot can be accomplished, where finance is concerned, the Wood Ox will need to be vigilant. The terms of financial agreements should be checked and professional advice obtained. Also, should the Wood Ox lend to another person or be tempted by a speculative venture, care is needed. This is not a year for risk or assumptions.

The Rooster year can, though, bring some personal highlights. For Wood Oxen with a partner, shared undertakings can be especially meaningful. Those who are parents will often delight in encouraging their children to master new feats and there will be some wonderful moments to share.

In view of the Wood Ox's commitments, it is, though, important that he remains well organized and, if concerned by any matter, forthcoming. Some Wood Oxen have a tendency to keep their thoughts to themselves, but in this significant year good communication will be helpful in addressing issues and furthering plans. Wood Oxen who have a reputation for being 'strong and silent', do bear this in mind.

For Wood Oxen who are alone and have perhaps had some personal turbulence in their life of late, the Rooster year can again offer positive change. Developments can be helped by the Wood Ox's own desire to move on and not let unsatisfactory situations linger. Wood Oxen who desire new friends, romance or greater fulfilment in their life will find that interests they pursue (or start) over the year can have a good social element. Affairs of the heart are favourably aspected and Wood Oxen who have been heavily involved in their work at the expense of their personal life should aim to address this. Actions taken now can make a real difference. May, June and mid-July to early October could be socially active months.

The Wood Ox's personal interests can also develop in encouraging ways and those who have ambitions to make more of a certain skill or specialist knowledge should look to take this forward, including promoting what they do.

All Wood Oxen should set aside time for recreation and ensure they take regular and appropriate exercise. With their often demanding lifestyle, they do need time to unwind and enjoy themselves.

At work, many Wood Oxen will have added considerably to their experience in recent years, particularly with changes to their role. However, the Wood Ox is ambitious and knows he is capable of contributing far more. As a result, when openings arise in his present place of work or he sees a position offering growth elsewhere, he should put himself forward. Once he indicates his desire to progress, encouraging developments can often follow on. Some senior personnel may also assist. This is very much a year for the Wood Ox to build on his experience and move forward.

For Wood Oxen keen to take their work in a different direction or seeking a position, again the Rooster year can open up fresh possibilities. By considering different ways in which they could use their skills, making enquiries and approaching employers and organizations, these Wood Oxen can gather useful information and be alerted to openings to pursue. Again, once the Wood Ox takes purposeful action, he will set in motion developments that can be potentially significant. April, June and late August to early November could see encouraging developments, but throughout the year the Wood Ox should seize his opportunities.

Although his work prospects are favourably aspected, he could, however, be troubled by the attitude of a colleague or find himself in a fraught situation. At such times, he should aim to keep the matter in perspective and not let it distract him from his duties. Every year brings its challenges and it is by meeting and overcoming them that the Wood Ox can show his qualities and potential.

Overall, the Rooster year can be a constructive one for the determined Wood Ox. In his personal life, plans (including for his accommodation) can often be successfully advanced and there will be special times to share with his friends and loved ones. For Wood Oxen who are alone, new friendships and possible romance can add sparkle to their life. Personal interests, too, can develop in an encouraging manner. The Rooster year also offers considerable scope for the Wood Ox's work prospects and will enable him to build on his experience and further his career. The accent this year is on growth and the Wood Ox can enjoy some well-deserved success.

Tip for the Year
Keep your lifestyle in balance and allow time to enjoy the rewards you work so hard for. Also, value your loved ones and close friends. They can benefit you in so many ways.

The Fire Ox

This year marks the start of a new decade in the Fire Ox's life, and as he enters his twenties, he will have hopes and plans he is keen to realize. And a lot will go in his favour, albeit in sometimes surprising ways.

Although the Fire Ox may have firm ideas about what he would like to do, he should not regard these as set in stone. The Rooster year can bring surprises and there will be new possibilities to consider. To benefit, the Fire Ox needs to be open-minded and make the best of situations *as they arise*.

His personal life will be especially busy. There will be fun times to be had with his friends and as a result of a change in circumstances (and sometimes location), there will be the opportunity to extend his social circle as well.

For many Fire Oxen, affairs of the heart will add considerable excitement to the year, with a chance meeting proving significant. Some romances are really set to blossom this year, and if others flounder, new ones will await. A lot will happen for a reason this year and will work out to the Fire Ox's longer-term advantage.

Fire Oxen who prefer to keep themselves to themselves may be selective in their socializing this year, but they should try not to miss out on the activities and social opportunities available to them. By participating, they will get much more from the year as well as add variety to their lifestyle. Reserved Fire Ox, take note and do try to engage more this year. It will be well worth it. Late April to the end of June and August and September could see the most social activity.

Throughout the year the Fire Ox can also derive much satisfaction from developing his personal interests, especially any that are creative. He could receive valuable encouragement from joining other enthusiasts and, if appropriate, getting instruction and additional equipment. The

Fire Ox has a curious streak to his nature and the Rooster year will provide him with new experiences to enjoy.

For Fire Oxen in education this can be an illuminating year. As they study subjects in greater depth, many will enjoy extending their skills and knowledge. They will be challenged, but, as they recognize, this is the way to learn and prove to themselves (and others) what they can do. Any Fire Oxen who have doubts about their current course or subject will find that by seeking advice they could be alerted to suitable alternatives. This is no year to close their mind to other options.

For Fire Oxen in work, the Rooster year is again one for exploring possibilities. Once they have proved their reliability and mastered what is required in their current position, these Fire Oxen should look to progress, either where they are or elsewhere. Those who decide to switch employer may find an entry into a different type of work with the potential for future development.

Fire Oxen seeking work should also keep alert for openings. For some, taking a course could lead to a position or they could learn of an attractive type of work in another way. By being actively involved in the job-seeking process, they will display their initiative and may secure that all-important rung on the employment ladder. Considerable effort will be required, but the Fire Ox's tenaciousness will often win through. April, June and September to mid-November could see interesting developments.

With socializing, personal interests and other commitments, the Fire Ox will need to keep a close watch on his spending, however, and try to remain within his budget. If entering into new agreements, tempted by a speculative venture or lending to another person, he should also exercise caution. There is a risk he could be misled. He should also safeguard valuable property. A loss could be upsetting.

Although his resources may be limited, the Fire Ox will have the chance to travel this year as well as attend some lively events. Last-minute offers or spur of the moment chances to go away could be much appreciated.

Many Fire Oxen will mark their twentieth birthday in fine style, with close friends and loved ones springing some surprises. Someone close may also use the opportunity to give the young Fire Ox advice. This may be surprising, but the words will be spoken with his best interests in mind.

Throughout the year it is important that the Fire Ox remembers he does have people ready to support him and their input is capable of making a difference to his current undertakings. Fire Oxen, take note and do be receptive.

Overall, the Year of the Rooster will be an often special one for the Fire Ox. There will be challenges and doubts to overcome, but the Fire Ox knows he has it within him to accomplish a great deal and his self-belief and resolve will take him forward. Both educationally and at work this can be an encouraging year. The Fire Ox's personal interests and social life can also bring him great pleasure, with new friendships being formed and opportunities opening up. The Rooster year is rich in possibility and will offer the Fire Ox the chance to move ahead and, importantly, prove himself in new ways.

Tip for the Year

Many of your activities and decisions now will shape what lies ahead for you. Use this year well. It can provide a significant platform for subsequent growth.

The Earth Ox

This will be a satisfying year for the Earth Ox, particularly as certain plans can now move forward. Rooster years favour organization and this suits the Earth Ox's temperament well. A further advantage will be that circumstances will often help. The Earth Ox will have a lot in his favour this year and his efforts will be well rewarded.

Accommodation matters will feature prominently, with some Earth Oxen deciding to move to somewhere which better suits their needs. Although this will involve great upheaval, these Earth Oxen will be pleased with the benefits gained. All Earth Oxen, irrespective of whether they move or remain where they are, will busy themselves with home projects, and whether decluttering, updating equipment or adding new comforts, they can accomplish a great deal. In addition, those who have gardens will again take pleasure in tending to their land, trying out new stock and enjoying the results.

The Earth Ox will also be glad of the input of family members in his various undertakings. Often others will have expertise which can be useful. And sharing tasks can generate a powerful synergy.

Although the year will see much practical activity, there will also be several social occasions to look forward to. The Earth Ox will often be tempted by events happening locally. By taking advantage of these, he can enjoy some good times. The Rooster year can be marked by some lively occasions.

Earth Oxen who are alone and perhaps feeling dispirited should aim to involve themselves in the activities that are available to them. By reaching out, they can inject new meaning into their life.

All Earth Oxen will also appreciate the chance to share news and interests with their friends. Many of these will be of long standing and the Earth Ox will value their opinions. Mid-April to the end of June and August and September are likely to see the most social activity.

Many Earth Oxen will also be keen to travel this year and by planning ahead could enjoy the chance to see places which have long appealed to them. There could be some spur of the moment trips too, perhaps due to late availability or a sudden invitation, and the Earth Ox should aim to make the most of what arises.

As always, he will take a keen interest in the activities of close family members and will offer advice when decisions are in the offing. He could also be thrilled by the achievements of a relative and admire the effort they have put in. Tenacity runs in the Earth Ox's family. July and September could see pleasing domestic developments and the latter part of the year could also be marked by the culmination of key projects.

The Earth Ox has a happy knack of using his time well and the Rooster year will be no exception. When not occupied with other matters, he will delight in his own interests. There will be ideas to pursue, new activities to try and sometimes equipment to master. The Earth Ox's enquiring nature will be well satisfied this year.

Although many Earth Oxen will prefer to concentrate on existing interests, those keen on a new challenge or seeking to add a new element to their lifestyle would do well to investigate courses available in their area or contact social groups.

A priority of many Earth Oxen this year will be to attend to their well-being. This could include making dietary modifications as well as starting suitable exercise programmes. With advice on the best way to proceed, the Earth Ox will often be pleased with the difference his new regime makes to his life.

Although a lot can go well, the Rooster year does, however, have its more awkward elements. Financial matters in particular require careful attention. Official forms need close and prompt attention, and if anything is unclear, questions should be asked and advice obtained. This also applies to more major transactions. Earth Oxen who move should keep watch on costs and obligations. And it would be prudent for all Earth Oxen to be on their guard this year, for there is a risk they could be misled or fall victim to a scam. Earth Oxen, take note and remain alert.

In general, though, the Year of the Rooster can be a gratifying one for the Earth Ox. Keen to carry out his plans, he will busy himself in many activities, often with beneficial results. In his home, this can be a year for extensive improvements and even a possible move. With joint effort and good co-operation, many hopes can now be realized. Personal interests can also prove satisfying, and the more the Earth Ox involves himself in what is going on around him, the more interesting his year can be. He needs to be careful in money matters and avoid risk. However, determination and thoroughness are key traits of the Earth Ox and they will often carry him through to a favourable outcome.

Tip for the Year

Pace yourself. Rushing or acting before you are ready could bring anxiety and pressure. Also, draw on the readiness of others to help and seek professional advice on important matters, especially those related to finance. With good support, you can make this a successful and personally satisfying year.

Famous Oxen

Hans Christian Andersen, Gemma Arterton, Johann Sebastian Bach, Napoleon Bonaparte, Albert Camus, Jim Carrey, Charlie Chaplin, George Clooney, Harlan Coben, Diana, Princess of Wales, Marlene Dietrich, Walt Disney, Jessica Ennis-Hill, Jane Fonda, Edward Fox, Michael J. Fox, Peter Gabriel, Gal Gadot, Elizabeth George, Richard Gere, Ricky Gervais, William Hague, Handel, King Harald V of Norway, Adolf Hitler, Dustin Hoffman, Anthony Hopkins, Billy Joel, former King Juan Carlos of Spain, Anna Kendrick, John Key, B. B. King, Keira Knightley, Mark Knopfler, Burt Lancaster, Bruno Mars, Queen Mathilde of Belgium, Chloë Moretz, Kate Moss, Carey Mulligan, Eddie Murphy, Jack Nicholson, Leslie Nielsen, Bill Nighy, Barack Obama, Gwyneth Paltrow, Oscar Peterson, Lionel Richie, Wayne Rooney, Nico Rosberg, Tim Roth, Rubens, Meg Ryan, Amanda Seyfried, Jean Sibelius, Bruce Springsteen, Meryl Streep, Lady Thatcher, Scott F. Turow, Vincent van Gogh, Sigourney Weaver, the Duke of Wellington, Arsène Wenger, Pharrell Williams, W. B. Yeats.

13 February 1926 to 1 February 1927 — *Fire Tiger*

31 January 1938 to 18 February 1939 — *Earth Tiger*

17 February 1950 to 5 February 1951 — *Metal Tiger*

5 February 1962 to 24 January 1963 — *Water Tiger*

23 January 1974 to 10 February 1975 — *Wood Tiger*

9 February 1986 to 28 January 1987 — *Fire Tiger*

28 January 1998 to 15 February 1999 — *Earth Tiger*

14 February 2010 to 2 February 2011 — *Metal Tiger*

The Tiger

The Personality of the Tiger

It's
the zest,
the enthusiasm,
the giving the little bit more,
that makes the difference.
And opens up so much.

The Tiger is born under the sign of courage. He is a charismatic figure and usually holds very firm views. He is strong-willed and determined and sets about most of his activities with tremendous energy and enthusiasm. He is very alert and quick-witted and his mind is forever active. He is a highly original thinker and is nearly always brimming with new ideas or full of enthusiasm for some new project or scheme.

The Tiger adores challenges and loves to get involved in anything that he thinks has an exciting future or that catches his imagination. He is prepared to take risks and does not like to be bound either by convention or the dictates of others. He likes to be free to act as he chooses and at least once during his life he will throw caution to the wind and go off and do the things he wants to do.

The Tiger does, however, have a somewhat restless nature. Even though he is often prepared to throw himself wholeheartedly into a project, his initial enthusiasm can soon wane if he sees something more appealing. He can also be rather impulsive and there will be occasions in his life when he acts in a manner he later regrets. If he were to think things through or be prepared to persevere in his various activities, he would almost certainly enjoy a greater degree of success.

Fortunately the Tiger is lucky in most of his enterprises, but should things not work out as he hoped, he is liable to suffer from severe bouts of depression and it will often take him a long time to recover. His life often consists of a series of ups and downs.

He is, however, very adaptable. He has an adventurous spirit and rarely stays in the same place for long. In the early stages of his life he is likely to try his hand at several different jobs and he will also change his residence fairly frequently.

The Tiger is very honest and open in his dealings with others. He hates any sort of hypocrisy or falsehood. He is also well known for being blunt and forthright and has no hesitation in speaking his mind. He can be rebellious at times, particularly against any form of petty authority, and while this can lead him into conflict with others, he is never one to shrink from an argument or avoid standing up for what he believes is right.

The Tiger is a natural leader and can rise to the top of his chosen profession. He does not, however, care for anything too bureaucratic or detailed, and he does not like to obey orders. He can be stubborn and obstinate and throughout his life he likes to retain a certain amount of independence in his actions and be responsible to no one but himself. He likes to consider that all his achievements are due to his own efforts and he will not ask for support from others if he can avoid it.

Ironically, despite his self-confidence and leadership qualities, he can be indecisive and will often delay making a major decision until the very last moment. He can also be sensitive to criticism.

Although the Tiger is capable of earning large sums of money, he is rather a spendthrift and does not always put his money to best use. He can also be most generous and will often shower lavish gifts on friends and relations.

The Tiger cares very much for his reputation and the image that he tries to project. He carries himself with an air of dignity and authority and enjoys being the centre of attention. He is very adept at attracting publicity, both for himself and the causes he supports.

The Tiger often marries young and he will find himself best suited to those born under the signs of the Pig, Dog, Horse and Goat. He can also get on well with the Rat, Rabbit and Rooster, but will find the Ox and Snake a bit too quiet and serious for his liking and will be highly irritated by the Monkey's rather mischievous and inquisitive ways. He will also find it difficult to get on with another Tiger or a Dragon – both partners will want to dominate the relationship and could find it difficult to compromise on even the smallest of matters.

The Tigress is lively, witty and a marvellous hostess at parties. She takes great care over her appearance and is usually most attractive. She can be a very doting mother and while she believes in letting her children have their freedom, she makes an excellent teacher and will ensure that her children are well brought up and want for nothing. Like her male counterpart, she has numerous interests and likes to have sufficient freedom to go off and do the things she wants to do. She has a most caring and generous nature.

The Tiger has many commendable qualities. He is honest, courageous and often a source of inspiration to others. Providing he can curb the wilder excesses of his restless nature, he is almost certain to lead a fulfilling and satisfying life.

The Five Different Types of Tiger

In addition to the 12 signs of the Chinese zodiac there are five elements and these have a strengthening or moderating influence on the signs. The effects of the elements on the Tiger are described below, together with the years in which they were exercising their influence. Therefore Tigers born in 1950 and 2010 are Metal Tigers, Tigers born in 1962 are Water Tigers, and so on.

Metal Tiger: 1950, 2010

The Metal Tiger has an assertive and outgoing personality. He is very ambitious, and while his aims may change from time to time, he will work relentlessly until he has obtained what he wants. He can, however, be impatient for results and become highly strung if things do not work out as he would like. He is distinctive in his appearance and is admired and respected by many.

Water Tiger: 1962

This Tiger has a wide variety of interests and is always eager to experiment with new ideas or satisfy his adventurous nature by going off to explore distant lands. He is versatile, shrewd and has a kindly nature. He tends to remain calm in a crisis, although he can be annoyingly indecisive at times. He communicates well with others and through his many capabilities and persuasive nature usually achieves what he wants in life. He is also highly imaginative and is often a gifted orator or writer.

Wood Tiger: 1974

The Wood Tiger has a friendly and pleasant personality. He is less independent than some of the other types of Tiger and more prepared to work with others to secure a desired objective. However, he does have a tendency to jump from one thing to another and can easily become distracted. He is usually very popular, has a large circle of friends and invariably leads a busy and enjoyable social life. He also has a good sense of humour.

Fire Tiger: 1926, 1986

The Fire Tiger sets about everything he does with great verve and enthusiasm. He loves action and is always ready to throw himself wholeheartedly into anything that catches his imagination. He has many leadership qualities and is capable of communicating his ideas and enthusiasm to others. He is very much an optimist and can be most generous. He has a likeable nature and can be a witty and persuasive speaker.

Earth Tiger: 1938, 1998

This Tiger is responsible and level-headed. He studies everything objectively and tries to be scrupulously fair in all his dealings. Unlike other Tigers, he is prepared to specialize in certain areas rather than get distracted by other matters, but he can become so involved in what he is doing that he does not always take into account the opinions of those around him. He has good business sense and is usually very successful in later life. He has a large circle of friends and pays great attention to both his appearance and his reputation.

Prospects for the Tiger in 2017

The Year of the Monkey (8 February 2016–27 January 2017) will have been a mixed one for the Tiger and it may have seemed as if he was putting in a lot of effort but not getting the results he wanted. Although there will have been successes, there will also have been frustrations and the remaining months of the year will continue to be busy and demanding.

At work many Tigers could face extra pressures, with situations not always helped by office politics or niggling delays. However, by doing his best, the Tiger can still achieve some impressive results. Late October and November could be particularly active and see some interesting possibilities arising.

The Tiger will be keen to make some large purchases at this time, including special gifts. By taking his time he could be both lucky and pleased with what he buys. However, receipts and guarantees need to be kept safe and financial paperwork attended to with care.

On a personal level, the Tiger will be in demand. In his domestic life there will be many arrangements to discuss and activities to fit in. To prevent certain weeks becoming frenetic, ideally plans should be agreed on in advance. Busy though his home life can be, the Tiger can look forward to many special times, with December and early January often lively.

There will also be many social opportunities, although when in company the Tiger will need to be attentive to the views of others. Without care, there is a risk of a misunderstanding or embarrassing *faux pas*. Tigers, be warned.

While not an easy year, the Monkey year will have seen a lot happen and there will be much the Tiger can build on as the new year approaches.

The Year of the Rooster starts on 28 January and is a promising one for the Tiger. During it he can make substantial progress, although he does need to remain mindful of others. This is no time to go out on a limb or be too independent. The Tiger can have a rebellious streak and if he is to fare well in the Rooster year, this needs to be watched.

At work, however, the Tiger's prospects are encouraging and the Rooster year can bring some good (and sometimes overdue) rewards, in particular for Tigers who have struggled during the last year or feel they have not been making the progress they deserve. In many a workplace the Tiger's experience and in-house knowledge will lead to him taking on an increased role, while Tigers who work in a creative environment could see their input leading to some potentially exciting developments.

The Tiger can help his position by working well with others and seizing any chances to raise his profile. Good connections can place him in a strong position when promotion opportunities arise or someone is required for more specialist tasks.

For Tigers who are keen to move elsewhere, as well as those seeking work, advice from agencies and professional organizations could be helpful, along with talking to colleagues and friends. March, May, August and November could see some potentially important developments.

Progress at work can lead to an increase in income and the financial position of many Tigers can improve over the year. However, while more money may flow into the Tiger's account, without care it can all too easily flow out again. In particular he should guard against impulse buying. Hasty purchases could be regretted later.

Travel is favourably aspected this year and by planning ahead many Tigers can look forward to some often fascinating journeys. Some will appreciate the chance to visit family and friends living some distance away. With his adventurous nature, the Tiger is likely to make the most of the travel opportunities the year will bring.

Although he will be kept busy, he should also make sure his interests do not get sidelined. Tigers have an inventive streak and the Rooster year encourages creativity. Once the Tiger sets to work on an idea or project, it can often develop in surprising (and pleasing) ways.

With his outgoing nature, the Tiger will also appreciate the social opportunities of the year and welcome the chance to meet others. Some can be especially supportive, although to benefit the Tiger does need to be willing to share his thoughts. February, June, September and December could see the most social activity, although at most times of the year there will be people to see, things to do and events to enjoy.

For the unattached, there will also be excellent opportunities to meet others and romantic prospects are promising. In some instances, a meeting that takes place in fortuitous circumstances could become significant.

Domestically, the Rooster year will also see considerable activity, and flexibility and co-operation will be needed. With work changes and increasing pressures likely, some weeks could be demanding, with everyone needing to rally round. Good communication will be of great value.

In addition, to get the most from the year, the Tiger and his loved ones would find it useful to have some plans to work towards, perhaps home projects, a holiday, a forthcoming anniversary or a special event. Rooster years favour planning and co-operative effort.

There will be demanding times in many a Tiger household this year, but gratifying and memorable ones too. June, August and September could be especially pleasurable.

Overall, the Rooster year offers great scope for the enthusiastic Tiger. Both professionally and personally he will welcome the opportunity to put his talents to more effective use. He has much to offer, but it is important he also draws on the support of those around him and responds to developments. This is not a time for going it alone. The year will, however, have many pleasing elements. Travel is favourably aspected and there will be good times to share both domestically and socially. Though this will be a busy year, it will encourage the Tiger to develop and use his strengths well.

The Metal Tiger

The Rooster likes to look ahead and plan and this is what the Metal Tiger would do well to do this year. By giving some thought to what he would like to see happen, he will not only be able to channel his energies more effectively but also accomplish a surprising amount.

In his planning, he should discuss his ideas with those close to him. This way not only will he be better able to gauge their reaction but his initial ideas can often broaden out as well as get underway. This is a year favouring concerted action. Projects could include neatening and refreshing certain rooms as well as adding new comforts. As they are started, they will have a tendency to mushroom and become more wide-ranging.

As well as practical improvements, the Metal Tiger can look forward to some special moments in his home life. Celebrations are possible, and whether these involve a wedding, birth, graduation or the career success of someone close, there will be reason for the Metal Tiger to feel justifiably proud. There will also be ways in which he can assist, either with arrangements or advice. In some instances, his expertise will be especially pertinent.

Another positive factor will be the mutual support seen in many a Metal Tiger's household. He himself will benefit from the guidance of others, particularly with some purchasing choices. Similarly, when problems arise (as they do in any year), it is important they are fully aired and opinions sought. If particularly complex, it may be worth the Metal Tiger seeking professional guidance or contacting a helpline.

June, August and September could see pleasing domestic developments, although there will be a lot to appreciate throughout the year.

Travel is also strongly indicated, and Metal Tigers who have family and friends living some distance away should take up any chances to visit them. Similarly, if able, the Metal Tiger should plan a holiday over the year. By choosing his destination with care, he will be able to fit in a surprising amount as well as see new sights and enjoy new thrills.

For Metal Tigers in work, the Rooster year will be one of decision. While some of these Metal Tigers will continue to make good use of their experience, others could decide to reduce their commitments or retire. Such transitions may not initially be easy, but by making the most of their opportunities (including any additional time now available), these Metal Tigers will quickly come to embrace what opens up for them. The Metal Tiger has an enquiring nature and invariably new ideas and possibilities will occur to him.

This will especially be the case with his interests. While he will continue to enjoy the pursuits he has followed for many years, he may also decide to experiment with new approaches or teach himself a new skill. Metal Tigers enjoy challenge and mental stimulation, and this Rooster year will bring a variety of ideas and opportunities their way. The Metal Tiger may also be inspired by contact with other enthusiasts and could find it worth joining a local club, society or class.

He could also enjoy some financial good fortune, perhaps through receiving a bonus or gift or seeing the fruition of a policy. A lucky few may even enjoy a competition win. However, while the aspects are favourable, the Metal Tiger will rarely be short of spending ideas. To get the best value from his purchases, he needs to take the time to check his requirements are being met and compare options and costs. The greater care, the better. He should also ensure he keeps paperwork safe and is thorough when completing forms. A loss or mistake could result in protracted correspondence. Metal Tigers, take note.

Socially, there will be quite a few convivial occasions for the Metal Tiger to look forward to over the year, with February, June, September and December seeing a lot of activity. While a lot will go well, should a difference of opinion arise or an issue concern the Metal Tiger, he will need to tread warily. Without care, something which starts in a minor way could become awkward. Also, if another person has reservations about one of his ideas, he should listen. There could be reasons for this which he may not have fully taken on board. Metal Tigers, take note and be mindful of others.

In general, the Year of the Rooster can be a constructive one for the Metal Tiger. He can accomplish a great deal and enjoy the benefits and good times that follow on. He can also look forward to a certain amount of luck this year and circumstances will often assist in what he sets out to do. Travel, too, can bring considerable pleasure, as can family news and projects. It is a year to join forces with others rather than act too independently, but overall it is a good one for the Metal Tiger, with many plans developing in encouraging ways.

Tip for the Year
Take action. With your ideas and sense of purpose, together with the support you enjoy, a lot can happen for you. But be sure to consult others and pay attention to their views.

The Water Tiger

The Water Tiger is thoughtful, forward looking and open-minded. And as the Rooster year starts, he will feel more energized than of late. For Water Tigers who have considered their recent progress lacklustre or who want to pursue certain ambitions, this is a year for concerted action.

For many Water Tigers, their aspirations will be work-related. Having proved themselves in their current capacity, these Water Tigers will be keen to take on new challenges. And this year circumstances can assist them. In some cases senior colleagues will move on, creating ideal promotion opportunities, and in others more specialist positions will need to be filled. Over the year many Water Tigers will have the chance to advance their career.

For those who feel prospects are limited where they are, as well as those seeking work, the Rooster year can present some interesting possibilities. However, the Water Tiger will need to take the initiative, including making direct contact with prospective employers and seeking advice from professional organizations as well as talking to others. Whether by word of mouth or a more formal enquiry, he can, with persistence, find new ways forward. His drive and enthusiasm can be used to telling effect this year. March, May, August and November will see encouraging developments.

In addition to furthering professional knowledge, this is also a year favouring personal development. If there is a subject that intrigues the Water Tiger, a skill he wants to learn or a pursuit he is considering taking up, this is the ideal time to do it.

Quite a few Water Tigers will also give some thought to their lifestyle. Those who lead a pressured existence may make a conscious decision to set more time aside for themselves and their family. Some may also consider taking more exercise, improving their diet and setting aside time for recreation. Many benefits can follow on from actions taken this year.

The encouraging aspects also extend to money matters. Many Water Tigers will enjoy a rise in income and possibly also receive something extra. However, the Water Tiger will still need to manage his outgoings carefully and consider and cost his purchases rather than rush.

With this being an excellent year for travel, he would do well to make provision for a holiday or aim to enjoy a few days away every so often. Visits to friends and relatives living some distance away could appeal.

The element of water strengthens a sign's effectiveness as a communicator and this is especially true of the Tiger. The Water Tiger has a good way with words and is able to empathize with many people. Over the year his skills will be in demand, with several friends seeking his advice over what could be difficult matters. Here the Water Tiger's understanding can be meaningful and pertinent. February, June, September and December could see the most social activity and give the Water Tiger the chance to extend his social circle.

However, while much will go well, no year is ever without its troubling moments and in this one the Water Tiger could become concerned by a friendship issue. This could stem from a difference of opinion or someone's changing attitude. When the Water Tiger detects a potential difficulty, he needs to tread carefully. Here his perceptive nature will be of great value.

Domestically, the Water Tiger will often have ideas he is keen to pursue. Whether updating appliances, freshening up certain areas or, if he has a garden, adding new stock, he will relish implementing improvements. At times his home will be abuzz with activity. He does, however, need to be realistic with timescales and focus on specific undertakings rather than overcommit himself. With such a lot happening, there will inevitably be fraught moments, but with care and consideration these will be minimal and not overshadow the accomplishments and enjoyable family times of the year. June, August and September could see some pleasing domestic developments, including perhaps celebrations.

Overall, the Rooster year holds good prospects for the Water Tiger and encourages him to make more of his strengths both professionally and personally. He will be in demand socially, while in his domestic life he can accomplish a great deal. Pressures and occasional rifts need to be watched, but with good use of his time and a good lifestyle balance, he can gain a lot from this favourable year.

Tip for the Year

Involve others in your thinking and planning. With their input and goodwill, so much more can open up for you. You have much to offer this year and can achieve some good results that you can build on in the future.

The Wood Tiger

Over the last few years the Wood Tiger will have learned a great deal and his patience and effort are about to be rewarded. This is very much a time for building *and* moving forward.

The Wood Tiger's work situation is especially well aspected and there will be good opportunities for him to move his career forward. Senior colleagues may make recommendations, offer new responsibilities and provide references and there could also be a lot going on behind the scenes that works out to the Wood Tiger's advantage.

While the majority of Wood Tigers will make progress with their current employer, for those who feel their long-term prospects could be bettered by a move elsewhere, as well as those seeking work, the Rooster year can bring some good possibilities. Contacts can be helpful here, as can the Wood Tiger's reputation. Similarly, if there is a particular type of work he wishes to do, he should approach companies and professional organizations directly. Initiative can open important doors this year. March, May, August and November could see key developments, but progress is possible throughout this encouraging year and when the Wood Tiger learns of an opening, he should act without delay.

Another factor in his favour is the good working relations he enjoys with those around him and over the year he should continue to meet others in his line of work. As has often been found, the more people you know, the greater your likelihood of learning about opportunities or knowing someone in a position to help you. And in the Rooster year it is the Wood Tiger's contacts, reputation and personal qualities that will lead to success.

Progress at work will often lead an increase in income and some Wood Tigers will also benefit from a gift or bonus payment. In view of this, the Wood Tiger will be keen to go ahead with several plans and purchases, often related to his accommodation. However, he should not act hastily. By waiting he could make savings or obtain something superior to his original choice.

Travel is strongly indicated this year and where possible the Wood Tiger should make provision for a holiday or at least aim to enjoy a break. With his busy lifestyle he does need a respite now and then and a change of scene can do him good.

Although he will have many commitments, it is also important he does not allow his personal interests to get sidelined. Not only can these provide an outlet for certain talents but they can also have a social element and/or provide additional exercise. If there are specific skills the Wood Tiger would like to learn, he should take action. The aspects are encouraging and substantial benefits can be gained.

The Rooster year will also see the Wood Tiger valuing his chances to meet up with his friends. Some will be especially helpful, and by talking over his hopes and activities, the Wood Tiger could be given the exact information or support he needs. In 2017 he will have many people rooting for him and keen to help. As a result of his active lifestyle, he will also have an excellent chance to extend his social network. February,

June, September and December could see the most social opportunities.

For Wood Tigers who start the year alone or dispirited, perhaps having suffered a recent disappointment, there can be encouraging developments in store. By pursuing their interests, participating in groups and taking advantage of what is available locally, they can make valuable new friendships. And where matters of the heart are concerned, a new romance could develop in exciting ways.

However, while much will go well, no year is without its problems and the Wood Tiger could have misgivings about a certain situation or find a minor difference of opinion irritating. Whenever possible, he should speak of his concerns rather than keep them bottled up. Also, at busy times, he may come across as preoccupied and this may lead to awkward moments. Wood Tigers, take note. This is a good year for you, but be vigilant and attentive, especially when pressures are great.

In his home life the Wood Tiger will again busy himself with many activities and will find that by combining his efforts with those of others, he can considerably enhance his home. He should also be prepared to offer advice and assistance, as other family members are likely to be involved in decision-making this year. His partner may be in a work-related quandary and if he is a parent there could be education choices to address. Senior relations too may be grateful for his help. The Wood Tiger's thoughtfulness will, however, be appreciated, as will activities he may suggest, such as a holiday, local trips and other treats. June, August and September could see active and often special times in the Wood Tiger home.

Overall, the Year of the Rooster will be a constructive one for the Wood Tiger. At work he has talents and experience to build on and by looking to further his position, he is set to do well. Importantly, what is achieved this year can be a springboard for future progress. He will also be encouraged by the good support he enjoys. With a busy lifestyle, he does need to preserve some time to enjoy with family and friends as well as in developing his interests. But he has a lot in his favour this year and his efforts can lead to some worthy accomplishments.

Tip for the Year

Develop your skills and knowledge. What you do now can prove to be an investment in your future. Also, value your good relations with those around you, for their support can be potentially significant as well as enrich your lifestyle.

The Fire Tiger

The Fire Tiger possesses great resolve and has a happy knack of making the best of situations. He is resourceful and ambitious and his talents will serve him well this year.

At work many Fire Tigers will have recently experienced change, including an increase in responsibility. Although they may consider they are still learning about the different aspects of their role, the changes are far from over. Rooster years can bring surprise developments and opportunities can arise in unexpected ways. Some Fire Tigers will be offered training that will enable them to take on other duties or concentrate on a more specialist area. Others will find colleagues moving on and creating roles to fill or, if in a large organization, see the chance for a transfer to another department. As the year starts, some Fire Tigers may not actually be seeking change, but openings *will* come their way.

For Fire Tigers who are keen to take on something different, as well as those seeking work, the Rooster year can again bring surprises. These Fire Tigers should keep alert for openings but also talk to friends, colleagues and contacts. By chance they could hear of an ideal opportunity. Others will apply for a position on the off-chance and then be presented with an interesting offer. The Rooster year can be marked by several fortunate developments. March, May, August and November could be significant months.

The Fire Tiger's prospects will also be helped by his ability to forge good working relations with his colleagues and throughout the year he should continue to make connections. Getting himself known can not only help his present position but his future too.

Progress at work can lead to an increase in income, but with all his plans and activities, as well as his existing commitments, the Fire Tiger's outgoings are likely to be high and he will need to manage his budget carefully. Some Fire Tigers may be involved in putting down accommodation deposits and this will require discipline. In addition, the Fire Tiger should draw on the knowledge of professionals where necessary. With assistance, and awareness of the implications, his financial decisions can be both easier and sounder.

Where personal interests are concerned, this is an excellent year for the Fire Tiger to develop his skills. What he does now can not only be personally satisfying but also lead to new possibilities. Whether his interests are creative, practical, outdoor-related or just pleasurable, he should allow himself the time to pursue them this year.

In addition, he would do well to give some thought to his well-being and, if lacking regular exercise, consider taking up an appropriate activity. Similarly, if his diet is deficient, he should aim to eat more nutritious food. To keep on good form, he is advised to look after himself this year.

Taking a holiday or break will also do him good. Travel is well aspected this year and can satisfy many a Fire Tiger's adventurous nature. Some travel opportunities could arise through work and/or last-minute offers. The festive season and new year are also likely to be busy times.

With his outgoing nature, the Fire Tiger knows many people and will once again find himself in demand this year. There will be a variety of things for him to do and take pleasure in. Unattached and lonely Fire Tigers will find that by taking up opportunities to go out, they can meet new people and put some sparkle back into their life. It will take effort, but be well worthwhile. The Rooster year has the capacity to surprise and delight, including romantically. February, June, September and December could see the most social activity.

Domestically, a lot is set to happen. For Fire Tigers with a partner this can be an especially busy year. Not only will both partners be contending with commitments and possible work changes, but there will be accommodation plans and purchases to decide on and sometimes other family members to assist. Some weeks will be demanding, but by being supportive and using his time well, the Fire Tiger can accomplish a lot and win the gratitude of those he helps out.

Hectic though parts of the year may be, it will also contain its memorable moments. There will be personal successes to enjoy, and if the Fire Tiger is a parent, he will delight in his child's progress. Here his enthusiasm and encouragement can be especially effective. Taking a holiday and visiting local attractions and places of interest could also bring pleasure to all concerned, and the Fire Tiger's ideas will often add variety to family life. June, August and September could be rewarding months.

No year is ever without its problems, however, and in this one the Fire Tiger will need to be open and communicative as well as show some patience, particularly at busy times. To be preoccupied or unresponsive could lead to awkward moments. Should a disagreement or other difficulty occur, rather than ignore it and risk it escalating, he should strive to resolve the issue. Fire Tigers, take note.

In many respects, the Rooster year will be an encouraging one for the Fire Tiger. At work there will be opportunities to develop skills and make progress, and personal interests too can develop well. The emphasis of the Rooster year is on growth. The Fire Tiger will be encouraged by the support he receives, with some connections proving especially helpful, and his domestic and social life can give rise to many good times. The Fire Tiger does need to ensure his lifestyle is balanced and to remain his attentive self, but overall, this is a good year for him and one in which to move forward.

Tip for the Year
Be receptive. Although some developments may surprise you, they could be of benefit. Be open-minded and investigate. A lot will happen for a reason this year and you have a lot to gain.

The Earth Tiger

This promises to be a full and active 12 months for the Earth Tiger and he would do well to remember the Chinese proverb 'Diligence leads to riches.' This year it really is worth him putting in the effort and striving to do his best.

For Earth Tigers in education there will be a lot to do. At times the demands will be considerable and some Earth Tigers will have doubts about what they are doing or struggle in certain areas. However, through their current work many will become aware of which strengths and subjects they want to focus on in the future and will even consider possible vocations. New courses or subjects can also open up possibilities.

It is important that these Earth Tigers make full use of the resources available to them, whether these are connected with their studying or their own interests. Often their place of education will have good facilities. Support, too, will be available and if the Earth Tiger has concerns at any time or finds himself wondering about future options, he should be forthcoming and seek advice. Being proactive and participating are key factors this year.

For Earth Tigers in work, the Rooster year can also bring the chance to prove themselves in new capacities. By making the most of their opportunities, these Earth Tigers can not only make progress but also see their commitment noticed and rewarded. Again, diligence leads to riches.

For Earth Tigers seeking work, this can be a challenging time with competition fierce. However, by showing initiative, including finding out more about the company and the duties involved, these Earth Tigers will often impress others and be offered that all-important opportunity. And once in a new position, if they involve themselves in their place of work, they could soon see their strengths being noticed and encouraged and other possibilities becoming available. March, May, August and November could see interesting developments.

The Earth Tiger will continue to derive pleasure from his personal interests over the year and, with his often inventive streak, will have ideas he is keen to carry out. Some Earth Tigers could greatly benefit from the guidance of experts, while others could be tempted by the challenge of new activities. This year it is very much a case of embracing and enjoying what occurs.

Travel is also positively indicated and the Earth Tiger will enjoy seeing new places and visiting lively attractions. August and September could be interesting months travel-wise.

With his active lifestyle, the Earth Tiger will have many outgoings, however, and if he is to do all he wants he will need to be disciplined in his spending and avoid succumbing to too many impulse buys. With care, he can manage well, though, and may be helped by a generous gift or surprise payment.

On a social level, he will find himself in demand. Much fun can be had with his circle of friends and there will be thoughts (and some secrets) to be shared and parties and other occasions to be enjoyed. Earth Tigers who may be feeling lonely or unsettled as a result of recent changes could see someone new entering their life and a potentially important friendship developing. Involvement will be rewarded this year and all Earth Tigers should make the most of the social groups, facilities and events on offer where they are. February, June, September and December could be particularly pleasing months.

As with every year, though, problems will sometimes arise and the Earth Tiger could have misgivings about a particular situation or the attitude of another person. If so, he needs to proceed carefully and, in some cases, exercise patience and wait for situations to settle down and reason to prevail. To respond hastily or act against his better judgement could cause difficulty. Earth Tigers, take note, and if troubled, act with care and allow time for the resolution of any worrying situation.

In view of the decisions and pressures he may face, it is also important that the Earth Tiger is forthcoming with family members and shares any matters on his mind. He may like to take responsibility for a great deal, but his loved ones do want to help and can sometimes assist in significant ways. In turn, the Earth Tiger will find that contributing to family life can help rapport as well as lead to some fine occasions. A key ingredient of this year is involvement and the more the Earth Tiger gives of himself, the more he will benefit.

Overall, the Rooster year will require discipline and commitment, but it will bring opportunities and what the Earth Tiger achieves can prove important in his future development. In addition, he can learn a lot about himself and his potential this year. His social life and personal interests can bring him considerable pleasure and a new friendship may become significant. With his verve, ideas and enquiring nature, the Earth

Tiger has much to offer and the Rooster year will help him develop his potential.

Tip for the Year
Resolve to do your best. A lot will be asked of you this year, but with diligence you will learn skills, acquire knowledge and benefit personally. You know in your heart that you are special – this is a year to show that and to work towards the riches that lie ahead.

Famous Tigers

Paula Abdul, Amy Adams, Kofi Annan, Sir David Attenborough, Christian Bale, Victoria Beckham, Beethoven, Jamie Bell, Tony Bennett, Tom Berenger, Chuck Berry, Usain Bolt, Jon Bon Jovi, Sir Richard Branson, Matthew Broderick, Emily Brontë, Garth Brooks, Mel Brooks, Isambard Kingdom Brunel, Agatha Christie, Suzanne Collins, Robbie Coltrane, Bradley Cooper, Sheryl Crow, Tom Cruise, Penelope Cruz, Lana Del Rey, Leonardo DiCaprio, Emily Dickinson, Drake, Dwight Eisenhower, Queen Elizabeth II, Enya, Frederick Forsyth, Jodie Foster, Megan Fox, Lady Gaga, Crystal Gayle, Ellie Goulding, Buddy Greco, Germaine Greer, Ed Harris, Hugh Hefner, William Hurt, Ray Kroc, Shia LaBeouf, Stan Laurel, Jay Leno, Groucho Marx, Karl Marx, Marilyn Monroe, Demi Moore, Alanis Morissette, Rafael Nadal, Robert Pattinson, Marco Polo, Beatrix Potter, Renoir, Nora Roberts, Kenny Rogers, the Princess Royal, Dylan Thomas, Julie Walters, H. G. Wells, Oscar Wilde, Robbie Williams, Tennessee Williams, Sir Terry Wogan, Stevie Wonder, William Wordsworth.

2 February 1927 to 22 January 1928 — *Fire Rabbit*

19 February 1939 to 7 February 1940 — *Earth Rabbit*

6 February 1951 to 26 January 1952 — *Metal Rabbit*

25 January 1963 to 12 February 1964 — *Water Rabbit*

11 February 1975 to 30 January 1976 — *Wood Rabbit*

29 January 1987 to 16 February 1988 — *Fire Rabbit*

16 February 1999 to 4 February 2000 — *Earth Rabbit*

3 February 2011 to 22 January 2012 — *Metal Rabbit*

The Rabbit

The Personality of the Rabbit

Whenever
Wherever
With whoever.
Always I try to understand.
Without this, one flounders.
But with understanding,
at least you have a chance.
A good chance.

The Rabbit is born under the signs of virtue and prudence. He is intelligent, well-mannered and prefers a quiet and peaceful existence. He dislikes any sort of unpleasantness and will try to steer clear of arguments and disputes. He is very much a pacifist and tends to have a calming influence on those around him. He has wide interests and usually a good appreciation of the arts and the finer things in life. He also knows how to enjoy himself and will often gravitate to the best restaurants and nightspots in town.

The Rabbit is a witty and intelligent speaker and loves being involved in a good discussion. His views and advice are often sought by others and he can be relied upon to be discreet and diplomatic. He will rarely raise his voice in anger and will even turn a blind eye to matters that displease him just to preserve the peace. He likes to remain on good terms with everyone, but he can be rather sensitive and takes any form of criticism very badly. He will also be the first to get out of the way if he sees any form of trouble brewing.

The Rabbit is a quiet and efficient worker and has an extremely good memory. He is very astute in business and financial matters, but his degree of success often depends on the conditions that prevail. He hates being in a situation which is fraught with tension or where he has to make sudden decisions. Wherever possible, he will plan his various activities with the utmost care and a good deal of caution. He does not like to take risks and does not take kindly to change. Basically, he seeks a secure, calm and stable environment, and when conditions are right he is more than happy to leave things as they are.

The Rabbit is conscientious and because of his methodical and ever-watchful nature he can often do well in his chosen profession. He makes a good diplomat, lawyer, shopkeeper, administrator or priest, and he excels in any job where he can use his superb skills as a communicator. He tends to be loyal to his employers and is respected for his integrity and honesty, but if he ever finds himself in a position of great power he can become rather intransigent and authoritarian.

The Rabbit attaches great importance to his home and will often spend a lot of time and money maintaining and furnishing it and fitting it with all the latest comforts – the Rabbit is very much a creature of comfort! He is also something of a collector and there are many Rabbits who derive much pleasure from collecting antiques, stamps, coins, *objets d'art* or anything else which catches their eye or particularly interests them.

The female Rabbit has a friendly, caring and considerate nature, and will do all in her power to give her home a happy and loving atmosphere. She is also very sociable and enjoys holding parties and entertaining. She has a great ability to make the maximum use of her time and although she involves herself in numerous activities, she always manages to find time to sit back and enjoy a good read or a chat. She has a great sense of humour, is very artistic and is often a talented gardener.

The Rabbit takes considerable care over his appearance and is usually smart and well turned out. He also attaches great importance to his relations with others and matters of the heart are particularly important to him. He will rarely be short of admirers and will often have several serious romances before he settles down. He is not the most faithful of signs, but he will find that he is especially well suited to those born under the signs of the Goat, Snake, Pig and Ox. Due to his sociable and easy-going manner he can also get on well with the Tiger, Dragon, Horse, Monkey, Dog and another Rabbit, but he will feel ill at ease with the Rat and Rooster, as both these signs tend to speak their mind and be critical in their comments and the Rabbit just loathes any form of criticism or unpleasantness.

The Rabbit is usually lucky in life and often has the happy knack of being in the right place at the right time. He is talented and quick-witted, but he does sometimes put pleasure before work and wherever possible will opt for the easy life. He can at times be a little reserved and suspicious of the motives of others, but generally will lead a long and contented life and one which – as far as possible – will be free of strife and discord.

The Five Different Types of Rabbit

In addition to the 12 signs of the Chinese zodiac there are five elements and these have a strengthening or moderating influence on the signs. The effects of the elements on the Rabbit are described below, together with the years in which they were exercising their influence. Therefore Rabbits born in 1951 and 2011 are Metal Rabbits, Rabbits born in 1963 are Water Rabbits, and so on.

Metal Rabbit: 1951, 2011

This Rabbit is capable, ambitious and has very definite views on what he wants to achieve in life. He can occasionally appear reserved and aloof, but this is mainly because he likes to keep his thoughts to himself. He has a quick and alert mind and is particularly shrewd in business matters. He can also be very cunning in his actions. He has a good appreciation of the arts and likes to mix in the best circles. He usually has a small but very loyal group of friends.

Water Rabbit: 1963

The Water Rabbit is popular, intuitive and keenly aware of the feelings of those around him. He can, however, be rather sensitive and take things too much to heart. He is very precise and thorough in everything he does and has an exceedingly good memory. He tends to be quiet and at times rather withdrawn, but he expresses his ideas well and is highly regarded by his family, friends and colleagues.

Wood Rabbit: 1975

The Wood Rabbit is likeable, easy-going and very adaptable. He prefers to work in a group rather than on his own and likes to have the support and encouragement of others. He can, however, be rather reticent in expressing his views and it would be in his own interests to become a little more open and let others know how he feels on certain matters. He usually has many friends, enjoys an active social life and is noted for his generosity.

Fire Rabbit: 1927, 1987

The Fire Rabbit has a friendly, outgoing personality. He likes socializing and being on good terms with everyone. He is discreet and diplomatic and has a very good understanding of human nature. He is also strong-willed and provided he has the necessary backing he can go far in life. He does, not, however, suffer adversity well and can become moody and depressed when things are not working out as he would like. He has a particularly good manner with children, is very intuitive and there are some Fire Rabbits who are even noted for their psychic ability.

Earth Rabbit: 1939, 1999

The Earth Rabbit is a quiet individual, but nevertheless very astute. He is realistic in his aims and prepared to work long and hard in order to achieve his objectives. He has good business sense and is invariably lucky in financial matters. He also has a most persuasive manner and usually experiences little difficulty in getting others to fall in with his plans. He is held in high esteem by his friends and colleagues and his views are often sought and highly valued.

Prospects for the Rabbit in 2017

The Year of the Monkey (8 February 2016–27 January 2017) will have been a mixed one for the Rabbit and although his efforts will have brought some rewards, he will have faced challenges. There could have been awkward situations to address and the Rabbit or someone close to him may have had a health worry. Monkey years test the Rabbit, but as this one draws to a close he will have resolved many issues and can look forward to some interesting possibilities arising.

The Rabbit's home and social life will see an increased level of activity, with arrangements to make, friends and relations to meet and domestic projects to complete. Often these will involve purchases for the home, and by drawing on the advice of his loved ones, the Rabbit will be pleased with what is acquired. Late November and early December could see a flurry of practical activity.

With expenditure on the home and other purchases too, this will be an expensive time, however, and the Rabbit would be well advised to keep track of his spending. Monkey years require financial vigilance.

Work-wise, the Rabbit could face a heavier workload with some tight deadlines to meet and/or additional demands. It will be an exacting time, but with focus and good use of his skills, he can achieve some impressive results which win him some plaudits. He should also actively pursue any career opportunities he sees, as potentially important developments can follow on.

The Monkey year will have asked a lot of the Rabbit, but despite its challenges he will have gained valuable skills and experience.

One of the Rabbit's talents is his ability to read situations and act accordingly. When he feels confident and excited by possibilities, he is prepared to act swiftly and take chances, but when he has reservations, he tends to hold back. And for parts of the Rooster year, this is exactly what he will opt to do. Rooster years bristle with activity and the Rabbit will not always be comfortable with the heady pace of this one. Rabbits like a certain freedom to express themselves, engage in creative thought or just get on with their activities unimpeded. Rooster years do not tend to suit their temperament. However, if the Rabbit exercises caution and responds well to the developments of this Rooster year, which starts on 28 January, it can still have unexpected delights for him.

One area which is particularly well aspected is the Rabbit's own personal development. With his enquiring mind, he is certainly inventive and enjoys using his skills in new ways, and during the year he should set time aside to develop areas of interest to him. Whether starting new projects, learning different techniques or upgrading equipment so that he can do more with it, by furthering his knowledge and skills, he can learn a great deal and enjoy himself in the process. Some Rabbits, including those who lead particularly busy lives, may decide to take up a new interest and will delight in learning new skills. Rooster years, despite their vexations, can be personally illuminating for the Rabbit.

If the Rabbit is sedentary for much of the day and/or keen to improve his fitness levels, he will also benefit from paying some attention to his well-being. By taking advice, and action, many could notice a real improvement as well as discover an exercise regime they especially enjoy.

At work, the aspects are more challenging. Some Rabbits may be concerned by office politics and proposed reorganization, while others may feel hindered by bureaucracy or other problems and that their initiative is being stifled. Parts of the year will be difficult and the Rabbit may opt to keep a low profile and just concentrate on the tasks in hand. This is a year for patience and knuckling down.

However, difficult though some months may be, Rooster years are not without opportunity, and Rabbits who are keen to move from where they are will find that enquiries made now may lead to new (and often different) positions being found. Progress will not necessarily be easy this year, but what the Rabbit is able to achieve can be significant in the longer term, especially with the opportunities that await in the following Dog year.

For Rabbits seeking work, securing a position will require great effort, but by having faith in themselves, many will prevail. Importantly, what is started now can be a platform to build on in the future. Amid difficulty there *is* opportunity, and the opportunities that come this year will often have long-term value. March, June, August and September could see important developments, but opportunities need to be seized quickly throughout the year.

Another area which requires care is finance. Although usually adept in money matters, the Rabbit needs to check the terms and implications of his transactions as well as keep his financial documents and guarantees safe. If lending to another person, care is needed, and should the Rabbit have concerns over a situation, including what he may be told, he should check the actual position. Rabbits, take note. This is no year to be lax.

With his amiable nature, the Rabbit enjoys company and his close social circle is important to him. Over the year he will particularly value the chance to talk to his friends and perhaps share his current vexations. In many instances, good friends will be able to respond in useful ways. In addition the Rooster year can bring some good social opportunities, especially local events and special occasions. April, July, October and December could be particularly active months, and for unattached Rabbits and those who are feeling lonely, the Rooster year may bring the gift of an important new friend and, for some, partner. On a personal level, the Rooster year can surprise and delight.

The Rabbit's home life will also be special. At home he can often escape the frustrations of work and other concerns, enjoy the company of his loved ones and content himself with satisfying pursuits. Sharing his thoughts will also help ease certain burdens and he will be reassured by the support of those around him. There will also be family activities to enjoy, often instigated by the Rabbit himself. His input and thoughtfulness can make an important difference to his household this year. April, August and December could be active and pleasurable months and bring travel possibilities.

Overall, the Rooster year will ask a lot of the Rabbit, but by proceeding carefully, he can steer his way round the more awkward aspects and gain new skills, friends and experience along the way. Progress will not be easy, but what is achieved now can be to the Rabbit's long-term benefit. More positively, he can take great pleasure in developing his interests, and his home and social life are favourably aspected. This may not be the easiest of years, but the Rabbit has a talent for making the best of his situation and, with vigilance, can do so now.

The Metal Rabbit

The Metal Rabbit is both efficient and thorough. Not only does he use his time well, but he takes an interest in many subjects. In the Rooster year he will find himself with a lot to do and a few problems mixed in with the more pleasurable activities. Rooster years can have awkward aspects which may test the skills and patience of the Metal Rabbit.

One area which will require particular care is finance. When considering any large outlay, the Metal Rabbit needs to check that his requirements are being met and only proceed when he is fully satisfied. Important paperwork also requires close attention and the Metal Rabbit should make sure policies (especially insurance ones) are kept up-to-date and are sufficient for his needs. This is a year for vigilance and scrutiny.

Although many Metal Rabbits are retired, those in work could see the Rooster year testing their skills and fortitude. Whether dealing with new approaches or tricky problems, the Metal Rabbit will not always find his duties straightforward. However, while some weeks could be demanding, the Metal Rabbit's years of experience will stand him in good stead and he can gain credit for his current efforts and, if he does now retire, be heartened by the esteem shown by colleagues and friends. March, June, August and September could be significant months, including for decision-making.

The Metal Rabbit has wide interests and over the year these can broaden out even further. For those who are considering learning a new skill, enrolling on a course or taking up a new pursuit, this is a year to take action. Local facilities could prove useful and cultural pursuits are well aspected, so the Metal Rabbit could particularly enjoy visits to museums, galleries and events held in his area.

He could also be inspired by projects he sets himself. Metal Rabbits who enjoy writing (and the Metal Rabbit is a good communicator) could take pleasure in what they produce, including sometimes their memoirs. Outdoor activities, too, can be of benefit, including visiting open spaces, travelling and, for the sports enthusiast, following sporting events.

Throughout the year the Metal Rabbit will also value his contact with his friends, including the chance to exchange news and test out ideas. At some time a close friend could have a concern or difficulty to address and here the Metal Rabbit's consideration can be much appreciated. When troubled himself, he should be equally open and let others assist. He does a lot for others and support needs to be reciprocal.

Many of the activities the Metal Rabbit engages in over the year will have a good social element and Metal Rabbits who would welcome more company will find that if they partake in what is available, they will have the chance to meet like-minded people and make some good friends. April, July, October and December could see the most social activity.

Domestically, this will also be a full and interesting year. As always, the Metal Rabbit will take a deep interest in the activities of family members and do much to support and advise. Younger relations could have some key decisions to take, particularly concerning a possible vocation, and here the Metal Rabbit's thoughts (and sometimes experience) can be a helpful guide. The Metal Rabbit can also look forward to some celebratory family occasions which, with his organizational skills, he will often help arrange.

There will also be several opportunities to travel, and sights seen and experiences shared while away can be among the year's highlights. April, August and December could be special months in many a Metal Rabbit household.

The Metal Rabbit will be keen to start several domestic projects too, including updating equipment and adding new comforts, but it is important that these are fully discussed and all viewpoints considered. While the Metal Rabbit is usually accommodating, any single-mindedness could cause some awkward moments. Metal Rabbits, take note.

The Metal Rabbit generally takes good care of himself and keeps active, but if he feels his level of exercise is deficient or diet lacking this year, he should seek advice on the best ways to improve. Similarly if he has any health concerns, he should get these checked out.

Despite the variable aspects, the Rooster year will certainly bring its rewarding times. There will be a lot to share with others and the Metal Rabbit's personal interests can also bring pleasure, particularly as new ideas and possibilities arise. Domestic projects, too, can be satisfying. However, paperwork and money matters require close attention. When faced with problems and concerns, the Metal Rabbit should proceed cautiously and draw on the support of those around him. Some of the Rooster year will challenge him, but the Metal Rabbit is adept and aware and despite the year's trickier elements, he will do a lot and, true to form, make the best of many a situation.

Tip for the Year

Avoid risk or haste. When making decisions, be thorough and ask questions. Also, look to develop your personal interests. These can be a good channel for your talents and develop in satisfying ways.

The Water Rabbit

The last few years will have been eventful for the Water Rabbit. There will have been successes but also disappointments. He may feel frustrated and consider he could have made more of certain strengths. However, he can take heart. He will have gained new insights as well as learned a lot about himself and his capabilities, and in the Rooster year this pattern will continue. While not always an easy year for the Water Rabbit, it can nevertheless be constructive *and* significant.

In his work the Water Rabbit could face uncomfortable moments. Rooster years bristle with activity and organizational changes may take place and demanding objectives be set. However, the Water Rabbit has experience and, despite misgivings, if he is willing to adapt and make the best of situations, his commitment may lead to a greater role and/or promotion. Also, if he detects new trends in his profession or industry, he should pay close attention to them. They can open up possibilities for the near future.

Many Water Rabbits will make important headway in their present place of work this year, but for those who desire change or are seeking work, new doors can open. By keeping alert for opportunities and considering other ways of using their skills, many of these Water Rabbits could take on a different position with the potential for future development. What happens this year will sometimes take the Water Rabbit out of his comfort zone but will also bring the incentive he needs. March, June, August to early October could see potentially significant developments.

Although the Water Rabbit may enjoy a rise in income this year, vigilance is required in financial matters. When entering into a new agreement or considering a substantial purchase, he should check the details and obligations and if in doubt seek further advice. Bureaucratic matters too could be problematic and need close attention. By nature the Water Rabbit is thorough, but extra care is advised this year. If he lends money or is tempted by a speculation, he should exercise caution and be aware of the implications. Water Rabbits, take note.

Some of the Water Rabbit's expenditure this year will be on his home. However, here again he should exercise care, as often alterations will become more extensive than envisaged. However, his eye for style and functionality will be on excellent form and some areas of his home will be considerably enhanced over the year. Project-wise, this can be a satisfying albeit expensive time.

Amid the practical activity, there will also be special occasions to enjoy. Personal successes can be particularly meaningful and the Water Rabbit will follow the progress of younger family members with keen interest. He will also appreciate the way many undertakings are shared. Support and advice can be of real value to him this year, especially during more difficult times. Domestically, this will be a full and promising year.

The Water Rabbit will also enjoy the social opportunities that arise over the year. There will be a good mix of things to do and by going out the Water Rabbit can bring balance to his lifestyle as well as have the chance to try out new pursuits. April, July, October and December could see the most social activity and it would reward Water Rabbits who are alone and/or feeling dispirited to find out about activities available in their area and participate in them. Pleasingly, new friendships and contacts can be made.

The encouraging aspects also extend to the Water Rabbit's interests. A new idea or way of developing an existing interest can prove particularly inspiring. The enquiring mind of many a Water Rabbit will be whetted by new pursuits this year. Contact with other enthusiasts may also be helpful.

The Water Rabbit should also give some consideration to his general level of exercise and diet this year, and if he has concerns, he should seek advice. To keep on good form he does need to look after himself.

If possible, he should also aim to take a break this year and should follow up travel ideas and invitations.

By the end of the year the Water Rabbit may be surprised by the amount he has managed to do. Admittedly, great effort will have been involved and there will have been problems to overcome. Rooster years do not make things easy for the Rabbit, but the Water Rabbit is blessed with tenacity and many other fine qualities and these will have enabled him to triumph over many of the year's frustrations. Work-wise, the talents of many Water Rabbits will have led to progress being made. But of key value this year will be the Water Rabbit's personal life, and his family, close friends and interests can all bring him joy. Overall, a demanding year, but still one of good possibility.

Tip for the Year
Enjoy time with those who are special to you and pursue your interests. Activities which highlight your talents can add an important ingredient to your year and are worth developing.

The Wood Rabbit

The element of wood helps to reinforce a sign's practical abilities and this is certainly evident in the Wood Rabbit. He is likes to keep himself active and is keen to make the most of his situation, and his qualities will serve him well in this busy year.

At work, many Wood Rabbits will have established themselves in a certain role and will have considerable experience behind them. Over the year, employers will often be keen to harness their skills by offering them greater duties or encouraging them to apply for promotion. The Wood Rabbit may not have anticipated what opens up for him, but will be encouraged to move his career forward. The new responsibilities he takes on will demand a lot of him and time will be needed to settle into any new role, but over the year he will have the chance to prove himself in new ways and, in the process, help his future prospects.

Most Wood Rabbits will remain with their present employer this year, but for those who feel their prospects could be improved by a move elsewhere or are seeking work, the Rooster year can have surprising developments in store. By chance, some of these Wood Rabbits may be alerted to a position which is very different from what they have done before but offers an ideal challenge. Others may seek out positions with particular employers. By keeping alert and exploring possibilities, many Wood Rabbits will secure the chance they desire this year. March, June and mid-August to the end of September could see important developments.

Progress made at work will lead to an increase in income for many Wood Rabbits, but financial matters require close attention. When considering large outlays, the Wood Rabbit should ideally budget ahead. Throughout the year he should be wary of risk and be particularly careful if tempted by anything speculative or lending to another person. In all instances he needs to check the facts, exercise caution and, if necessary, seek professional advice. It is better to be safe than sorry.

However, while the Wood Rabbit will need to keep watch on his spending, if possible he should make provision for travel. With the pressures of the year, a break will do him a lot of good.

Also, while often busy, he should set aside time for his interests and recreational pursuits. These will not only help keep his lifestyle in balance but may give him the benefit of additional exercise and be an outlet for certain talents. With his practical disposition, he could have specific ideas he is keen to develop or become enthused by new equipment or pursuits. The Rooster year is one of interesting possibilities.

It is also an excellent year for the Wood Rabbit to network and raise his profile. April, July, October and December could see pleasing social events and other occasions. Wood Rabbits who are lonely will find that by taking an interest in activities in their area and perhaps joining community groups, important new friendships can be made.

However, while the aspects are encouraging, the Wood Rabbit could find himself assisting a friend or relation in a difficult situation this year. As a Rabbit, he dislikes awkwardness and will have concerns, but the support he gives can be of real value. Other people regard him highly and their opinion will be justified this year.

The Wood Rabbit always attaches great importance to his home life and in view of the pressures arising this year, this can be a welcome refuge. At home he will enjoy sharing activities with his loved ones and initiating projects, including some pleasing enhancements to his home and garden (if he has one). Once again his attentiveness and input can bring interesting experiences to his household. April, August and December could be lively and gratifying months.

Generally, the Rooster year will be a busy one for the Wood Rabbit. While it will bring its pressures, it will also contain excellent opportunities to develop particular strengths. At work, interesting (if unanticipated) opportunities can come the Wood Rabbit's way and the emphasis will be on personal and professional development. Money matters require care and the Wood Rabbit should proceed cautiously if he finds himself in a difficult situation. But his personal interests and social and domestic life are all well aspected. A demanding but constructive year.

Tip for the Year
Enjoy quality time with your loved ones and share plans and activities. These can bring you much pleasure. Career prospects can also develop encouragingly, but, as with so much this year, it will be a case of venturing forth and making the most of emerging opportunities.

The Fire Rabbit

This will be a significant year for the Fire Rabbit. Not only does it mark the start of a new decade in his life but its developments will have long-term value. Its importance should not be underestimated.

Of especial value to the Fire Rabbit will be the love and support of those around him. Personally and domestically, there will be exciting events in store, which can include achieving a cherished aim. Throughout the year the Fire Rabbit will enjoy sharing activities with his loved ones and his almost infectious enthusiasm will help carry a lot forward.

In addition to the pleasure shared activities will bring, many Fire Rabbits will spend time on their home, adding features, improving décor and stamping their personality on where they live. Domestically, this can be a full and satisfying time.

With purchasing decisions to make and many thoughts to consider, particularly if setting up his first home, the Fire Rabbit should draw on the assistance of family members and close friends. Some of these could help in important ways and this is very much a year for pooling together. April, August and December could be meaningful times and see plans significantly advanced. However, the Fire Rabbit does need to be realistic in what is doable at any one time. To spread his energies too widely can not only be exhausting but also undermine some of what he wants do. Ideally, he should prioritize and concentrate on one thing (or maybe a few) at a time.

Loved ones will be keen to commemorate the Fire Rabbit's thirtieth birthday and there may be some surprises and generous treats in store. Some of this Rooster year will be very special to the Fire Rabbit.

His social life will also see considerable activity, and while he may have to cut back on going out because of his commitments, he will still enjoy himself when he can. Personal interests and work changes can bring him into contact with new people, and Fire Rabbits who are alone could meet someone who quickly becomes special. Rooster years can have their fortuitous developments. April, July, October and December are likely to see the most social activity.

However with a lot to do, share and enjoy, the Fire Rabbit's spending will be high and he is also likely to take on new commitments. He does need to keep close watch on this and check the terms of any new obligations. Also, if tempted by anything speculative or having misgivings over any transaction, he should be wary and seek advice. This is no year to be lax or take risks. Fire Rabbits, take note.

Although the Fire Rabbit will be kept busy this year, he should also try to preserve time for his interests and recreational pursuits. These may not only be a good channel for certain ideas and talents but skills acquired now may open up possibilities for the near future. Some Fire Rabbits may also regard their thirtieth year as a new chapter in their life and decide to try something different. Again, by following through his ideas, the Fire Rabbit can ultimately gain a great deal.

This also applies to his work situation. For the many Fire Rabbits pursuing a particular career, there will be excellent opportunities to build on their experience and move to a new level. Sometimes what opens up may be different from what the Fire Rabbit expected but allow him to learn about other aspects of his industry. What occurs this year may (initially) be daunting, but it will mark an important stage in his ongoing development.

There will, though, be some Fire Rabbits who are keen to make a more major change and to develop their skills in other ways. For these Fire Rabbits, as well as those seeking work, the Rooster year can be challenging but significant. New openings will be difficult to come by, but by widening the scope of their search and remaining persistent, many of these Fire Rabbits will obtain a position which may be different from what they have done before but offer good prospects. March, June, August and September could see encouraging developments.

The Fire Rabbit can help his situation by working closely with his colleagues and being active in his place of work. If applicable, joining a professional organization could be of benefit to him.

With expectations high and duties demanding, the Rooster year will ask a lot of the Fire Rabbit work-wise, but in return it can offer a platform on which he can build and make his thirties a fruitful decade.

Overall, the Fire Rabbit can take a lot from this Rooster year. His personal and home life in particular can see achievements celebrated, plans fulfilled and occasions enjoyed. The Rooster year favours personal development and the Fire Rabbit has much to gain by furthering his interests or starting something new. At work new responsibilities and additional experience can provide him with the skills necessary for future progress. This will be a busy year, with some months a whirl of activity (and excitement), but with good use of his time and the support of others, the Fire Rabbit can give this new decade in his life a positive start.

Tip for the Year

Pursue your aims with determination. By concentrating your efforts, you can achieve a great deal. Also, value your loved ones and enjoy the special occasions this year will bring. You have a lot in your favour and can really make the most of your potential.

The Earth Rabbit

One of the key features of the Rooster year is its long-term effects. Although it is not always an easy one for Rabbits, what many accomplish during it can be a necessary prerequisite for future success. This will especially be the case for Earth Rabbits born in 1999.

In their education there will be much happening and many decisions to take. Many of these Earth Rabbits will have important exams to prepare for and should work steadily, leaving ample time for revision and coursework. Keeping in mind what certain results can make possible will help these Earth Rabbits remain focused. Their efforts now are an investment in their future.

Many of them will think deeply about the direction of their education and possible vocation. In this they should be open-minded and talk to their family and to experts, but also think carefully about what *they* want to do. This can be a significant time and help shape the next few years. A few Earth Rabbits may alter their original intentions over the course of the Rooster year, due to advice received and how they fare in certain subjects. This is a year to be open to possibility.

In view of the pressures and decisions many young Earth Rabbits will face this year, it is also important they share their thoughts with family members. The more open they are, the more helpfully others can respond. A close relation could give the Earth Rabbit some especially pertinent advice. He needs to listen well.

For Earth Rabbits who start university or move to a new educational establishment during the year, this can be an exciting yet daunting time. There will be new environments and routines to adjust to, new people to meet and much to study. The Earth Rabbit likes to feel settled and secure and will find some of the year demanding, but as he recognizes, upheaval is sometimes necessary in order to progress. By joining in with various activities, he will soon settle down and become a part of his new environment.

For Earth Rabbits who decide to seek work, again the year will bring important developments. These Earth Rabbits should actively pursue any openings that interest them, and even if what they obtain is different from what they originally intended, it will not only give them useful experience but also be a platform on which to build. The key this year is to make a positive start and show others their potential.

For those already in a position, this can be an encouraging time. Having proved themselves in their present capacity, many of these Earth Rabbits will be offered training and greater responsibilities. Some may decide to further their career by seeking a more remunerative position elsewhere. The Rooster year offers excellent possibilities for the keen and ambitious. Opportunities can arise suddenly and will need to be grasped quickly. March, June, August and September could see potentially significant developments.

In money matters, however, the Earth Rabbit will need to be careful. He may already be trying to do a great deal on a limited budget and he should avoid risks and be especially careful if tempted by anything speculative. Also, when making large purchases, he should consider his options rather than proceed hurriedly.

One of the most encouraging aspects of the year concerns the Earth Rabbit's interests and he should aim to take these further in some way. Whether developing skills and ideas or trying a new activity, with some aims in mind he will not only enjoy himself but be inspired to do more. For Earth Rabbits nurturing special skills (and maybe having aspirations for those skills), it could be to their advantage to seek expert guidance.

Throughout the year the Earth Rabbit will also appreciate the camaraderie of his circle of friends. Those in similar positions can offer one another support and there will also be much fun to be had. As a result of changes in their situation, many Earth Rabbits will also make a new group of friends this year, and the Earth Rabbit's quiet yet genial nature will make him popular company. April, July, October and December could see the most social activity.

There will also be travel opportunities for many Earth Rabbits and they will welcome the chance to visit some exciting attractions. Travelwise, the Rooster year can contain some memorable highlights.

For Earth Rabbits born in 1939, the Rooster year will also have its pleasures. These Earth Rabbits will derive considerable satisfaction from their interests, especially any which encourage self-expression and/or some form of artistry. Some may enjoy recording (including writing about) various reminiscences, and their ideas and deft touches can bring pleasure both to themselves and others.

Many of these Earth Rabbits will see family numbers increase, possibly with the birth of great-grandchildren, and there will also be the achievements of close relations to celebrate. During the year the Earth Rabbit will once again dispense valued advice and assistance.

The more senior Earth Rabbit does, though, need to be careful when dealing with official correspondence and financial matters. If he has uncertainties, he should seek guidance. Earth Rabbits, take note.

The Year of the Rooster will have its highlights for all Earth Rabbits and their ideas and interests will develop well and often give rise to other possibilities. For the Earth Rabbit born in 1999, decisions made now will determine future directions. There will be many pressures and a lot will be asked of the Earth Rabbit, but he knows he has it in him to succeed and the events of the year will prepare him well for what lies ahead. Overall, a constructive and significant time.

Tip for the Year
Nurture your talents. And for the younger Earth Rabbit, have self-belief. If you act with determination, your accomplishments this year can be of far-reaching value.

Famous Rabbits

Margaret Atwood, Drew Barrymore, David Beckham, Harry Belafonte, Ingrid Bergman, St Bernadette, Jeff Bezos, Kathryn Bigelow, Michael Bublé, Nicolas Cage, Lewis Carroll, John Cleese, Confucius, Marie Curie, Johnny Depp, Novak Djokovic, Albert Einstein, George Eliot, W. C. Fields, James Fox, Cary Grant, Ashley Greene, Edvard Grieg, Oliver Hardy, Seamus Heaney, Tommy Hilfiger, Bob Hope, Whitney Houston, Helen Hunt, John Hurt, Anjelica Huston, Enrique Iglesias, E. L. James, Henry James, Sir David Jason, Angelina Jolie, Michael B. Jordan, Michael Keaton, John Keats, Enda Kenny, Lisa Kudrow, Gina Lollobrigida, George Michael, Sir Roger Moore, Andy Murray, Mike Myers, Brigitte Nielsen, Graham Norton, Michelle Obama, Jamie Oliver, George Orwell, Brad Pitt, Emeli Sandé, Elisabeth Schwarzkopf, Neil Sedaka, Jane Seymour, Maria Sharapova, Neil Simon, Frank Sinatra, Sting, Quentin Tarantino, Charlize Theron, J. R. R. Tolkien, KT Tunstall, Tina Turner, Luther Vandross, Sebastian Vettel, Queen Victoria, Muddy Waters, Orson Welles, Walt Whitman, Will-i-Am, Robin Williams, Kate Winslet, Tiger Woods.

3 February 1916 to 22 January 1917 — *Fire Dragon*

23 January 1928 to 9 February 1929 — *Earth Dragon*

8 February 1940 to 26 January 1941 — *Metal Dragon*

27 January 1952 to 13 February 1953 — *Water Dragon*

13 February 1964 to 1 February 1965 — *Wood Dragon*

31 January 1976 to 17 February 1977 — *Fire Dragon*

17 February 1988 to 5 February 1989 — *Earth Dragon*

5 February 2000 to 23 January 2001 — *Metal Dragon*

23 January 2012 to 9 February 2013 — *Water Dragon*

The Dragon

The Personality of the Dragon

I like giving things a go.
Sometimes I succeed,
sometimes I fail.
Sometimes the unexpected happens.
But it is the giving things a go
and the stepping forward
that makes life so interesting.

The Dragon is born under the sign of luck. He is a proud and lively character and has a tremendous amount of self-confidence. He is also highly intelligent and very quick to take advantage of any opportunity. He is ambitious and determined and will do well in practically anything he attempts. He is also something of a perfectionist and will always try to maintain the high standards he sets himself.

The Dragon does not suffer fools gladly and will be quick to criticize anyone or anything that displeases him. He can be blunt and forthright in his views and is certainly not renowned for being either tactful or diplomatic. He does, however, often take people at their word and can occasionally be rather gullible. If he ever feels that his trust has been abused or his dignity wounded, he can sometimes become very bitter and it will take him a long time to forgive and forget.

The Dragon is usually very outgoing and is particularly adept at attracting attention and publicity. He enjoys being in the limelight and is often at his best when he is confronted by a difficult problem or tense situation. In some respects he is a showman and he rarely lacks an audience. His views are highly valued and he invariably has something interesting – and sometimes controversial – to say.

He also has considerable energy and is often prepared to work long and unsocial hours in order to achieve what he wants. He can, however, be rather impulsive and does not always consider the consequences of his actions. He also has a tendency to live for the moment and there is nothing that riles him more than to be kept waiting. The Dragon hates delay and can get extremely impatient and irritable over even the smallest of hold-ups.

The Dragon has an enormous faith in his abilities, but he does run the risk of becoming over-confident and unless he is careful he can sometimes make grave errors of judgement. While this may prove disastrous at the time, he does have the tenacity and ability to bounce back and pick up the pieces again.

The Dragon has such an assertive personality, so much willpower and such a desire to succeed that he will often reach the top of his chosen profession. He has considerable leadership qualities and will do well in positions where he can put his own ideas and policies into practice. He is usually successful in politics, show business, as the manager of his own department or business, and in any job that brings him into contact with the media.

The Dragon relies a tremendous amount on his own judgement and can be scornful of other people's advice. He likes to feel self-sufficient and there are many Dragons who cherish their independence to such a degree that they prefer to remain single throughout their lives. However, the Dragon will often have numerous admirers and many will be attracted by his flamboyant personality and striking looks. If he does marry, he will usually marry young, and will find himself particularly well suited to those born under the signs of the Snake, Rat, Monkey and Rooster. He will also find that the Rabbit, Pig, Horse and Goat make ideal companions and will readily join in with many of his escapades. Two Dragons will also get on well together, as they will understand each other, but the Dragon may not find things so easy with the Ox and Dog, as both will be critical of his impulsive and somewhat extrovert manner. He will also find it difficult to form an alliance with the Tiger, for the Tiger, like the Dragon, tends to speak his mind, is very strong-willed and likes to take the lead.

The female Dragon knows what she wants in life and sets about everything she does in a determined and positive manner. No job is too small for her and she is often prepared to work extremely hard to secure her objectives. She is immensely practical and somewhat liberated. She hates being bound by routine and petty restrictions and likes to have sufficient freedom to go off and do what she wants to do. She will keep her house tidy, but is not one for spending hours on housework – there are far too many other things that she prefers to do. Like her male counterpart, she has a tendency to speak her mind.

The Dragon usually has many interests and enjoys sport and other outdoor activities. He also likes to travel and often prefers to visit places that are off the beaten track rather than head for popular tourist destinations. He has a very adventurous streak in him and providing his financial circumstances permit – and the Dragon is usually sensible with his money – he will travel considerable distances during his lifetime.

The Dragon is a very flamboyant character and while he can be demanding of others and in his early years rather precocious, he will have many friends and will nearly always be the centre of attention. He has charisma and so much confidence that he can often become a source of inspiration to others. In China he is the leader of the carnival and he is also blessed with an inordinate share of luck.

The Five Different Types of Dragon

In addition to the 12 signs of the Chinese zodiac there are five elements and these have a strengthening or moderating influence on the signs. The effects of the elements on the Dragon are described below, together with the years in which they were exercising their influence. Therefore Dragons born in 1940 and 2000 are Metal Dragons, Dragons born in 1952 and 2012 are Water Dragons, and so on.

Metal Dragon: 1940, 2000

This Dragon is very strong-willed and has a particularly forceful personality. He is energetic, ambitious and tries to be scrupulous in his dealings with others. He can also be blunt and to the point and usually has no hesitation in speaking his mind. If people disagree with him or are not prepared to co-operate, he is more than happy to go his own way. He usually has very high moral values and is held in great esteem by his friends and colleagues.

Water Dragon: 1952, 2012

This Dragon is friendly, easy-going and intelligent. He is quick-witted and rarely lets an opportunity slip by. However, he is not as impatient as some of the other types of Dragon and is prepared to wait for results rather than expect everything to happen at once. He has an understanding nature and is willing to share his ideas and co-operate with others. His main failing is a tendency to jump from one thing to another rather than concentrate on the job in hand. He has a good sense of humour and is an effective speaker.

Wood Dragon: 1964

The Wood Dragon is practical, imaginative and inquisitive. He loves delving into all manner of subjects and can quite often come up with some highly original ideas. He is a thinker and a doer and has the drive and commitment to put many of his ideas into practice. He is more diplomatic than some of the other types of Dragon and has a good sense of humour. He is very astute in business matters and can also be most generous.

Fire Dragon: 1916, 1976

This Dragon is ambitious, articulate and has a tremendous desire to succeed. He is a hard and conscientious worker and is often admired for his integrity and forthright nature. He is very strong-willed and has considerable leadership qualities. He can, however, rely a bit too much on his own judgement and fail to take into account the views and feelings of others. He can also be rather aloof and it would certainly be in his own interests to let others join in more with his various activities. He usually enjoys music, literature and the arts.

Earth Dragon: 1928, 1988

The Earth Dragon tends to be quieter and more reflective than some of the other types of Dragon. He has a wide variety of interests and is keenly aware of what is going on around him. He also has clear objectives and usually no problems in obtaining support and backing for any of his ventures. He is very astute in financial matters and often able to accumulate considerable wealth. He is a good organizer, although he can at times be rather bureaucratic and fussy. He mixes well with others and has a large circle of friends.

Prospects for the Dragon in 2017

The Year of the Monkey (8 February 2016–27 January 2017) will have been a curious one for the Dragon and while he will have set about his activities with characteristic verve, his results could have been mixed. In some cases support may have been lacking and in other instances he may have put in a lot of effort but had little to show in return. Monkey years, while on the surface abuzz with activity, can be tricky ones.

In the remaining months of this Monkey year the Dragon will need to remain watchful and co-operative. While he may like to make his own decisions, he should liaise with those around him and discuss plans and arrangements. Being too single-minded could deny him some good opportunities. Dragons, take note.

At work, increasing pressures could exasperate the Dragon and make some duties difficult. However, such situations can display his skills and resourcefulness and help his prospects. Often what is accomplished now can prepare him for the opportunities arising in 2017.

The closing months of the year are invariably expensive and ideally the Dragon should make early provision for extra outlay and more substantial purchases. He should also attend to paperwork carefully.

The Monkey year can, though, give rise to some lively times and there will be domestic and social occasions to enjoy. September, December and early January can be especially active, although, with a lot happening, it is again important that the Dragon communicates well with others and makes plans in advance.

For Dragons enjoying romance, as well as those who are unattached, affairs of the heart may also add some sparkle to the latter part of the year. Monkey years, despite their tribulations, are capable of pleasant surprises and the end of year will often bring some special times.

The Year of the Rooster starts on 28 January and is a very encouraging one for the Dragon. He can make good headway and, being born under the sign of luck, could benefit from some fortuitous developments. Any Dragons who are nursing disappointment or feeling frustrated by their present situation will find the Rooster year can bring a fresh outlook.

The aspects are especially encouraging for the Dragon's work situation. Often as a result of the skills he has recently demonstrated, he may now be encouraged to take on greater responsibilities and make more of his strengths. He could be well placed when promotion opportunities occur and make impressive progress over the year.

Dragons who are particularly keen to move on to something else will also find that developments can move swiftly. In some instances colleagues and friends may be helpful in alerting them to openings and/ or giving them ideas to consider. The Rooster year can bring interesting opportunities and many of these Dragons will feel more energized than they have for some time.

Dragons seeking work should keep informed of developments in their area. An existing employer may be expanding or new companies recruiting, and the Dragon's initiative and personal qualities may result in many a prospective employer being interested in what he has to offer. March, May, September and November could see encouraging developments.

Another positive feature of the year will be the way the Dragon can further his professional skills. Often training will be available at his place of work, but if he feels another skill or qualification would help his prospects or there is a subject that appeals to him, he should set time aside for personal study. Professional development is an area all Dragons should consider carefully this year.

The encouraging aspects also apply to the Dragon's personal interests. Inspired by his own ideas and often encouraged by others, he can derive considerable pleasure from them this year. Dragons whose busy lifestyle has led to personal interests being set aside should consider starting something new. This can inject an enjoyable element into their lifestyle.

In money matters, progress made at work can result in a rise in income and some Dragons could also receive a bonus payment or sum which is overdue. To fully benefit the Dragon should watch his spending and budget for key requirements, but with good financial management he can proceed with many of his plans. In particular, new entertainment and media devices could be appealing.

The Dragon should also make provision for travel this year. He may enjoy the chance to see sights he has long wanted to see. Some Dragons will also take advantage of last-minute offers and invitations to visit people living some distance away. Travel-wise, the Rooster year will satisfy the adventurous nature of many a Dragon.

However, while the aspects are generally encouraging, the Rooster year also has its more cautionary elements. In particular the Dragon will need to be attentive to those around him. If he becomes too preoccupied by his own activities, strains and tensions may arise. Pressures and tiredness could also lead to disagreements and this is not a year to take feelings for granted or make assumptions. Dragons, take note. Without care and attention you may find the Rooster year putting certain relationships to the test, but by being aware *and giving your time*, you will see some relationships strengthened.

Although this is a year for increased mindfulness of others, it will not be without its social opportunities and the Dragon can look forward to some lively occasions. April, June, August and October could be busy and interesting and see good connections being forged, but where romance is concerned, care and time are advised. New relationships should be built up steadily (and often potentially successfully) rather than hurried.

The Dragon should also make sure work and other commitments do not impinge on his home life. At times he may find it difficult to balance his busy lifestyle, but preserving time to share with his loved ones can make an important difference. In addition, plans, purchases and travel can all add pleasure to the year. Rooster years may require extra attention to key relationships, but there will be a lot happening in this one and a lot to value.

Overall, the Year of the Rooster is an important one for the Dragon. At work there will often be the opportunity to learn new skills and take on interesting duties. Finances can also see improvement, and carefully considered plans and purchases (including travel) will bring pleasure. The Dragon will, though, need to take care in his relations with others and devote time to those who are special to him. Preoccupation, inattention and indiscretion could all rebound on him. Provided he takes note of these cautionary aspects, however, he is set to do well this year.

The Metal Dragon

This will be a year of considerable possibility for the Metal Dragon and by setting about his activities with his customary resolve, he can look forward to accomplishing a great deal.

For the Metal Dragon born in 2000, this can be an especially interesting year. As they advance in their education, these Metal Dragons will be able to put their newly acquired knowledge to greater use. They can make important strides this year and some of what they do will highlight talents and indicate possibilities for the future. A lot will be expected of the young Metal Dragon, but what he learns now will have far-reaching value. Above all, Rooster years are illuminating, and results obtained in exams and tests will indicate the Metal Dragon's strengths as well as sometimes be a wake-up call that more effort is required in certain areas. It is by being stretched that the Metal Dragon will learn and understand.

In his studying, it is important that he tells others of any concerns rather than struggles on in silence. Once he talks to others, whether tutors or family, useful guidance can be given. Similarly, if he has other difficulties or anxieties, he should voice these too. This is no time to be headstrong or obtuse if he is to benefit from the support available to him.

The young Metal Dragon will derive a lot of pleasure from his interests this year and, inspired by ideas and projects, will be keen to take these further. This is very much a time to enjoy and explore his capabilities, and expert guidance can be of considerable value.

Many Metal Dragons will also be keen to supplement their funds over the year and will take on work in their spare time. Although the tasks given may be routine, by demonstrating their reliability, they can gain the opportunity to do more. The Metal Dragon often has an enterprising spirit and this will not only reward him now but as he continues through life.

Some Metal Dragons will enter the world of work this year, and again, by showing commitment, they will be encouraged and often trained for a greater role. These are early but potentially significant days.

The Metal Dragon's enterprise this year will help financially and while he will need to watch his spending levels, by managing his situation well and saving towards more substantial purchases, he will be pleased with how he fares. Financially, this is a rewarding and sometimes lucky year.

Metal Dragons often have a wide circle of friends and over the year there will be fun times to share, news to exchange and parties and other occasions to look forward to. April, June, August and October could be especially active months. However, the year will also have its trickier moments. A difference of opinion could sour a close relationship, a promising romance could be cut short and a particular situation could worry the young Metal Dragon. At such times he will need to tread warily and be careful not to exacerbate situations or go against his better instincts. Metal Dragons, take note and over the year be attentive and aware.

Metal Dragons born in 1940 can also derive considerable pleasure from their activities this year and will often delight in how their interests develop. In some cases, joining others or enlisting the help of relations will give a particular project added momentum. In addition to more creative activities, many senior Metal Dragons will carry out domestic projects they have had in mind for some time, including sorting out accumulated items. Some could find themselves benefiting financially, perhaps from selling items that are no longer required or unearthing something of unexpected value. Some may also enjoy a competition win or receive a surprise gift.

The senior Metal Dragon will also appreciate the family occasions held during the year and will find the successes of close relations a source of great pride. He could also offer guidance when concerns arise, often involving the situation of another person. All years have their ups and downs and this one will be no exception.

However, although the Rooster year will have its vexing areas, overall it is a highly encouraging one for the Metal Dragon. Whether born in 1940 or 2000, he will find his personal interests developing well and often proving a satisfying outlet for his talents. For the younger Metal Dragon, progress made in his education will prepare him for the more advanced work ahead. Support is there for him and he should avail himself of it if required. Being born under the sign of luck, all Metal Dragons can look forward to some fortunate developments over this active and favourable year.

Tip for the Year

Pay attention to your relations with others and value those who are special to you. Also, watch your independent tendencies. The more you consult others, the more you can benefit.

The Water Dragon

When the Water Dragon comes to look back on this Rooster year he may well be astonished by all that has happened. This promises to be an action-packed 12 months. To get the best from it, the Water Dragon will need to liaise closely with those around him rather than be too independent. If he remembers this and acts with his characteristic verve, however, much will go in his favour.

His domestic life is set to be particularly busy, with quite a few ambitious home projects underway. And some undertakings could mushroom and become even more extensive than originally planned. Water Dragons, take note.

In addition to all the practical activity, the Water Dragon will spend time helping and advising others. With those around him likely to be involved in potentially significant decision-making, his judgement will be appreciated. There will inevitably be concerns, too, and here frank discussion and sometimes professional input can assist. This can be a time of change and it may be that in the wake of uncertainty, another option arises. This Rooster year can be a time of swift-moving developments. June, August and early September are likely to be particularly active times. Some Water Dragons could also see their family increase in numbers with the birth of grandchildren.

The Rooster year can also give rise to some interesting travel possibilities and the Water Dragon should not only consider taking a holiday but also take up any chances to have a short break and/or visit others.

The financial aspects are encouraging and will enable certain plans to go ahead. The Water Dragon's judgement will be on good form and when he has a purchase or plan in mind, once he starts to look at possibilities, he could find himself able to take advantage of favourable buying opportunities. In addition, if in receipt of funds he does not immediately need, by saving and investing wisely, he could come to be grateful for his actions in later years.

The Water Dragon has an enquiring nature and over the year may well decide to take certain interests forward or start something new. Although his interests can be widespread, he may find creative projects particularly satisfying. Water Dragons who retire this year or are recently retired may find a new objective or interest adding a pleasing element to their year. In addition some may be tempted to start a keep-fit discipline or try Pilates, *Tai Chi* or something similar. By following up their ideas, they can derive much pleasure from what they do over the year.

The Water Dragon's various activities will also give him opportunities to go out and spend time with others. During the year he will enjoy a variety of social occasions and other forms of entertainment. April, June, August and October could see the most social activity.

The Rooster year does, however, have its awkward elements. It may be that a particular friendship is strained following a disagreement or that a romance flounders due to lack of care and attention. Rooster years can be unforgiving of lapses and preoccupation and during them minor matters have a tendency to escalate. Water Dragons, take note and take extra care.

At work the Rooster year can bring important developments, especially as quite a few Water Dragons will take the decision to retire or substantially reduce their work commitments. Considerable adjustment will be needed, but these Water Dragons will relish the additional time this opens up and will have ideas and projects they are keen to get underway. The Rooster year can bring surprises and some of these Water Dragons will find new ways to use their experience (and sometimes still to earn).

For Water Dragons who remain in employment, the Rooster year can present complex challenges which will exercise their minds and skills.

For all Water Dragons, March, May, September and November could see key work developments.

Overall, the Year of the Rooster will be busy but fulfilling for the Water Dragon. Whether taking decisions concerning his work, developing new or existing interests or undertaking home improvement projects, he is likely to be active and inspired. In quite a few instances, he will also benefit from moments of luck. Domestically, there will be much happening and the Water Dragon will often give sterling support to his loved ones. When the inevitable problems arise, he should try to deal with them quickly, lest they escalate. Friendships and romances require special attention this year if they are to proceed smoothly. However, in many respects this will be a constructive year for the Water Dragon and he may be amazed by all he manages to achieve.

Tip for the Year
Take action. Your efforts can reward you well. Also, value those around you and *do communicate with them*. With support, goodwill and co-operation, you will find so much more will happen.

The Wood Dragon

There is a Chinese proverb which reminds us, 'Hoist your sail when the wind is fair. Seize the opportunity.' This advice is very apt for the Wood Dragon this year. This is a favourable year for him and by following up his ideas he can fare well. Pleasingly, recent activities can often be taken further and goals he has been working towards for some time can be reached.

In his work this can be a significant year. Although many Wood Dragons will have experienced change in recent times, this period of transition is far from over. Indeed, what many have been engaged in recently can be regarded as preparation for growth. In 2017 important opportunities can now arise. And whether these come through senior positions becoming available or initiatives requiring experienced staff, the Wood Dragon will often be excellently placed to benefit. Some Wood Dragons may also be helped by long-standing colleagues either recommending them for a particular role or putting in a good word on their behalf. In fact there may be much going on behind the scenes that is to their advantage. Depending on their line of work, a few Wood Dragons may also find themselves headhunted.

Wood Dragons who are feeling staid in their present role or seeking a position which better suits their current circumstances, as well as those seeking work, will also benefit from the encouraging aspects of the year. With characteristic drive and initiative, they may well succeed in taking on a new role in which they can not only quickly impress others but also make greater use of their strengths. Many Wood Dragons will be on inspired form as a result of fresh opportunities this year. March, May, September and November could see encouraging developments, but throughout the year the Wood Dragon should seize opportunities as they arise.

Progress made at work can help financially and many Wood Dragons will also benefit from the receipt of extra funds or a gift. This financial upturn will persuade many to go ahead with plans and purchases they have been considering for some time as well as enjoy some travelling. However, to get the best value, they should consider their choices carefully rather than proceed hurriedly. Also, if they are able to add to their savings or a pension policy, they could benefit in years to come.

The Rooster year can also be marked by some special family occasions, including the chance to spend time with some relations the Wood Dragon does not often see. As always, he will take a caring interest in the progress of family members and will offer pertinent advice as well as assist in additional ways. At the time he may not realize just how valuable his input can be. June, August and early September could see exciting times in many a Wood Dragon household.

This is also an excellent year for shared activities and it is important the Wood Dragon communicates well with those close to him rather than keeping his thoughts (and concerns) to himself. Although Dragons have an independent streak, greater openness will not only be good for relationships but also lead to more appropriate advice being given. Particularly in the Wood Dragon's domestic life, good communication will make an important difference this year.

Although involved in many activities, the Wood Dragon should also not allow his own interests to become sidelined. These not only help him relax and keep his lifestyle in balance but may also give him the benefit of additional exercise. Some activities related to his interests could also give rise to travel, especially during the summer and at the end of the year. For all Wood Dragons, some 'me time' this year can be of particular value.

With his active lifestyle, the Wood Dragon is in contact with many people and the Rooster year will contain a variety of interesting social occasions for him to attend. However, if a disagreement should arise, speedy resolution or compromise may be needed to help prevent it from escalating or souring a situation. Care is advised.

For the lonely and unattached Wood Dragon, personal interests and changes in his situation can lead to meeting others, although where romance is concerned, he should proceed slowly. Rushing or putting pressure on a relationship in the early stages could bring disappointment. Wood Dragons, take note, for affairs of the heart require careful handling this year.

However, the Wood Dragon is both versatile and shrewd and his talents will reward him well in the Rooster year. With his experience and reputation, he can make excellent headway in many areas. As he has so often found, when he puts his mind to something, he often prevails, and so it will be this year. It is a case of 'hoisting his sail' and catching the favourable winds. With commitment and the desire to move forward, he can enjoy this time of splendid possibilities.

Tip for the Year
Seize the moment and make more of yourself. You have much to offer. Do, though, keep your lifestyle in balance and be attentive in your relationships with others.

The Fire Dragon

The element of fire gives a sign more energy and drive and this can certainly be evident in the Fire Dragon. Never one to sit on the sidelines, he likes to play his part and in 2017 he will have some fine opportunities to do so.

An important feature of the Rooster year is that it will enable the Fire Dragon to move forward. This is a time to take his ideas further. He will often be assisted by circumstances and may see ideal openings arising. This year he will have a lot on his side.

At work many Fire Dragons will have seen considerable change in recent years and their duties becoming more extensive. These Fire Dragons will have the chance to improve further upon their present position, either with their current employer or by transferring to a more appealing and remunerative role elsewhere. In many instances, some adjustment to the Fire Dragon's skill-set may be required, but this is a year favouring progress.

The Fire Dragon will be helped by close colleagues. Not only will some offer advice when he is taking decisions but they may also alert him to potentially useful openings. He will have many rooting for him and his reputation will help his prospects.

For Fire Dragons keen on more substantial change, as well as those seeking work, again the Rooster year can open up some good possibilities. Effort will be required, but with resolve and initiative, many Fire

Dragons will secure the chance they have been seeking, and with it a platform they can build on. March, May, September and November could see important developments.

Progress at work will also help financially. However, to benefit the Fire Dragon will need to be disciplined, otherwise anything extra could be absorbed by everyday spending and not used to best advantage. Ideally, if he has specific purchases or plans in mind, he should make early provision for them. And if he is able to contribute more to a pension policy or savings plan, this too could be of benefit. With good financial management, he can not only be satisfied with his acquisitions this year but also help his long-term position.

Travel is well aspected and if there is a destination that appeals to him, the Fire Dragon should make enquiries and see what is possible. Some spur of the moment breaks or weekends away, unexpected though they may be, can also be much appreciated.

Although the Fire Dragon enjoys a busy lifestyle, if sedentary for much of the day he may benefit from taking advice on additional exercise. Improving his diet may also help. Extra attention to his well-being can often make a difference to how he feels.

Personal interests too can be helpful to the Fire Dragon this year. He may be inspired by giving himself a new objective, following through an idea or joining other enthusiasts. This is a time to enjoy his talents and, if applicable, promote what he does.

In his home life, this can be a pleasing year. There will be mutual interests, shared occasions and personal successes to enjoy. The Fire Dragon and other family members will also be faced with some important decision-making, especially when opportunities arise and work situations change. These do need to be talked through and the implications discussed.

Home projects and purchases should also be considered jointly. That way everyone will enjoy the results more fully. June, August and early September will often be lively and special months domestically.

With his active lifestyle, the Fire Dragon is in contact with many people and the Rooster year will bring good opportunities to meet more. Professionally in particular, this can be an excellent time to network and forge new connections. The Fire Dragon should also take up social invitations as well as go to events that appeal to him. April, June, August and October could see the most social activity. However, should a disagreement arise, the Fire Dragon should try to resolve it rather than ignore it. Little niggles, a *faux pas* or a clash of opinion could escalate and sour relations, and this needs to be watched. Similarly, new romantic attachments need care and attention if they are to endure. Fire Dragons, take heed.

In many respects the Rooster year offers considerable scope for the Fire Dragon. For any who start the year dissatisfied with their present situation, it can bring welcome change. The Fire Dragon needs to take action, but some good possibilities will arise over the course of the year. In his home life, shared decision-making and activities can be of benefit. Minor disagreements and romantic situations require care and mindfulness, but overall the aspects are positive and many an enterprising Fire Dragon will make the most of the Rooster year and enjoy himself in the process.

Tip for the Year
Make your experience and talents count by looking to further your position. Also, value your relations with others. Not only can their support be invaluable, but there will be lots to share and enjoy in this full and successful year.

The Earth Dragon

The Earth Dragon can fare well in this encouraging year. However, to get the best from it, he will need to liaise closely with others. Although he may like to make his own plans, with backing and good advice from those around him, his successes can be all the more substantial.

Earth Dragons nurturing particular aims will find that if they work steadily towards them, important developments can follow on. As the Chinese proverb states, 'A journey of 1,000 miles begins with a single step.' In 2017, it is important for the Earth Dragon to take some steps – even strides – towards his goals.

Over the year many Earth Dragons will be giving some thought to accommodation matters. For those who are settled where they are, there will be improvements to make and appliances to acquire. By taking time and seeking advice (and, if applicable, waiting for favourable buying opportunities), they will be able to proceed with many of their plans. Quite a few Earth Dragons will consider moving this year and will spend time viewing possibilities and working out the financial implications. Here again the Earth Dragon should seek advice. His plans can be considerably advanced this year, and many realized, but it will require effort and support. June, August and early September could be potentially significant months.

With so much happening and/or under consideration, the Earth Dragon will need to watch his financial situation. With high outgoings and sometimes deposits to put down, he needs to be disciplined with his everyday spending. The better his control, the better his position. However, many Earth Dragons will be helped this year by a rise in income and some will benefit from a generous gift. While this is a year for financial care, it can have an element of good fortune too.

In view of his financial situation, the Earth Dragon will be more selective in the times he goes out socializing. However, he should not deny himself the chance to meet friends or go to events related to his interests. Contact with other people can do him good as well as add balance to his lifestyle. April, June, August and October could see the most social activity.

While a lot is set to go well, one area which requires particular care is romance, particularly new relationships and those still in the early stages. Without proper attention, affairs of the heart could be problematic for the Earth Dragon this year. In the Rooster year it is a case of exercising care, enjoying the present and letting any romance build up steadily (which many will), without pressure.

An important feature of the Earth Dragon character is that he is always keen to add to his knowledge and skills. Although occupied with many activities this year, he could find some projects related to his interests particularly satisfying and be enthused by new ideas and knowledge. No matter whether he prefers creative, practical or more outdoor pursuits, over the year he should allow himself some 'me time' to develop his own interests. Much pleasure can follow on, and often other benefits too.

His work situation will also encourage him to develop his skills. If following a particular career, he is likely to find his employers keen for him to take on more responsibilities and offering the chance of further training. This is a year for him to build and grow. In addition, many a workplace will see changes, with new systems, technology and products being introduced. If the Earth Dragon familiarizes himself with these and keeps himself informed about developments in his industry, his increasing knowledge can not only serve him well now but also be to his future advantage.

The Earth Dragon can further assist his situation by actively contributing to his place of work, including getting to meet other colleagues. The more involved he is, the more others can appreciate his value and potential.

The majority of Earth Dragons will make progress with their present employer this year, but some will take on greater responsibilities elsewhere. The career ambitions of many will be recognized and rewarded, with March, May, September and November seeing some key developments.

For Earth Dragons seeking work, the Rooster year may spring some surprises. Although the job-seeking process may be wearying, by keeping themselves informed and talking to others, these Earth Dragons could be alerted to employers looking to recruit and/or positions in which they can use their skills in other ways. By acting with determination and showing initiative at interview, many will be able to secure a position offering the potential for growth. This is a year rewarding effort.

A key feature of the Rooster year is that once the Earth Dragon takes action, circumstances will often assist him. With his skills and sense of purpose, a lot can open up for him this year and he can end it with many achievements to his credit. Personal plans, accommodation matters and key purchases will often proceed in pleasing ways, although the Earth Dragon needs to draw on the support of others rather than act single-handedly. He will also derive much satisfaction from furthering his interests and his work position. The accent this year is on growth, and important gains, both now and in the near future, can follow on. While care is needed with romance, overall this is a year of opportunity for the Earth Dragon.

Tip for the Year

Seize the moment and act, while drawing on the support of those around you. You have it within you to do a great deal this year, but do act with determination and aim to make the most of your opportunities. The long-term benefits can be considerable.

Famous Dragons

Adele, Maya Angelou, Jeffrey Archer, Joan Armatrading, Joan Baez, Count Basie, Sandra Bullock, Michael Cera, Courteney Cox, Bing Crosby, Russell Crowe, Benedict Cumberbatch, Roald Dahl, Salvador Dali, Charles Darwin, Neil Diamond, Bo Diddley, Matt Dillon, Christian Dior, Placido Domingo, Fats Domino, Dan Fogler, Sir Bruce Forsyth, Sigmund Freud, Tyson Fury, Rupert Grint, Che Guevara, James Herriot, Paul Hogan, Joan of Arc, Boris Johnson, Sir Tom Jones, Immanuel Kant, Martin Luther King, John Lennon, Abraham Lincoln, Elle MacPherson, Michael McIntyre, Hilary Mantel, Queen Margrethe II of Denmark, Liam Neeson, Florence Nightingale, Nick Nolte, Sharon Osbourne, Al Pacino, Pelé, Edgar Allan Poe, Vladimir Putin, Nikki Reed, Keanu Reeves, Ryan Reynolds, Sir Cliff Richard, Rihanna, Shakira, George Bernard Shaw, Martin Sheen, Blake Shelton, Alicia Silverstone, Ringo Starr, Karlheinz Stockhausen, Emma Stone, George Strait, Shirley Temple, Maria von Trapp, Andy Warhol, Mark Webber, the Earl of Wessex, Mae West, Sam Worthington.

23 January 1917 to 10 February 1918 — *Fire Snake*

10 February 1929 to 29 January 1930 — *Earth Snake*

27 January 1941 to 14 February 1942 — *Metal Snake*

14 February 1953 to 2 February 1954 — *Water Snake*

2 February 1965 to 20 January 1966 — *Wood Snake*

18 February 1977 to 6 February 1978 — *Fire Snake*

6 February 1989 to 26 January 1990 — *Earth Snake*

24 January 2001 to 11 February 2002 — *Metal Snake*

10 February 2013 to 30 January 2014 — *Water Snake*

The Snake

The Personality of the Snake

I think
And think some more.
About what is,
About what can be,
About what may be.
And when I am ready,
Then I act.

The Snake is born under the sign of wisdom. He is highly intelligent and his mind is forever active. He is always planning and always looking for ways in which he can use his considerable skills. He is a deep thinker and likes to meditate and reflect.

Many times during his life he will shed one of his famous Snake skins and take up new interests or start a completely different job. The Snake enjoys a challenge and he rarely makes mistakes. He is a skilful organizer, has considerable business acumen and is usually lucky in money matters. Most Snakes are financially secure in their later years, provided they do not gamble – the Snake has the distinction of being the worst gambler in the whole of the Chinese zodiac!

The Snake generally has a calm and placid nature and prefers the quieter things in life. He does not like to be in a frenzied atmosphere and hates being hurried into making a quick decision. He also does not like interference in his affairs and tends to rely on his own judgement rather than listen to advice.

At times the Snake can appear solitary. He is quiet, reserved and sometimes has difficulty in communicating with others. He has little time for idle gossip and will certainly not suffer fools gladly. He does, however, have a good sense of humour and this is particularly appreciated in times of crisis.

The Snake is certainly not afraid of hard work and is thorough in all that he does. He is very determined and can occasionally be ruthless in order to achieve his aims. His confidence, willpower and quick thinking usually ensure his success, but should he fail it will often take a long time for him to recover. He cannot bear failure and is a very bad loser.

The Snake can also be evasive and does not willingly let people into his confidence. This secrecy and distrust can sometimes work against him and these are traits that all Snakes should try to overcome.

Another characteristic of the Snake is his tendency to rest after any sudden or prolonged bout of activity. He burns up so much nervous energy that he can, if he is not careful, be susceptible to high blood pressure and nervous disorders.

It has sometimes been said that the Snake is a late starter in life and this is mainly because it often takes him a while to find a job in which he is genuinely happy. However, he will usually do well in any position which involves research and writing and where he is given sufficient freedom to develop his own ideas and plans. He makes a good teacher, politician, personnel manager and social adviser.

The Snake chooses his friends carefully and while he keeps a tight control over his finances, he can be particularly generous to those he likes. He will think nothing of buying expensive gifts or treating his friends or loved ones to the best theatre seats in town. In return, he demands loyalty. The Snake is very possessive and can become extremely jealous and hurt if he finds his trust has been abused.

The Snake is also renowned for his good looks and is never short of admirers. The female Snake in particular is most alluring. She has style, grace and excellent (and usually expensive) taste in clothes. A keen socializer, she is likely to have a wide range of friends and the happy knack of impressing those who matter. She has numerous interests and her opinions are often highly valued. She is generally a calm person and while she involves herself in many activities, she likes to retain a certain amount of privacy in her undertakings.

Affairs of the heart are very important to the Snake and he will often have many romances before he finally settles down. He will find that he is particularly well suited to those born under the signs of the Ox, Dragon, Rabbit and Rooster. Provided he is allowed sufficient freedom to pursue his own interests, he can also build up a very satisfactory relationship with the Rat, Horse, Goat, Monkey and Dog, but he should try to steer clear of another Snake as they could very easily become jealous of each other. The Snake will also have difficulty in getting on with the honest and down-to-earth Pig and will find the Tiger far too much of a disruptive influence on his quiet and peace-loving ways.

The Snake certainly appreciates the finer things in life. He enjoys good food and often takes a keen interest in the arts. He also enjoys reading and is invariably drawn to subjects such as philosophy, political thought, religion or the occult. He is fascinated by the unknown and his enquiring mind is always looking for answers. Some of the world's most original thinkers have been Snakes, and although he may not readily admit it, the Snake relies a lot on intuition and is often psychic.

The Snake is certainly not the most energetic member of the Chinese zodiac. He prefers to proceed at his own pace and to do what he wants. He is very much his own master and throughout his life he will try his hand at many things. He is something of a dabbler, but at some time – usually when he least expects it – his efforts and hard work will be recognized and he will invariably meet with the success and the financial security he so desires.

The Five Different Types of Snake

In addition to the 12 signs of the Chinese zodiac there are five elements and these have a strengthening or moderating influence on the signs. The effects of the elements on the Snake are described below, together with the years in which they were exercising their influence. Therefore Snakes born in 1941 and 2001 are Metal Snakes, Snakes born in 1953 and 2013 are Water Snakes, and so on.

Metal Snake: 1941, 2001

This Snake is quiet, confident and fiercely independent. He often prefers to work on his own and will only let a privileged few into his confidence. He is quick to spot opportunities and will set about achieving his objectives with an awesome determination. He is astute in financial matters and will often invest his money well. He has a liking for the finer things in life and a good appreciation of the arts, literature, music and food. He usually has a small group of extremely good friends and can be generous to his loved ones.

Water Snake: 1953, 2013

This Snake has a wide variety of interests. He enjoys studying all manner of subjects and is capable of undertaking quite detailed research and becoming a specialist in his chosen area. He is highly intelligent, has a good memory and is particularly astute when dealing with business and financial matters. He tends to be quietly spoken and a little reserved, but he does have sufficient strength of character to make his views known and attain his ambitions. He is very loyal to his family and friends.

Wood Snake: 1965

The Wood Snake has a friendly temperament and a good understanding of human nature. He is able to communicate well and often has many friends and admirers. He is witty, intelligent and ambitious. He has numerous interests and prefers to live in a quiet, stable environment where he can work without too much interference. He enjoys the arts and usually derives much pleasure from collecting paintings and antiques. His advice is often highly valued, particularly on social and domestic matters.

Fire Snake: 1917, 1977

The Fire Snake tends to be more forceful, outgoing and energetic than some of the other types of Snake. He is ambitious, confident and never slow in voicing his opinions, and he can be very abrasive to those he does not like. He does, however, have many leadership qualities and can win the respect and support of many with his firm and resolute manner.

He usually has a good sense of humour, a wide circle of friends and a very active social life. He is also a keen traveller.

Earth Snake 1929, 1989

The Earth Snake is charming, amusing and has a very amiable manner. He is conscientious and reliable in his work and approaches everything he does in a level-headed and sensible way. He can, however, tend to err on the cautious side and never likes to be hassled into making a decision. He is adept in dealing with financial matters and is a shrewd investor. He has many friends and is very supportive towards the members of his family.

Prospects for the Snake in 2017

The Monkey year (8 February 2016–27 January 2017) is a fast-moving one and the Snake, who likes to proceed in a measured way, could feel ill-at-ease with some of its developments. In the closing months, the pace shows no sign of abating.

At work there will be additional pressures as new demands are placed on the Snake and challenging objectives set. Problems, too, could test his skills, but there will be the opportunity for him to prove himself in new ways and progress *is* possible. September and October could be key months, with good opportunities for some Snakes.

The Snake's financial prospects could see some improvement toward the end of the year, and by planning carefully he can make some useful purchases for himself, his family and his home.

He will also find his social life becoming busier, though while he will enjoy many occasions, he could be concerned by the attitude or situation of another person. Care and diplomacy will be required and the Snake will need to be aware of any awkward undercurrents.

A lot is set to happen in his home life, and with many arrangements to fit in, it is important that there is good co-operation between family members. Some flexibility is also advised, as there may be surprise invitations, sometimes involving travel, and unexpected events. December and early January will be particularly active times.

The Snake may not have welcomed the heady pace of the Monkey year, but it will have allowed him to add to his skills and profit from some interesting opportunities and he can take heart as the Rooster year approaches.

The Year of the Rooster begins on 28 January and will be an encouraging one for the Snake. Rather than feel buffeted by events, he will appreciate the structure and order that characterize Rooster years and will be better able to plan ahead. And with conditions more conducive to his temperament, he can expect to make good headway.

For Snakes who start the year dissatisfied with their situation, this is a time to focus on the present rather than what has gone before. With resolve, important corners can be turned, new starts made and prospects improved. Rooster years support the Snake and encourage him to make more of his personal strengths.

This will be especially the case in his work. With the skills he has built up and the ways he has proved himself in recent times, he will often be excellently placed to now take on a greater role. In some instances, he will have the chance to take on a position which he has been working towards for some time, and his progress will be both deserved and appropriate. For Snakes working in large organizations, other openings could be tempting and some could transfer to a substantially different role and even relocate. Such are the aspects that any Snake who takes on a new role in the early months of the year could find additional duties being offered later on. These can be significant times for the Snake, with the accent on career progression.

Snakes who are currently unfulfilled at work and would welcome a change should actively seek out another position. Once they start to make enquiries, developments can often move swiftly.

For those currently seeking work, the Rooster year can also open up interesting possibilities. By considering different ways of using their skills, many of these Snakes could secure a position which is different from what they have done before but offers potential for the future.

Some openings could be discovered by chance or through a friend alerting the Snake. February, May, September and November could see important developments.

A particular strength of the Snake is that he likes to keep himself up-to-date with developments in his industry. To help, if training courses are available in his place of work, he should put himself forward or, if he feels another skill could be to his advantage, he should seek to gain it. Evening or online courses could help. With this being a year of growth, many Snakes can benefit from positive action.

This also extends to personal interests. Whether developing an existing interest or becoming absorbed in something new, all Snakes should allow time for recreation this year. It is always important for the Snake to unwind, gather his thoughts and spend time in ways he wants. Often personal interests can be a good outlet for particular talents. And for an enterprising few, they will offer prospects of monetary return.

Progress at work, too, can bring a welcome increase in income. However, the Snake could carry out some expensive undertakings this year, and while money may flow into his account, it could quickly flow out too. Throughout the year the Snake does need to watch his spending and budget ahead.

Also, if able, he should make provision for travel. A change of scene can do him good as well as offer the chance to try new activities.

Being a private person, the Snake attaches great importance to his immediate family circle and over the year there will be pleasing developments in his home life. April, July and December could see much domestic activity and some pleasing news, but at most times of the year there will be activities to enjoy. The Rooster year is rich in possibility. The one proviso is that at busy times, the Snake should prioritize rather than overcommit himself. Rooster years favour good planning.

While the Snake tends to only let a select few into his confidence, during the year he could have reason to be grateful to a close friend. When he is facing decisions in particular, someone he knows well could have the contact and experience to be of particular help. Although the Snake likes to rely on his own efforts (and keep his own counsel), with the aspects being so encouraging he does need to open up and consult others more readily. Snakes, take note, for the input of others can make an important difference this year.

For the unattached, the year can also have good romantic possibilities and a chance meeting may prove significant. However, true to form, rather than rush, many a Snake will be content to let romance develop gradually. Over the year, many relationships will develop in meaningful ways. April and July to the end of September could be good months for meeting others.

Overall, the Year of the Rooster will be a busy but favourable one for the Snake. At work there will be opportunities to pursue, and when inspired, the Snake is a formidable force. His interests, too, will often enthuse him and his fertile mind will explore many ideas. He will benefit from the support of those around him as well, although he does need to be open and prepared to consult others. In his home life there will be a lot to share and enjoy. The Rooster year is often one when the Snake's strengths come into their own, and his rewards can be substantial and well deserved.

The Metal Snake

The Metal Snake has a determined nature and when he sets himself an objective, he does his best to see it through. In the Rooster year, his resolve will reward him well.

For the Metal Snake born in 2001, a lot is set to happen. In his education there could be a bewildering amount to learn in a diverse range of subjects. Often the pressures will be considerable, but by rising to the challenges and keeping in mind the benefits good results can bring, many of these Metal Snakes will make excellent progress and in some subjects surpass expectations.

Although the Metal Snake relies a lot on his own efforts, throughout the year he also needs to be receptive to advice and, if struggling with a certain topic, seek guidance. He may be self-willed, but in this important year he needs to draw on support when necessary.

As well as making progress in his education, he should also make good use of the recreational facilities available to him. Sometimes these can not only help advance his interests but also lead to some fun times. By being involved, the young Metal Snake can improve his confidence levels, and for those who keep themselves to themselves (and some Metal Snakes are loners), the Rooster year will offer the chance to display some of their qualities.

In the Metal Snake's home life too, rather than remain for a long time in his room, he should be involved. This will not only be good for the rapport he shares with those around him, but if other family members are more aware of how he feels and what he has to do, they will be better able to advise and support. In addition, many Metal Snakes can look forward to some pleasing family occasions, including visiting some lively attractions. The late summer could be especially active.

Although the young Metal Snake knows many people, he prefers to keep his social circle relatively small. Over the year he will again value the comradeship and support of his trusted close friends. Some shared interests could develop in surprising ways and open up new possibilities.

Sometimes, however, the Metal Snake will have doubts over a certain situation or find himself in a personal predicament. At such times, he should be open rather than keep his anxieties to himself. Often talking through problems or contacting a helpline can help resolve matters.

With his interests and the various purchases he will want to make, he will need to manage his resources well this year. But by waiting, saving and keeping alert, he could make some pleasing acquisitions, and often at competitive prices. Some Metal Snakes may also find ways to earn something extra. Financially, the Metal Snake can fare well this year and do a surprising amount on an often limited budget.

For Metal Snakes who decide to seek work or take an apprenticeship rather than continue in education, this can be a time of important possibility. The positions they are offered may initially be routine, but once they have had the chance to familiarize themselves with what is required, their commitment will be rewarded with more varied duties. With purpose and the desire to make the most of his situation, the Metal Snake can do well this year and sow significant seeds for later.

Metal Snakes born in 1941 will also be keen to move certain plans forward. With the input of loved ones or friends, backed by their own resolve, they can enjoy some pleasing accomplishments. Whether their ideas concern their accommodation or other projects, by taking action they can achieve a lot. Interests which draw on the Metal Snake's creativity will also delight him and a key feature of this Rooster year is that once activities are started, they can become more extensive than originally envisaged.

Another pleasing feature of the year will be the progress of close family members. Domestically, the summer could be a busy time, with some good news to enjoy.

Many more senior Metal Snakes could also benefit from an additional payment this year. This could persuade them to go ahead with certain plans. However, when involved in any large outlay, the Metal Snake needs to check the facts and only proceed when he is satisfied that his requirements are being met.

For all Metal Snakes, whether born in 1941 or 2001, this is a constructive year and their efforts can be well rewarded. Timely opportunities and the support of others can also contribute. For Metal Snakes born in 2001, their commitment, both in their education and other activities, can help them get a lot out of the present as well as assist their future prospects. Determined, resourceful and keen, the Metal Snake can highlight his personal qualities and reap important benefits. A pleasing and practical year.

Tip for the Year

Remember there is no time like the present, and now is the time to make the most of your situation. Also, draw on the support and expertise of those around you. With a helping hand, so much more can happen.

The Water Snake

For some while now the Water Snake may have been nurturing particular hopes and dreams. And the Rooster year will give him the chance to realize them. This can be an active and satisfying year for him.

As with all Snakes, the Water Snake likes to keep his thoughts close to his chest, but in order to profit from the developments of the year, he needs to be forthcoming. If he talks through his ideas with his family and those who have relevant experience, he can be greatly assisted. This auspicious year is no time to go it alone. Independent Water Snakes, take careful note!

One particularly well-aspected area is personal interests. Some Water Snakes may delight in creative projects, others in practical activities, while others may prefer to travel or practise a fitness discipline. Whatever the Water Snake enjoys doing, this is a year to give time to it. For Water Snakes who have recently retired or who reduce their work commitments over the year, it is also a time to consider taking up other activities or improving existing skills. Many benefits can result, including reduced stress levels and additional exercise.

For Water Snakes in work, the year can also bring important developments. Staff may move and organizations change, and the Water Snake, with his experience, could find himself taking on a more extensive role, overseeing changes or smoothing out problem areas. The skills of many Water Snakes, sometimes including diplomatic ones, will be tested this year. But while there will be demanding times, the Water Snake will often take pride in the way he can draw on his extensive experience. Some Water Snakes will take their career to new levels and enjoy the culmination of many years of loyal commitment. February, May, September and November could be significant months.

There will also be some Water Snakes who decide to retire or cut back on what they do. Again this may be something they have been considering for some time and the Rooster year may encourage them to act in ways they think is right for them. The year offers choice and opportunity. In view of the implications involved, the Water Snake should seek the opinion of those he trusts. Talking through his situation can often help clarify his thoughts as well as reassure him he is making the right decision.

The Water Snake will also give much consideration to his financial situation over the year. The aspects are favourable and he may receive a bonus or gift or benefit from a policy. This may encourage him to proceed with plans and purchases he has been contemplating. Whether adding comforts to his home, buying equipment for his interests or enjoying a holiday, his foresight and budgeting can reward him well. He does, however, need to attend to paperwork promptly and keep important documents safe. A delay or loss could inconvenience him and take time to rectify. Water Snakes, take note.

Once again the Water Snake will greatly appreciate his home life this year. As he is a rather private person, his home is a welcome sanctuary for him and over the year he will enjoy making improvements to it as well as following the activities of those who are special to him. As a result of some of his own decisions, and possibly those of his partner too, there can be significant changes to routine this year and he will appreciate the benefits (and sometimes additional time) that follow on. April, July and December could be particularly pleasing months.

The Water Snake may be selective in his socializing, but the Rooster year can offer a varied selection of things to do and he would do well to keep informed of what is happening locally. For Water Snakes who are feeling lonely, perhaps as a result of recent change, joining a group or helping in their community could be good ways to meet like-minded people. The Rooster year encourages participation. April and July to the end of September could see the most social activity.

Although the Rooster year is generally encouraging for the Water Snake, every year has its more challenging moments and this one will be no exception. Some weeks will be stressful, especially as changes occur and decisions are needed. Also, the Water Snake cannot afford to ignore minor matters. He may sometimes adopt the philosophy of 'least said, soonest mended', but if he does not address niggling issues, they can gnaw away at him and start to overshadow an otherwise good year. Whenever he has concerns, he does need to be forthcoming and look to resolve matters. Water Snakes, take note.

The Water Snake relies a lot on instinct and this year he will feel the time is right for taking key decisions. And with the aspects favourable, he can look forward to accomplishing a great deal. In his personal interests (which are especially well aspected) and his work, he can enjoy some very gratifying results. He will also be pleased with the way he can proceed with many plans and purchases. His home life will be busy and meaningful and there will be plans and successes to share. The Water Snake has waited a long time for such an encouraging year and he should use it well.

Tip for the Year
'It is the hopes you nourish that so often flourish.' *Now* is the time to nourish your hopes, take your plans further and explore possibilities. With willingness and your traditionally game nature, you can make this a personally significant and rewarding year.

The Wood Snake

Rooster years reward good planning, and early on in the year the Wood Snake would do well to consider his aims for the next 12 months. Having objectives in mind will not only help him to channel his energies more effectively but also make him more aware of opportunities and additional factors that can help in his quest. Rooster years are supportive of Snakes and the purposeful Wood Snake can benefit from this one.

Though sometimes reticent, it is also important that the Wood Snake talks his ideas over with those who are close to him. Many people are keen to support him, but for that to happen he does need to be open and receptive. In addition, some flexibility would not come amiss if he is to make the most of the year. Once plans are started, other possibilities can open up and these need to be taken into account.

Some of the Wood Snake's thinking will concern his work situation. Although he may have achieved a lot in recent years, he will often be hankering to realize key ambitions. As a result, he may well look to further his position this year, either by putting in for a greater role where he is or looking elsewhere. This is not a time to stand still.

For Wood Snakes who feel their prospects could be improved by a move elsewhere, as well as those seeking work, the Rooster year can again have important implications. By keeping alert for opportunities and talking to employment advisers, many of these Wood Snakes will see their initiative rewarded with a new position which has potential for the future. The purposeful Wood Snake can do well this year. February, May, September and November could see significant developments.

The Wood Snake can also fare well in financial matters. Not only will he often enjoy an increase in income but he could receive an additional payment or gift. Enterprising Wood Snakes may also find a way to supplement their earnings through putting an interest or skill to good use. However, to make the most of any upturn, the Wood Snake should save up for key plans and purchases. If he is able, setting funds aside for the longer term would also be worth considering.

Although the Wood Snake will have many commitments, it is also important that he doesn't neglect his personal interests. The Rooster year encourages the Wood Snake to make greater use of his talents and this can be a stimulating time.

In addition, for Wood Snakes who are sedentary for large parts of the day and may lack regular exercise, some attention to their lifestyle could be of benefit as well as sometimes introduce them to new pursuits.

The Wood Snake can also look forward to some good travel opportunities and if there is a destination or special event that appeals to him, he should make early enquiries. It is by following up his ideas that he can make things happen.

His domestic life is pleasingly aspected, and with joint effort, many plans can be realized. Whether carrying out practical projects (and the Rooster year could see many) or considering major purchases, the Wood Snake will find that the more everyone is involved in the process, the more satisfying home life will be. In addition, certain changes could impact on domestic routine and these also need to be addressed jointly. April, July and December could be fine and active months domestically, but throughout the year there will be a good many pleasing family occasions.

With his various commitments, the Wood Snake tends to be selective in his socializing, but in the Rooster year a few special events will tempt him into going out. Some could be related to his interests, but he could also receive invitations to parties and other occasions and welcome chances to meet his friends. April and July to the end of September could be lively months.

Unattached Wood Snakes and those who have had recent personal difficulties should also aim to go out when they can. Action on their part can not only bring opportunities to meet others but also add new interests to their lifestyle.

Overall, the Year of the Rooster can be a successful one for the Wood Snake. This is a year for setting goals and then working purposefully towards them. To fully benefit, some flexibility will be needed, but with work prospects encouraging, personal interests satisfying and good times to enjoy both domestically and socially, this is a year of possibility for the Wood Snake.

Tip for the Year
Seek out opportunities and make the most of them. You can do a lot this year and fortune will favour the bold and enterprising.

The Fire Snake

This year marks the start of a new decade in the Fire Snake's life and he will have ambitions and plans in mind. With his talents, backed by the support of others and fortuitous circumstances, he will also have much in his favour.

For any Fire Snake who feels he has drifted of late or has not been making the most of his potential, this is a year to focus on the present rather than what has gone before. With resolve, many of these Fire Snakes will see changes taking place which will have a positive bearing on several aspects of their life.

At work many Fire Snakes will feel they have reached an important juncture. Having proved themselves in their present capacity, quite a few will be keen to move forward in their career. In some cases, openings will arise in their present place of work, senior personnel will be keen to offer support and the Fire Snake's reputation will stand him in excellent stead.

Other Fire Snakes will be keen to take their career in a new direction. These Fire Snakes, and those seeking work, should make contact with employers and professional organizations as well as seek advice from experts and other contacts. With initiative, many will be offered a position with good scope for development. February, May, September and November could see key developments.

Progress made at work will also help financially. Many Fire Snakes will enjoy a welcome rise in income and some will also benefit from the receipt of extra funds. Financially, this can be a much improved year, although with his existing commitments and the plans he would like to carry out, the Fire Snake does need to watch his everyday spending and be wary of too many unplanned purchases. Without care, these can mount up. He should also be thorough with paperwork, including checking the terms of any new agreement and keeping policies and receipts safe. Lapses or mistakes could take time to resolve. Fire Snakes, take note and remain vigilant.

With this being their fortieth year, many Fire Snakes will delight in travel, perhaps treating themselves to a holiday and to a destination they have long wanted to visit. Here again, advance planning will help. Fire Snakes who choose not to go away may find their birthday marked by surprises as loved ones arrange special occasions and give thoughtful gifts. The affection and generosity shown the Fire Snake may touch him deeply.

In addition to his own birthday, there will be several reasons for celebration in his home life. Whether marking his own career progress or that of a close relation, an academic success or personal news, the Fire Snake can enjoy several special occasions. He will also be encouraged by the way many of his ideas now develop. However, while he will be keen to get certain plans underway, he should resist the temptation of committing himself to too much at once. April, July and December could be special months domestically.

The Fire Snake will also be grateful for the support and input of his friends this year. When considering changes or needing advice, he could find the expertise and first-hand knowledge of another person particularly helpful. The Rooster year can give rise to quite a few social occasions, and for the unattached Fire Snake, a fortuitous sequence of events could mark the start of a potentially significant romance. April and July to early October could see the most social opportunities.

Although the Fire Snake will be juggling many commitments, he should also allow time for his personal interests, as he could be inspired by new ideas and challenges. In addition, if a new activity appeals to him, he should find out more. Action taken this year can open up interesting possibilities.

In general, the Fire Snake's resolve and skills will reward him well this year. In his work, new responsibilities can mark an important stage in his development. He will be encouraged by the support he receives and this too can aid his progress. He has a lot in his favour this year but this is very much a time to take the initiative and seize opportunities. With determination, the Fire Snake can make his fortieth year a significant one and it can bring him many special times to enjoy.

Tip for the Year

Rooster years favour planning and follow-through. By pursuing your goals, you can achieve a great deal now and build on your success in the future. Enjoy the year and your relations with those who are special to you. This year has great possibilities.

The Earth Snake

The Earth Snake has a talent for reading situations well and timing his actions accordingly. When he has reservations or thinks an outcome uncertain, he will hold back, but when he feels conditions are right, he will proceed with considerable fortitude. And in this Rooster year he will feel positive about a great deal and achieve some favourable results.

His personal life is especially well aspected. Earth Snakes with a partner will enjoy setting about projects on their home, continuing to stamp their personalities on it and getting it as they want, as well as developing shared interests. In several of his undertakings, including when buying appliances or new equipment, the Earth Snake could be fortunate in securing his purchases on favourable terms or in being assisted in some way. Timing and luck can feature strongly this year. Earth Snakes who are keen to move may also be fortunate in finding somewhere suitable and will enjoy establishing themselves in a new base. A key feature of this Rooster year is that action can bring results.

Affairs of the heart are splendidly aspected and Earth Snakes currently enjoying romance could see their relationship continue to grow and develop in significance, while for the unattached, a chance encounter could lead to meeting their future partner. This year many Earth Snakes will benefit from fortuitous developments which have far-reaching consequences.

Throughout the year the Earth Snake will also appreciate the support of his close friends. Not only will some have first-hand knowledge he can draw on when making decisions or carrying out plans, but sometimes they will be in an ideal position to assist. There will also be celebrations to share and a good mix of things to do. These can be lively times and even Earth Snakes who are more introverted will find that participating in what is going on around them can add richness to their year. April and July to early October could see the most social opportunities.

The Earth Snake should also look to develop his personal interests. Some of his ideas could be particularly inspiring. Creative pursuits are favourably aspected and if the Earth Snake is tempted by a new activity, he should find out more. Again, by following up his ideas, he can reap some rewards.

Travel, too, will be tempting and if possible the Earth Snake should aim to take a holiday this year. Even if not travelling too far in distance, good planning can lead to him visiting impressive attractions as well as enjoying new experiences. Additional travel opportunities could arise at short notice and the unexpectedness add to the fun.

Some consideration to his well-being would also be beneficial for the Earth Snake this year and if he feels some additional exercise, a keep-fit discipline or a change in diet could be to his advantage, he should seek advice on how to go about it. It could make a noticeable difference to how he feels.

At work this can be a significant year. By nature the Earth Snake is thorough and his recent work will not only have won him many plaudits but also given him valuable experience. Having proved himself, he may well feel ready to take his career to the next level. Here again, chance and timing can help, with an ideal promotion opportunity opening up in his place of work or a suitable position falling vacant elsewhere. Important headway can be made this year and many Earth Snakes will welcome the challenge they now take on.

For Earth Snakes who are not feeling fulfilled in their present line of work, as well as those seeking a position, again the Rooster year can have important developments in store. By not being too restrictive in the type of positions they seek, many of these Earth Snakes could secure an opening that allows them to develop their skills in other ways. Although this may initially be daunting, by putting in the effort, these Earth Snakes can not only make an early impression but also open up other possibilities. February, May, September and November could see potentially important developments.

The Earth Snake's progress at work will help financially and enable him to proceed with many plans and purchases. However, he does need to manage his outgoings well. This can be an expensive time and funds need to be apportioned accordingly. But if the Earth Snake considers his more major transactions carefully, he may identify some favourable buying opportunities as well as make more appropriate choices. Again, timing and instinct can serve him well.

Overall, this is a favourable year for the Earth Snake, with often special times in his personal life. In his work and personal interests, he can benefit from the opportunities that arise and the skills that he learns. The key factor is that this is a year for *action* and any Earth Snakes who let chances go by could undermine both their present and future prospects. It is the *now* that counts, and for the Earth Snake, it offers the opportunity to make more of his potential as well as enjoy many pleasing developments.

Tip for the Year
You know in yourself you are capable of achieving great things. Believe … begin … become. Make the most of the year and add to your skills. What you do now can have far-reaching value.

Famous Snakes

Jason Aldean, Muhammad Ali, Ann-Margret, Avicii, Kim Basinger, Ben Bernanke, Björk, Tony Blair, Michael Bloomberg, Michael Bolton, Brahms, Pierce Brosnan, Mark Carney, Casanova, Jackie Collins, Tom Conti, Robert Downey Jr, Bob Dylan, Elgar, Michael Fassbender, Sir Alexander Fleming, Mahatma Gandhi, Greta Garbo, Art Garfunkel, J. Paul Getty, Johann Wolfgang von Goethe, Princess Grace of Monaco, Tom Hardy, Stephen Hawking, Audrey Hepburn, Jack Higgins, Dakota Johnson, James Joyce, Stacy Keach, Ronan Keating, J. F. Kennedy, Chaka Khan, Carole King, Rory McIlroy, Mao Tse-tung, Chris Martin, Henri Matisse, John Mayer, Alfred Nobel, Mike Oldfield, Jacqueline Onassis, Sarah Jessica Parker, Pablo Picasso, Daniel Radcliffe, Franklin D. Roosevelt, J. K. Rowling, Jean-Paul Sartre, Franz Schubert, Charlie Sheen, Paul Simon, Delia Smith, Ben Stiller, Taylor Swift, Juno Temple, Madame Tussaud, Shania Twain, Dionne Warwick, Mia Wasikowska, Charlie Watts, Kanye West, Oprah Winfrey.

11 February 1918 to 31 January 1919 — *Earth Horse*

30 January 1930 to 16 February 1931 — *Metal Horse*

15 February 1942 to 4 February 1943 — *Water Horse*

3 February 1954 to 23 January 1955 — *Wood Horse*

21 January 1966 to 8 February 1967 — *Fire Horse*

7 February 1978 to 27 January 1979 — *Earth Horse*

27 January 1990 to 14 February 1991 — *Metal Horse*

12 February 2002 to 31 January 2003 — *Water Horse*

31 January 2014 to 18 February 2015 — *Wood Horse*

The Horse

The Personality of the Horse

There are many worn paths,
but the most rewarding
is the one you decide on and forge yourself.

The Horse is born under the signs of elegance and ardour. He has a most engaging and charming manner and is usually very popular. He loves meeting people and likes attending parties and other large social gatherings.

The Horse is a lively character and enjoys being the centre of attention. He has many leadership qualities and is much admired for his honest and straightforward manner. He is an eloquent and persuasive speaker and has a great love of discussion and debate. He also has a particularly agile mind and can assimilate facts remarkably quickly.

He does, however, have a fiery temper and although his outbursts are usually short-lived, he can often say things that he will later regret. He is also not particularly good at keeping secrets.

The Horse has many interests and involves himself in a wide variety of activities. He can, however, get involved in so much that he can often waste his energies on projects that he never has time to complete. He also has a tendency to change his interests rather frequently and will often get caught up in the latest craze or 'in thing' until something more exciting turns up.

The Horse also likes to have a certain amount of freedom and independence. He hates being bound by petty rules and regulations and as far as possible likes to feel that he is answerable to no one but himself. But despite this spirit of freedom, he still likes to have the support and encouragement of others in his various enterprises.

Due to his many talents and likeable nature, the Horse will often go far in life. He enjoys challenges and is a methodical and tireless worker. However, should things go against him and he fail in any of his enterprises, it will take a long time for him to recover and pick up the pieces again. Success to the Horse means everything. To fail is a disaster and a humiliation.

The Horse likes to have variety in life and will try his hand at many different things before he settles down to one particular job. Even then, he will probably remain alert to see whether there are any better opportunities for him to take up. He has a restless nature and can easily get bored. He does, however, excel in any position that allows him sufficient freedom to act on his own initiative or brings him into contact with a lot of people.

Although the Horse is not particularly bothered about accumulating great wealth, he handles his finances with care and will rarely experience any serious financial problems.

He also enjoys travel and loves visiting new and faraway places. At some stage during his life he will be tempted to live abroad for a short period of time and due to his adaptable nature will find that he will fit in well wherever he goes.

The Horse pays a great deal of attention to his appearance and usually likes to wear smart, colourful and rather distinctive clothes. He is very attractive to others and will often have many romances before he settles down. He is loyal and protective to his partner, but despite his family commitments he still likes to retain a certain measure of independence and have the freedom to carry on with his own interests and hobbies. He will find that he is especially suited to those born under the signs of the Tiger, Goat, Rooster and Dog. He can also get on well with the Rabbit, Dragon, Snake, Pig and another Horse, but he will find the Ox too serious and intolerant for his liking. He will also have difficulty in getting on with the Monkey and the Rat – the Monkey is very inquisitive and the Rat seeks security, and both will resent the Horse's rather independent ways.

The female Horse is usually most attractive and has a friendly, outgoing personality. She is highly intelligent, has many interests and is alert to everything that is going on around her. She particularly enjoys outdoor pursuits and often likes to take part in sport and keep-fit activities. She also enjoys travel, literature and the arts, and is a very good conversationalist.

Although the Horse can be stubborn and rather self-centred, he does have a considerate nature and is often willing to help others. He has a good sense of humour and will usually make a favourable impression wherever he goes. Provided he can curb his slightly restless nature and keep tight control over his temper, he will go through life making friends, taking part in a multitude of different activities and generally achieving many of his objectives. His life will rarely be dull.

The Five Different Types of Horse

In addition to the 12 signs of the Chinese zodiac there are five elements and these have a strengthening or moderating influence on the signs. The effects of the elements on the Horse are described below, together with the years in which they were exercising their influence. Therefore Horses born in 1930 and 1990 are Metal Horses, Horses born in 1942 and 2002 are Water Horses, and so on.

Metal Horse: 1930, 1990

This Horse is bold, confident and forthright. He is ambitious and a great innovator. He loves challenges and takes great delight in sorting out complicated problems. He likes to have a certain amount of independence and resents any outside interference in his affairs. He has charm and a certain charisma, but he can also be very stubborn and rather impulsive. He usually has many friends and enjoys an active social life.

Water Horse: 1942, 2002

The Water Horse has a friendly nature and a good sense of humour and is able to talk intelligently on a wide range of topics. He is astute in business matters and quick to take advantage of any opportunities that arise. He does, however, have a tendency to get easily distracted and can change his interests – and indeed his mind – rather frequently, and this can often work to his detriment. He is nevertheless very talented and can often go far in life. He pays a great deal of attention to his appearance and is usually smart and well turned out. He loves to travel and also enjoys sport and other outdoor activities.

Wood Horse: 1954, 2014

The Wood Horse has a most agreeable and amiable nature. He communicates well with others and is able to talk intelligently on many different subjects. He is a hard and conscientious worker and is held in high esteem by his friends and colleagues. His opinions are often sought and, given his imaginative nature, he can often come up with some very original and practical ideas. He is usually widely read and likes to lead a busy social life. He can also be most generous and often holds high moral views.

Fire Horse: 1966

The element of Fire combined with the temperament of the Horse creates one of the most powerful forces in the Chinese zodiac. The Fire Horse is destined to lead an exciting and eventful life and to make his mark on his chosen profession. He has a forceful personality and his intelligence and resolute manner bring him the support and admiration of many. He loves action and excitement and his life will rarely be quiet. He can, however, be rather blunt and forthright in his views and does not take kindly to interference in his own affairs or to obeying orders. He is a flamboyant character, has a good sense of humour and will lead a very active social life.

Earth Horse: 1918, 1978

This Horse is considerate and caring. He is more cautious than some of the other types of Horse, but is wise, perceptive and extremely capable. Although he can be rather indecisive at times, he has considerable business acumen and is very astute in financial matters. He has a quiet, friendly nature and is well thought of by his family and friends.

Prospects for the Horse in 2017

Never one to be idle, the Horse generally fares well in the active Monkey year (8 February 2016–27 January 2017). In the closing months, he will set about his many activities with his customary verve and can look forward to some pleasing accomplishments. However, to be most effective he should avoid spreading his energies too widely.

At work, whether dealing with heavy workloads or challenging situations, many Horses can do their reputation a lot of good. In addition, some could be involved in a change of duties and will be keen to establish themselves in their new role. October and early November could bring important developments.

On a personal level, the Horse will find himself in demand, with an increasing number of social opportunities. Affairs of the heart are favourably aspected and Horses who are enjoying romance or who meet someone now will find this can add special meaning to the latter part of the year.

Domestically, too, there will be much to think about and arrange. Where home purchases and gift-buying are concerned, the Horse can make some pleasing acquisitions, although when entering into agreements, he does need to check the small print. Horses, take note.

Overall, the Horse will have fitted a lot into the Monkey year and while there will have been pressures, his successes will have been richly deserved.

The Year of the Rooster begins on 28 January and will be a challenging one for the Horse. Horses are independent-minded and like a certain freedom of action, while Rooster years favour structure. As a result, there will be times when the Horse could feel hampered and some of his activities could prove problematic. However, by being aware of what is going on around him and adapting accordingly, he can still make steady progress.

At work, many Horses will have recently experienced changes in their role or will take on a new position as the Rooster year begins. For these

Horses, this can be an excellent year to establish themselves and learn about the different aspects of their industry. By immersing themselves in their situation, many will be able to make this a more fulfilling time than might otherwise be the case. Working closely with colleagues and being an active member of any team will also help their reputation. All Horses, whether new to their position or established, should also take advantage of any training that is available to them and keep up-to-date with developments in their field. This way, when opportunities arise, they will be better prepared to seize them.

The majority of Horses will remain with their present employer, but for those who are keen to move on, or seeking work, the Rooster year can have great significance. While finding a new position will not be easy, by widening their search and making plenty of enquiries (here their persistence can be telling), many of these Horses will secure a position which offers considerable change. Some adaptation will be required and the Rooster year can be demanding, but it will also give these Horses an excellent chance to prove themselves. What many take on this year can in fact be regarded as groundwork for future success. March, July, October and November could see encouraging developments.

Although the Horse may enjoy a modest rise in income over the year, he will need to manage his finances carefully, particularly as he could have to repair or replace appliances as well as face additional expenses. As a result, he should keep a close watch on spending and, where possible, make early provision for forthcoming expenses. Where large purchases are concerned, he also needs to check the costs and implications. Without vigilance, problems can arise. Horses, take note and be thorough.

More positively, this is a good year for travel and the Horse should aim to make provision for a holiday as well as take advantage of any short breaks or weekends away. A change of scene can do him good and, with his thirst for adventure, often be fun too.

Although he will have many demands on his time, recreational pursuits can also be a satisfying outlet for his ideas. If he feels that enrolling on a course, joining a local group or setting time aside for practice and study would be useful, he should do so. Focused effort can reward him well this year.

With his often demanding lifestyle, he should also give some consideration to his own well-being and, if he lacks regular exercise or his diet is poor, seek medical advice on ways to improve.

With his outgoing nature, the Horse enjoys company and will once again welcome opportunities to go out. However, while much will go well, petty jealousy, a disagreement or the awkward attitude of another person could be disappointing. There could be occasions when the Horse feels let down this year. In tricky situations he should proceed carefully, aim to address matters of concern and keep everything in perspective. And if certain friendships fall away, new ones will surely take their place. Despite the awkward aspects, his social life can still bring some lively and enjoyable occasions, with May, June, August and October likely to see the most activity.

The Horse's home life can a very special part of his year. As the Rooster year starts, the Horse and his family members could find it helpful to discuss plans for the months ahead. Whether these are personal and family goals, individual hopes or home improvements, talking them through can result in a course of action. Rooster years favour planning and concerted effort. In addition, shared interests, individual successes and travel can all bring special times. March and August are likely to see the most domestic activity. However, openness between family members is essential throughout the year, especially in view of the pressures and tribulations it may bring.

The Horse is a doer and always keen to make the most of his situation. However, the Rooster year can be challenging for him. Some situations will be troubling, but by focusing on his situation and looking to build on his skills, he can prepare himself for the more substantial successes soon to come, especially in the following Dog year. This may not be the easiest of years, but the determined Horse can gain skills and insights he can take forward. And he can also enjoy quality time with his loved ones as well as take pleasure in his interests and travels.

The Metal Horse

This will be a full year for the Metal Horse. Importantly, he will be able to build on recent achievements and make reasonable progress, but some developments could be problematic. While not a bad year, it will not always be straightforward.

One feature of the Metal Horse's personality is his strong will. When he sets his mind to something, he is not one to change it. And while his resolve can often work in his favour, in the Rooster year he should avoid being intransigent. To make the most of certain situations and avoid some of the year's trickier moments, he will need to be flexible. Metal Horses, take note.

At work the Metal Horse could find himself having to adapt his role. Although he may have misgivings about this, this is not a time to distance himself from what is going on or appear obtuse. In 2017 it is a case of making the most of situations *as they are.*

And there will still be benefits to be had. Not only will many Metal Horses have the chance to gain experience in another capacity, but they can also learn more about their line of work and so improve their prospects for later.

The majority of Metal Horses will remain with their present employer over the year, but for those who are discontented where they are, keen to progress in other ways or seeking work, the Rooster year can have significant developments in store. In their quest, these Metal Horses should consider different ways of using their strengths. With some thought, and input from others, they could find themselves setting their career on a new path. In many cases, brighter prospects lie ahead, especially in the following Dog year. March, July and mid-September to early December could see key developments.

To help their situation, all Metal Horses should take advantage of any training available to them as well as involve themselves in their workplace. By being active they will benefit both their present situation and their future prospects.

Although many Metal Horses will increase their income too, this will be an expensive year. Some may need to put down deposits and all will have existing commitments and be keen to make certain purchases. If plans are to be carried out, control will be required. This is no year to proceed on an ad hoc basis or succumb to too many unplanned purchases. Neither is it a time to be lax. The Metal Horse should be thorough with paperwork and if he takes on a new agreement, check the terms with care. Mistakes could prove costly and inconvenient.

While the Metal Horse will need to budget carefully, travel can bring him great pleasure and, even if not travelling too far in distance, he should aim to take a holiday during the year. If he is able to combine his travelling with a special event, he can make his time away all the more meaningful.

Personal interests can also reward him well. Many Metal Horses will feel on inspired form this year. They could also be encouraged by other enthusiasts or the possibilities of new equipment. The Metal Horse often has a deep interest in a particular area and this year he should allow himself the chance to enjoy and further his knowledge.

Socially, although the Rooster year has its encouraging aspects, it also has its more cautionary ones. If the Metal Horse finds himself in a fraught situation or sees signs of impending difficulty, he needs to exercise care and ideally try to defuse the situation. Some issues could easily escalate and cast a shadow over the year. The Metal Horse could also be troubled by a difference of opinion, a petty jealousy or a friend holding back in a moment of need. This is a year for awareness and, where necessary, an accommodating approach. Metal Horses, take note.

The Rooster year can, though, give rise to some lively times and the Metal Horse will enjoy many of the year's varied social occasions. For the unattached and those who may have had recent personal difficulties, someone special may appear at just the right time. Tricky though the Rooster year may be, it can bring pleasant surprises and in many ways have long-term significance. May, June, late July to early September and October could see the most social activity.

The Metal Horse's home life will also be busy. Keen to go ahead with improvements, he may throw himself into practical activities, and projects that are started early on in the year can often lead to others. The Metal Horse may be kept occupied throughout the year, often sharing tasks with other people and enjoying himself in the process. Metal Horses who move will quickly make their new home their own.

While the practical Metal Horse will be on inspired form, he could face complex matters at home. Whether these affect his or his partner's work position, domestic finances or another aspect of his domestic life, it is important that any concerns are talked through. Domestically, it is a year for sharing, planning and valuing quality time together.

In general, the Year of the Rooster will be a busy and demanding one for the Metal Horse. At work he may be under pressure and uneasy about developments taking place. However, by being prepared to adapt (rather than resist), he can benefit. He will need to be careful in money matters, and if a disagreement arises over the year, try to defuse the situation and keep matters in perspective. However, while Rooster years have their trickier aspects, the Metal Horse can often successfully steer his way round these and demonstrate his skills in the process. And importantly, what he learns now can prepare him for future success.

Tip for the Year
Be prepared to adapt and make the most of the opportunities that come your way, especially if they further your skills and knowledge. Rooster years can leave an important legacy. Also, enjoy time with your loved ones and share your thoughts with them.

The Water Horse

The Water Horse has an enquiring mind and over the Rooster year he will involve himself in many satisfying pursuits. In addition he can look forward to some special times in the company of others, although, as with all years, there will be difficulties to address. Some will call for deft handling.

Water Horses born in 1942 will have plans they will be particularly keen to implement. Whether these relate to home improvements, solving a domestic problem, making a key purchase or something else they want to do or see, they should discuss their thoughts with others. It is also important they are not too rigid in their thinking. Sometimes discussion can result in better alternatives and/or once they start to look at the choices available they can find alternatives which better meet their needs. As with all Horses this year, flexibility and attention to detail are advised.

The Water Horse will particularly delight in some acquisitions for his home. He will also take pleasure in projects that he and other household members undertake, and combined effort can make a real difference this year. In addition, many Water Horses will enjoy some of the activities that are planned in advance. These could include family occasions, visits to relations and revisiting favourite areas or places of interest.

The Water Horse will also take great interest in the activities of family members. The bonds he shares with grandchildren and great-grandchildren are often special. However, while there will be times of joy, there could also be concerns. A relation could come under intense pressure as major decisions are called for and the Water Horse could be worried over a close friend as well. The support he feels able to give may be of more value than he may realize. In turn he should not keep any of his own anxieties hidden. If he speaks of these, he can *and will* be helped. Water Horses, take note and do be forthcoming.

In money matters, the Water Horse will need to be vigilant. Some activities will involve considerable outlay and he needs to keep a check on his position, including any obligations he takes on. If he has any doubts, he should get matters clarified before proceeding. He should also deal with financial correspondence carefully. Mistakes or delayed responses could take time to rectify. Water Horses, take note.

As well as bureaucratic problems, Rooster years can bring difficulties concerning the attitude of another person. Here the Water Horse will need to deal with the situation as best he can rather than ignore it. Again, he should remember that support and advice are available.

Overall, though, the Rooster year will be a satisfying one for the senior Water Horse, especially in the way his plans evolve, and he will find that acting in combination with others will lead to some good outcomes.

For the Water Horse born in 2002, the Rooster year will be a busy one. In his education, he will have much material to cover, and while he will have his preferred subjects, there will be some which give rise to anxiety. Here, though, his own attitude can make a difference. By rising to challenges and not closing his mind to particular subjects, he can make important strides.

The young Water Horse should also make the most of the opportunities available to him. Whether involving himself in extra activities at school or taking advantage of additional tuition, including in recreational pursuits, if he participates in what is going on around him, he will often get more pleasure *and value* from the year.

He will also enjoy fun times with his many friends. However, friendships do evolve and differences in outlook or altered circumstances could cause a possible rift this year. As well as the good times, there could be some painful ones. All are part of life's rich learning experience.

Throughout the year the young Water Horse will, however, enjoy the support of many of those around him and whenever he is troubled he should speak to others rather than worry alone. Pleasingly, problems will often be short-lived and not detract from the pleasures and achievements of the year.

For all Water Horses, whether born in 1942 or 2002, this will be a constructive year. It is a time to plan, take ideas forward and make the most of the present. As with all years, there will be difficulties to address, but these can often be overcome. This may not be the easiest of years for the Water Horse, but he can accomplish a lot.

Tip for the Year
Be open-minded and receptive. By making the most of what happens this year, you can take many of your ideas forward and enjoy some satisfying outcomes.

The Wood Horse

This will be an important year for the Wood Horse and as it starts he should give some thought to his hopes and objectives for it. With something to work towards, he can make this a constructive time. However, while a lot can happen, throughout the year the Wood Horse will need to be aware of what is going on around him and show some flexibility. He may be purposeful, but circumstances are apt to change and he needs to adapt accordingly.

At work many Wood Horses will be content to continue in their present role and focus on duties they know well. However, new procedures, management changes and other issues could all prove challenging. Some weeks will be particularly difficult, but the Wood Horse will be helped by his experience, and by keeping situations in perspective, he will be able to ride out the pressures and emerge with much to his credit. When situations settle, there could also be the opportunity for him to take on specific tasks, including perhaps mentoring junior colleagues.

There will, though, be some Wood Horses who decide to look for something less stressful, more convenient and with hours that better suit their lifestyle. For these Wood Horses, as well as those currently seeking a position, the Rooster year can have significant developments in store. Although their quest will not be easy, events can move in curious ways and chance plays a big part this year. Whenever the Wood Horse scents an opportunity, he should be quick to pursue it. What he takes on now could provide the opportunity he has been seeking for some time. A few Wood Horses may decide to go freelance, too, or start their own enterprise. Work-wise, this Rooster year is one of interesting possibilities. March, July, October and November could see important developments.

In most of his activities the Wood Horse will be well supported, although he does need to be mindful of the views (and sensitivities) of his colleagues. If a disagreement does occur, he should not let it distract him from his duties. Rooster years can test the Wood Horse, but in the process highlight his many qualities.

Another area which will require care is finance. In view of the plans and purchases he is considering, the Wood Horse will need to keep a close watch on spending and make early provision for large outlays. Also, when attending to paperwork he will need to be thorough and check anything that is unclear. This is no year for risks or assumptions. If necessary, professional advice should be sought.

More positively, travel is favourably aspected and the Wood Horse should try to make provision for a holiday during the year. Advance planning could see some exciting plans taking shape and long-held hopes being realized.

Although busy, the Wood Horse should also make sure recreational pursuits are not ignored. These can give him the chance to develop his ideas and use his talents in other ways, and he could become interested in a new activity over the year. Here again he should be receptive to the year's emerging possibilities.

In addition, he should give some consideration to his level of exercise and the quality of his diet. With advice, he could find positive changes making a real difference to how he feels.

With his amiable nature, the Wood Horse enjoys meeting others and will be tempted by many social events this year. Some could prove unexpectedly significant, with friends offering helpful advice or information that is relevant to plans he is considering. May, June, August and October could be particularly active months.

However, while much is set to go well, should a minor disagreement occur or the Wood Horse be concerned about the situation of another person, he should speak openly and, if appropriate, seek advice. Here instinct can be a helpful indicator.

The Wood Horse's home life will see interesting developments and it is important that there is good communication when plans are being made. Whether making purchases, smartening up living areas, undertaking garden projects or making the most of what is happening locally, the Wood Horse can enjoy seeing his projects take shape. Again, though, plans can be subject to change, especially as the Wood Horse becomes aware of better alternatives or has fresh ideas, and flexibility will be required.

There will also be family successes to celebrate and a loved one could enjoy, after much time and effort, a personal triumph. Short breaks and trips and a possible holiday will also do everyone good. March, August and December could see gratifying times in many a Wood Horse household.

Overall, the Year of the Rooster will be a busy one for the Wood Horse, but with care and his customary resolve, he will be pleased with how many of his activities develop. At work there will increased pressures but also good opportunities. Travel and personal interests can be pleasing and in his home and social life the Wood Horse will enjoy shared activities and be encouraged by the support of those around him. However, he will need to be vigilant in money matters and should try to defuse any awkward situation that arises over the year. If applicable, he should also obtain further advice. There can be exacting times in the Rooster year, but problems are there to be dealt with and their resolution can highlight the Wood Horse's qualities. This will be a demanding year for him, but it will also be one of interesting and potentially significant opportunities.

Tip for the Year
Be aware of what is happening around you and adapt accordingly. Also, spend quality time with your loved ones and enjoy your personal interests. With good lifestyle balance and the desire to make the most of your opportunities, you can make good gains despite the sometimes awkward conditions.

The Fire Horse

The Horse personality and the fire element are a powerful mix and the Fire Horse is a dynamic character. In the Rooster year he will set about his activities with typical resolve and gain often important results. But there is a big 'but'. The Fire Horse likes a certain independence and can also be dogmatic. During 2017 he needs to exercise care, remembering it is the Rooster that rules the year and calls the tune.

Almost all areas of the Fire Horse's life will see considerable activity but his work in particular will be significant, as there will be scope for him to further his career.

For Fire Horses who work in large organizations, there could be an opening in a different department or location, or the opportunity to become involved in a specific project. The Rooster year will encourage the Fire Horse to make more of himself, but adjustment will be required, and for some, moving away from familiar roles.

Fire Horses seeking work should widen their search as well as keep themselves informed about developments in their area. The arrival of a new employer or expansion of an existing one could lead to new opportunities. March, July and mid-September to November could see key developments.

Throughout the year the Fire Horse also needs to involve himself in his place of work. By liaising well with his colleagues and raising his profile, he can help both his present situation and his future prospects. However, while the aspects are encouraging, there could be difficult moments. Delays, a systems failure or an awkward colleague could all be troubling, and when faced with difficulties, the Fire Horse needs to remain focused and aim to resolve the problem as quickly as he can. Rooster years can be problematic, but it is often in the surmounting of difficulties that reputations are made.

Progress at work will reward many Fire Horses financially, but Rooster years can be expensive ones and the Fire Horse will need to keep a close watch on his spending. To succumb to too many unplanned purchases could curtail other activities later on. Also, when making large purchases or entering into new agreements he should check the terms and implications. This is no year for risk or rush.

With his enquiring nature, the Fire Horse enjoys a wide range of interests and could be tempted to take up something new this year. This could be an extension of an existing interest or something a friend is enthusiastic about.

Travel is also favourably aspected and all Fire Horses should aim to go away at some time during the year. There could also be a lot happening in their locality and if anything appeals to the Fire Horse, or is suggested by a loved one, he should follow it up.

He will also welcome the social opportunities of the year, including a special occasion involving someone close to him. He may help with the arrangements and his imaginative input will be appreciated. In turn, he himself will value the support of his close friends when making decisions and should listen carefully to their words. This is no time to close his mind to what could be helpful advice. May, June, August and October could see much social activity. However, while a lot is set to go well, many Fire Horses could also find themselves involved in an irritating matter. At such times, the Fire Horse should proceed tactfully and aim to defuse any tension. His judgement can serve him well.

His home life will see considerable activity. Here pooling ideas and combining talents can lead to satisfying outcomes, including home improvements that benefit all concerned. This is a year favouring collective effort. There will also be some domestic highlights, including celebrating achievements, travelling and enjoying some of the more spontaneous occasions that arise. The Rooster year is capable of surprises. Throughout, the Fire Horse's attentiveness will be appreciated and add a great deal to his home life. March, August and December could be busy and special months.

At the end of the year, the Fire Horse may look back over the last 12 months and be astonished at all he has managed to do. The year may have demanded a lot of his skills and fortitude, and he will have needed to be aware and nimble-footed, but he can emerge from it with some good and often far-reaching gains to his credit.

Tip for the Year
Put in the effort and rise to the challenges – and opportunities – of the year. Situations may not always be easy, but in dealing with them you can demonstrate your personal strengths and learn new skills. Your successes this year will be hard won but richly deserved.

The Earth Horse

There is a Chinese proverb which the Earth Horse would do well to remember this year: 'Slow and steady wins the race.' With careful planning and steady effort, he can achieve a great deal and sow the seeds for later success. This may not be the smoothest of years, but it can have far-reaching significance.

One key feature of the Rooster year is that it favours planning, and as it starts, the Earth Horse should consider his objectives for the months ahead. By having some aims in mind, he will be more alert to opportunities as well as to timely developments. Serendipity can be a useful friend this year.

At work many Earth Horses will decide to focus on their current role and the duties they know well. For those who have experienced recent change, this is an ideal time to become more established in their role and involve themselves in their workplace. With commitment, they can greatly enhance their reputation.

However, while the aspects are encouraging, there will be challenging times too. Problems, disagreements and complex issues will make some weeks difficult and patience and resourcefulness will be required. The skills of many Earth Horses will be tested, but in the process they can gain experience they can build on in the future.

For Earth Horses who are not fulfilled where they are, as well as those seeking work, the Rooster year can mark an important stage in their career. By considering their strengths and how best they can use them, these Earth Horses can become aware of positions which would suit them well. Training and refresher courses could be required, but by keeping alert and pursuing openings that interest them, many of these Earth Horses will get that all-important foothold in a new company or industry. March, July and mid-September to early December could see encouraging developments.

Although progress made at work will bring an increase in income, financial matters require care this year. Spending needs to be watched and early provision made for forthcoming expenses. With larger purchases, the Earth Horse should consider his options with care. The more time he allows, the more satisfactory his decisions will be. He also needs to be thorough when attending to paperwork and to keep receipts, guarantees and documents safe. Mislaying a document could be to his disadvantage. Earth Horses, take note.

More positively, with travel well aspected, the Earth Horse should aim to take a holiday during the year. Short breaks and special events could also appeal to him. The early summer could see good travel possibilities.

The Earth Horse should also set some time aside for his personal interests. These can not only be good ways for him to relax – which is important given his demanding lifestyle – but also develop in new ways this year. For the inquisitive and keen Earth Horse, these can be stimulating times.

Some of the Earth Horse's interests can also have a good social element. Existing friends and work changes can also extend his contacts this year and he is set to impress many new people. May, June, August and October could see the most social activity.

For unattached Earth Horses, a chance meeting can add excitement to their year, although relationships should be built up steadily rather than rushed. The Rooster year can also set traps for the unwary. A *faux pas*, misunderstanding or lack of attentiveness on the Earth Horse's part could result in tensions, and if he detects any awkward undercurrents in a relationship, he needs to proceed carefully. To ignore them could be to exacerbate them. Earth Horses, take note.

The Earth Horse's home life will see much decision-making taking place, perhaps involving his own or his partner's work situation or the educational options open to younger relations. To help, the Earth Horse should speak openly about his preferences and any reservations. With good communication, important decisions can be taken much more easily.

The Earth Horse will also be eager to go ahead with certain home projects, and here again, if he shares his thoughts and allows time, a lot can happen. Domestically, this can be a satisfying year and one marked by notable personal achievements. March and August could be particularly active months.

In general, the Year of the Rooster can be a constructive one for the Earth Horse. By focusing on his objectives and adapting to circumstances, he can further his knowledge *and* help his future prospects. Personal interests, too, can develop well. Money matters require care, however, and the Earth Horse also needs to be attentive in his relations with others. Uncharacteristic slips or lapses can undermine his position. However, travel, social occasions and an active home life can bring him considerable pleasure and be especially important in light of some of the year's pressures. 'Slow and steady wins the race' and the Earth Horse will advance steadily this year and work towards the opportunities that lie ahead.

Tip for the Year

Take advantage of any training and/or other chances to extend your skills. By investing in yourself, you will be opening up important possibilities for the future. Also, keep your lifestyle in balance and preserve time for the things you enjoy. You deserve some 'me time' this year.

Famous Horses

Roman Abramovich, Neil Armstrong, Rowan Atkinson, Samuel Beckett, Ingmar Bergman, Leonard Bernstein, Joe Biden, Helena Bonham Carter, David Cameron, James Cameron, Jackie Chan, Chopin, Sir Sean Connery, Billy Connolly, Kevin Costner, Clint Eastwood, Thomas Alva Edison, Harrison Ford, Aretha Franklin, Bob Geldof, Samuel Goldwyn, Rita Hayworth, Jimi Hendrix, François Hollande, Janet Jackson, Jean-Claude Juncker, R. Kelly, Calvin Klein, Ashton Kutcher, Petra Kvitová, Jennifer Lawrence, Lenin, Annie Lennox, Sir Paul McCartney, Nelson Mandela, Angela Merkel, Ben Murphy, Sir Isaac Newton, Louis Pasteur, Jodi Picoult, Gordon Ramsay, Rembrandt, Jean Renoir, Theodore Roosevelt, Helena Rubenstein, Adam Sandler, David Schwimmer, Martin Scorsese, Kristen Stewart, Barbra Streisand, Kiefer Sutherland, Patrick Swayze, John Travolta, Malcolm Turnbull, Usher, Vivaldi, Emma Watson, Billy Wilder, Brian Wilson, the Duke of Windsor, Caroline Wozniacki, Jacob Zuma.

1 February 1919 to 19 February 1920 — *Earth Goat*

17 February 1931 to 5 February 1932 — *Metal Goat*

5 February 1943 to 24 January 1944 — *Water Goat*

24 January 1955 to 11 February 1956 — *Wood Goat*

9 February 1967 to 29 January 1968 — *Fire Goat*

28 January 1979 to 15 February 1980 — *Earth Goat*

15 February 1991 to 3 February 1992 — *Metal Goat*

1 February 2003 to 21 January 2004 — *Water Goat*

19 February 2015 to 7 February 2016 — *Wood Goat*

The Goat

The Personality of the Goat

Amid the complexities of life,
it is the ability to appreciate that is so special.

The Goat is born under the sign of art. He is imaginative, creative and has a good appreciation of the finer things in life. He has an easy-going nature and prefers to live in a relaxed and pressure-free environment. He hates any sort of discord or unpleasantness and does not like to be bound by a strict routine or rigid timetable. He is not one to be hurried against his will, but despite his seemingly relaxed approach to life, he is something of a perfectionist and when he starts work on a project he is certain to give his best.

The Goat usually prefers to work in a team rather than on his own. He likes to have the support and encouragement of others and if left to deal with matters on his own he can get very worried and tend to view things rather pessimistically. Wherever possible, he will leave major decision-making to others while he concentrates on his own pursuits. If, however, he feels particularly strongly about a certain matter or has to defend his position in any way, he will act with great fortitude and precision.

The Goat has a very persuasive nature and often uses his considerable charm to get his own way. He can, however, be rather hesitant about letting his true feelings be known and if he were prepared to be more forthright he would do much better as a result.

The Goat tends to have a quiet, somewhat reserved nature, but when he is in company he likes he can often become the centre of attention. He can be highly amusing, a marvellous host at parties and a superb entertainer. Whenever the spotlight falls on him, his adrenaline starts to flow and he can be assured of giving a sparkling performance, particularly if he is allowed to use his creative skills in any way.

Of all the signs in the Chinese zodiac, the Goat is probably the most gifted artistically. Whether it is in the theatre, literature, music or art, he is certain to make a lasting impression. He is a born creator and is rarely happier than when occupied in some artistic pursuit. But even in this he does well to work with others rather than on his own. He needs inspiration and a guiding influence, but when he has found his true *métier*, he can often receive widespread acclaim.

In addition to his liking for the arts, the Goat is usually quite religious and often has a deep interest in nature, animals and the countryside. He is also fairly athletic and there are many Goats who have excelled in some form of sporting activity or who have a great interest in sport.

Although the Goat is not particularly materialistic or concerned about finance, he will find that he will usually be lucky in financial matters and will rarely be short of the necessary funds to tide himself over. He is, however, rather self-indulgent and tends to spend his money as soon as he receives it rather than make provision for the future.

The Goat usually leaves home when he is young but he will always maintain strong links with his parents and the other members of his family. He is also rather nostalgic and is well known for keeping mementoes of his childhood and souvenirs of places that he has visited. His home will not be particularly tidy, but he knows where everything is and it will be scrupulously clean.

Affairs of the heart are particularly important to the Goat and he will often have many romances before he finally settles down. Although he is fairly adaptable, he prefers to live in a secure and stable environment and he will find that he is best suited to those born under the signs of the Tiger, Horse, Monkey, Pig and Rabbit. He can also establish a good relationship with the Dragon, Snake, Rooster and another Goat, but he may find the Ox and Dog a little too serious for his liking. Neither will he care particularly for the Rat's rather thrifty ways.

The female Goat devotes all her time and energy to the needs of her family. She has excellent taste in home furnishings and often uses her considerable artistic skills to make clothes for herself and her children. She takes great care over her appearance and can be most attractive to others. Although she is not the most organized of people, her engaging manner and delightful sense of humour create a favourable impression wherever she goes. She is also a good cook and usually derives much pleasure from gardening and outdoor pursuits.

The Goat can win friends easily and people generally feel relaxed in his company. He has a kind and understanding nature and although he can occasionally be stubborn, he can, with the right support and encouragement, live a very satisfying life. And the more he can use his creative skills, the happier he will be.

The Five Different Types of Goat

In addition to the 12 signs of the Chinese zodiac there are five elements and these have a strengthening or moderating influence on the signs. The effects of the elements on the Goat are described below, together with the years in which they were exercising their influence. Therefore Goats born in 1931 and 1991 are Metal Goats, Goats born in 1943 and 2003 are Water Goats, and so on.

Metal Goat: 1931, 1991

This Goat is thorough and conscientious in all that he does and is capable of doing very well in his chosen profession. Despite his confident manner, he can be a great worrier and he would find it helpful to discuss his concerns with others rather than keep them to himself. He is loyal to his family and employers and will have a small group of particularly close friends. He has good taste and is usually highly skilled in some aspect of the arts. He is often a collector of antiques and his home will be very tastefully furnished.

Water Goat: 1943, 2003

The Water Goat is very popular and makes friends with remarkable ease. He is good at spotting opportunities but does not always have the necessary confidence to follow them through. He likes to have security both in his home life and work and does not take kindly to change. He is articulate, has a good sense of humour and is usually very good with children.

Wood Goat: 1955, 2015

This Goat is generous, kind-hearted and always eager to please. He usually has a large circle of friends and involves himself in a wide variety of activities. He has a very trusting nature but can sometimes give in to the demands of others a little too easily and it would be in his interests if he were to stand his ground more often. He is usually lucky in financial matters and, like the Water Goat, is very good with children.

Fire Goat: 1967

This Goat usually knows what he wants in life and often uses his considerable charm and persuasive personality to achieve his aims. He can sometimes let his imagination run away with him and has a tendency to ignore matters that are not to his liking. He is rather extravagant in his spending and would do well to exercise a little more care when dealing with financial matters. He has a lively personality, many friends, and loves attending parties and social occasions.

Earth Goat: 1919, 1979

This Goat has a considerate and caring nature. He is particularly loyal to his family and friends and invariably creates a favourable impression wherever he goes. He is reliable and conscientious in his work but sometimes finds it difficult to save and never likes to deprive himself of any little luxury he might fancy. He has numerous interests and is often very well read. He usually derives much pleasure from following the activities of the various members of his family.

Prospects for the Goat in 2017

The Year of the Monkey (8 February 2016–27 January 2017) will have been a generally encouraging one for the Goat and in its closing months he will continue to see a lot happen.

In his work there could be challenging objectives to meet. With changes likely to be taking place, including staff movements, there will be a lot to consider and many Goats will face a heavier workload. But despite the pressures, they can achieve some impressive results. And those who take on new responsibilities will find this can give them experience and insights they can build on in the future.

The last quarter of the year will also see much spending and the Goat should keep track of his outgoings. It could be easy to overspend at this time.

More positively, he can look forward to a good mix of social occasions, especially in December. His home life will also be busy, with some weeks awhirl with activities, commitments, relations and friends. In view of this, it is important that the Goat both consults others and listens to them. Assumptions and misunderstandings could bring problems.

In general, the Monkey year will have been a full and interesting one for the Goat and he will have reaped some good benefits to take forward into the new year.

The Year of the Rooster starts on 28 January and will be one of considerable significance for the Goat. He may not like the demands and chivvying that characterize the Rooster year – the Rooster can be a hard taskmaster – but he will be encouraged to make more of himself and can make this an important time of reappraisal.

As he will find, this is no time to idle or take a back seat. Rooster years are action-driven and important developments are in store. For Goats who start the year discontented, now is the time for concerted action. Improvements can follow on, though it does rest with the Goat to seize the moment and *act with resolve*.

At work, many Goats will have established themselves in a particular career. Developments in their place of work can now provide them with the chance to move ahead. Training may be offered, vacancies may be opened up by staff movements or new objectives, and in many instances the Goat will welcome the chance to have greater influence as well as use his creative and communicative skills.

The majority of Goats will remain where they are this year and prove themselves in a greater capacity, but for those keen to further themselves in other ways or seeking work, the Rooster year can again be significant. Persistence and an open mind will be required, but these Goats could find a new position that offers the chance to develop their skills. February, April, September and October could see encouraging developments.

Work-wise, the most important factor this year for all Goats is to build on their strengths. In view of the encouraging aspects of the next few years, what is accomplished now can have important future value.

This emphasis on development also applies to the Goat's personal interests. Many Goats will put their talents to more effective use this year and creative pursuits can be particularly satisfying. Support and further guidance will spur the Goat on. Indeed, he should not act in isolation but draw on the support and expertise available to him. Also, Goats who lead a pressurized lifestyle should aim for a better balance this year. Personal interests can often be the tonic they need.

Quite a few Goats will also enjoy some financial good fortune this year. Progress at work can often lead to an increase in income and many Goats will also benefit from a gift or bonus payment. With many outgoings and expensive plans, however, the Goat will still need to manage his finances carefully. Too many unplanned purchases could quickly eat into extra resources. This is a year for control.

The Goat enjoys company and will have a varied mix of things to do over the year. He could be attracted to events to do with his interests and enjoy the chance to meet other enthusiasts. Several new friends and potentially important acquaintances can be made this year, with March, July, September and December seeing the most social opportunities. However, the good-natured and easy-going Goat *must not allow himself to be put upon*. If he has reservations about a particular situation or does not want to do something, he should let his views be known. This is no time to stay silent.

For the unattached, a chance meeting, often stemming from a shared interest, could bring especial joy this year. Affairs of the heart can be both surprising and delightful.

The Goat's home life will see a lot of activity, and with the Goat and others facing work choices and mulling over ideas, it is important that there is good communication and the Goat lets his views be known. During the year family members will have good reason to appreciate his talents. Whether empathizing over a personal problem or providing a listening ear (something the Goat is good at), arranging family activities or carrying out home improvements, he can make this a full and constructive year. The summer months could be especially active. For a few Goats, a move is possible. This is certainly an excellent year to explore possibilities.

Overall, the Year of the Rooster will be a significant one for the Goat, so much so that by the end of it he may be astonished at all the changes that have taken place. It is very much a time to build on strengths and be open to possibility. New duties at work can often being a platform for later growth, while personal interests can be inspiring as well as improve lifestyle balance. Spending needs to be watched, especially as the Goat will have domestic plans and an often lively social life. But throughout the year he will be well supported, especially if he talks openly about his hopes and plans. He has a lot in his favour this year, but to make the most of it he needs to seize the moment and *act with determination*.

The Metal Goat

This will be an eventful year for the Metal Goat and while there will be times when he will feel outside his comfort zone, the emphasis is on progress. The Rooster year favours careful planning and if the Metal Goat has particular goals in mind, he should work towards them. If he acts purposefully, a lot can open up for him.

Accommodation could feature prominently, as quite a few Metal Goats could relocate this year. Those who are discontented where they are or would like a move to somewhere more suitable should explore possibilities, while those who marry or settle down with another person this year will delight in setting up their home.

However, with often considerable accommodation costs, major purchases and (probably) a lively lifestyle, this will be an expensive year for the Metal Goat and he needs to manage his resources well and avoid too many impulse buys. Also, when taking on new obligations, he needs to clarify the terms and, if appropriate, obtain professional advice.

Though his outgoings will be considerable, the adventurous and inquisitive Metal Goat may still decide to make provision for travel as well as take up any chances to visit special attractions. By making enquiries early on, he can see exciting plans taking shape.

Personal interests are also favourably aspected and the Metal Goat should make sure they are not sidelined due to all the activity. Not only can they be a good outlet for his ideas and creative talents but they can also bring social opportunities and sometimes the chance of additional exercise. Metal Goats who enjoy creative pursuits should look to develop their ideas and skills this year. They could be heartened by the interest shown in what they produce. And if a new interest tempts the Metal Goat, he would do well to find out more. Rooster years reward an earnest attitude.

The Metal Goat will also enjoy the social opportunities of the year and will have the chance to extend his social network. He will be popular company and enjoy a varied mix of occasions throughout the year. March, July, September and December could be particularly busy, and for the unattached and those who have had recent personal upset, someone met by chance could very quickly become special.

For Metal Goats with a partner, the Rooster year promises to be busy. Again accommodation matters and major purchases could feature. Quite a few Metal Goats could also have reason for a personal celebration during the year. The summer is likely to be an active and potentially exciting time.

At work the Metal Goat is always keen to make the most of himself and new opportunities will beckon (sometimes in a different location). There will be new procedures to master, colleagues to get to know and routines to adapt to, but by applying himself, the Metal Goat can demonstrate his skills and highlight his potential.

For Metal Goats who are seeking work or keen to move on from what they currently do, the Rooster year can again offer good opportunities. By keeping alert for vacancies and seeking professional advice, many of these Metal Goats will find an opening which will use their skills in new ways. Again, this could involve considerable adjustment, but it could be the very challenge they need. February, April, September and October could see important developments.

The Year of the Rooster offers the Metal Goat great possibilities, although its demands can be considerable. Progress at work will bring often daunting challenges but give the Metal Goat the chance to prove himself in new ways, while personal and domestic plans will involve much time and effort, but can be rewarding. This is very much a year for action and to make the most of it the Metal Goat needs to act.

Tip for the Year

Have faith in yourself. You know you have much to offer and you enjoy good support. Look to make the most of your potential this year. It may at times be challenging but your achievements will be well deserved and something to build on in following years.

The Water Goat

This will be a satisfying year for the Water Goat, although he will need to act with determination, otherwise there is a risk he may drift through it and not achieve the results he would like. The Rooster year rewards planning *and commitment*.

For the Water Goat born in 1943, the year will bring some interesting possibilities, but to benefit he needs to be active and involved. If there are ideas he would like to put into practice, now is the time to take them forward. *He* needs to be the instigator this year.

With accommodation matters featuring prominently for Goats this year, Water Goats who have thoughts of moving, perhaps to accommodation that better suits their needs, should see what is available. Once the possibility has been raised, plans can quickly gather momentum.

Whether the Water Goat moves or remains where he is, he may well spend time over the year reviewing the contents of his home and disposing of items that are no longer needed as well as updating equipment. This can be a practical and satisfying time.

In view of the plans he may have for his accommodation, along with his other commitments, he will need to manage his resources well. Transactions should not be rushed and terms should be checked. Paperwork should also be handled with care. Oversights or delays could be to the Water Goat's disadvantage. Water Goats, take note and be thorough.

Throughout the year the Water Goat should also draw on the support of those around him and if involved in anything strenuous or potentially hazardous, obtain the services of a professional. Some of his ideas could be quite ambitious and he should not attempt to carry them out himself or alone.

In addition to the often considerable practical activity of the year, the Water Goat will enjoy helping family members and will have some celebrations to look forward to. These could include the academic or career success of a younger relation. Some Water Goats will also see their family increase in numbers. The Water Goat's family often means a great deal to him and he treasures these precious bonds.

Travel is well aspected and the Water Goat will appreciate any holidays and trips he takes. He may have the chance to go to places he has long wanted to see as well as benefit from some invitations and special offers. However, to make the most of his trips, he would do well to plan ahead and work out his itinerary. The summer could be an especially active time, not only for travel but also for family successes and the realization of key plans.

The Water Goat enjoys wide interests and over the year will take pleasure in the way ideas evolve and skills can be put to more effective use. With his rich imagination and creative flair, he will find this an inspiring time.

He will also welcome the social opportunities of the year, particularly the chance to talk over his ideas with his friends. A long-standing friend could offer advice worth heeding. March, July, September and December could see the most social activity.

For the Water Goat born in 2003, the Rooster year again calls for commitment and action. In his education, the young Water Goat should rise to the challenges given. Even though he may have his preferred subject areas, he should not close his mind to those he finds less appealing. Rooster years are not ones for idling either, and the greater the effort the young Water Goat makes, the bigger the potential reward.

Over the year there will also be different activities to try and new skills to learn. By being open to what is available, the Water Goat stands to benefit both now and in the future.

The young Water Goat should also draw on the support of those around him. This will not only help him understand more, but also lead to more assistance being offered. And if he would like to buy equipment or other items, he should take advice rather than rush into a purchase. Similarly, in his home life he should play his part rather than withdraw or act independently. The greater his participation, the better.

The Water Goat usually has a close circle of friends and will enjoy sharing interests and some lively times. New interests can also lead to new (and enduring) friendships, especially for Water Goats who are rather reserved (and there are some). Rooster years are encouraging but they do require the young Water Goat to reach out and make the most of his opportunities.

For all Water Goats, whether born in 1943 or 2003, this can be a constructive year. The effort they put into their plans and activities can bring some satisfying results, and circumstances can often help the process along. The Water Goat will be helped by the support of others, particularly his family and friends, and he has a lot in his favour this year. However, he does need to take action and seize his opportunities.

Tip for the Year
Be open and forthcoming. By talking over your plans and hopes, you can set a lot in motion. Also, follow up your ideas and make good use of your skills. These can be constructive and satisfying times for you.

The Wood Goat

As the Rooster year begins, the Wood Goat may have certain plans for it and feel in determined form. Encouragingly, the aspects are on his side, but there is a 'but'. During the year he will need to show flexibility and adapt to situations as they arise. He should also draw on the opinion of those around him and, if considering anything with important implications, talk to professionals. With good advice, he will feel more satisfied that what he has decided on is the right way forward. Indeed, as a Goat he welcomes support, and he will have it in many of his undertakings this year.

One area which will exercise the minds of many Wood Goats is their work situation. Although they may have made headway in recent times, some will feel jaded or unfulfilled and be hankering to do something else. By considering their situation, they could come up with some interesting possibilities. Colleagues and contacts could also make suggestions worth considering. By keeping alert and following up their ideas, many of these Wood Goats will have the opportunity to do something different this year and in the process make more of a particular talent.

For Wood Goats who remain where they are, there can also be important choices to make. The roles of quite a few of these Wood Goats will change over the year, perhaps as the result of an internal review, changes in personnel or new directives. Some weeks could bring uncertainty and a few Wood Goats will decide to move and/or reduce their work commitments as a result. The majority, however, will continue and adapt accordingly. Importantly, what happens will give many of these Wood Goats the chance to make greater use of their expertise and extend their role. Work-wise, Rooster years can be volatile, but they do allow the Wood Goat to turn change to his advantage. February, April, September and October could see important developments.

Another area which can bring new possibilities is the Wood Goat's interests. During the year many Wood Goats will have the chance to spend more time on activities they enjoy and some will set themselves a new project. In some cases, local facilities or classes could help, and by taking advantage of these, the Wood Goat could have something to look forward to on a regular basis.

He will also enjoy his travelling this year and whether planning a holiday or arranging visits to special attractions (including some locally), he will be able to fit in a surprising amount. For Wood Goats who are interested in history or culture, the Rooster year can hold some particular delights.

It will, though, be an expensive time and the Wood Goat will need to budget carefully. Also, when entering into agreements, he should check the terms and implications. This is no year to be lax or take risks.

Domestically, it promises to be a busy time. Often inspired by his ideas and keen to make improvements to his home, the Wood Goat is likely to embark on several ambitious projects, sometimes simultaneously. Although the results will be pleasing, the disruption could be far more considerable than initially envisaged. At times the Wood Goat should keep his zealous nature in check and *tackle one project at a time* rather than engage in several at once. Drawing on support will also help.

A few Wood Goats may move this year and while their new home could offer many advantages, again the process could be exhausting. The Wood Goat does need to pace his activities this year.

Amid the practical activity, there will also be a great deal to appreciate. Not only will the Wood Goat enjoy celebrating personal successes, but shared interests can also lead to some good family times. The summer in particular could see some special occasions.

The Wood Goat also sets great store by his circle of friends, and while he may not see some as often as he would like, he will value the contact he has with them. They could make useful suggestions this year and/or assist in some other way. The Wood Goat's interests can have a pleasing social element too and the support of other enthusiasts will be encouraging. Wood Goats who are alone or who have had some recent personal difficulty will find that pursuing their interests can be an excellent way to meet others, and for some, an important new friendship or romance could be born this year. March, July, September and December could see the most social activity.

In general, the Year of the Rooster will be active and significant for the Wood Goat. However, to get the best from it, he will need to forge ahead with his plans and make the most of his opportunities. As he will find, once he takes those all-important initial steps, possibilities can arise and circumstances conspire to give impetus to his plans. Whether carrying out domestic plans, developing personal interests or taking advantage of changes (and chances) at work, he can make important gains in this year of possibility.

Tip for the Year
Act with determination. A lot can happen for you now and fortune will favour the bold and enterprising.

The Fire Goat

This will be a significant year for the Fire Goat. Not only does it mark the start of a new decade in his life but it will usher in important change. A great deal is possible this year and by making the most of his strengths and opportunities, the Fire Goat can do very well and lay the foundation for future success.

Throughout the year the Fire Goat will be aided and encouraged by others, although to benefit fully, he does need to be forthcoming. This is no time for him to nurture hopes but keep them to himself. If he talks over his ideas and plans with those around him, he can obtain valuable assistance. The Fire Goat does a lot for others and this year he should let others do a lot for him.

Domestically, this promises to be a special year, especially as the Fire Goat's loved ones will be keen to commemorate his fiftieth birthday and possibly spring some carefully thought-out surprises. The affection shown him can mean a great deal to the Fire Goat and the surprises can add excitement to his year. Many Fire Goats will also have the opportunity to meet up with some people they do not often see, and they will appreciate this.

The Rooster year is also likely to see quite a few pleasing developments in the Fire Goat's home, with several family successes to celebrate.

Also, as certain relations face key moments, perhaps interviews, exams or personal decisions, the Fire Goat's empathy will be particularly valued. He has a talent for understanding others and bringing out the best in them, and this will be evident several times during the year. May, July and August in particular could see some family highlights, including some travel possibilities.

The Rooster year will also see much practical activity, with the Fire Goat keen to improve the décor of certain rooms and update equipment. A few Fire Goats will move this year as well. The Rooster year encourages action and will see the fulfilment of quite a few Fire Goat hopes.

With his many contacts, the Fire Goat will have a good mix of things to do socially and Fire Goats who are lonely should go out and make the most of what is available. This can add a new dimension to their lifestyle and in many cases result in new friendships and romance. March, July, September and December could see the most social activity.

With his enquiring nature, the Fire Goat has a good range of interests and new ones could attract him this year. Many Fire Goats will be on inspired form and will try something different or set themselves a particular challenge for their fiftieth year. Again, family and friends can be encouraging, and Fire Goats who enjoy creative pursuits could find that any work they put forward is well received. Fire Goats with writing aspirations in particular, take note.

Although the Fire Goat generally keeps himself active, he may aim to introduce more exercise into his lifestyle over the year as well as improve the quality of his diet. With advice and persistence, he will notice the benefits.

At work, the Rooster year can give rise to some significant developments which may catch the Fire Goat by surprise. Unanticipated staff movements can open up promotion possibilities and he may have the chance to take on a more specialist role. Admittedly, this will bring new pressures too, especially as the Fire Goat accustoms himself to what is required, but he will relish the opportunity to make more of particular strengths. This can be a demanding but fulfilling year.

The majority of Fire Goats will make important headway with their present employer, but some will feel their fiftieth year is a time for fresh challenges. For these Fire Goats, and those seeking work, it would be worth talking to employment experts, friends and other contacts, as these could alert them to an ideal opening or a type of work worth investigating. This is a year to be open to possibility. In many cases, these Fire Goats will succeed in gaining the change (and incentive) they need. Events can work in fortuitous ways this year, and while possibilities can arise at almost any time, February, April and September to early November could be key months.

There will also be some Fire Goats who, keen to make more of their specialist knowledge, are tempted by the idea of self-employment. These Fire Goats, too, may well feel their fiftieth year is an ideal one in which to proceed. By seeking professional advice and being thorough in setting up their undertaking, they can make important headway. Work-wise, the Rooster year is one of good possibility.

Financially, although the Fire Goat will enjoy moments of luck this year and receive what could be generous gifts from others, this is a time for vigilance. Costly purchases need to be carefully considered and forms, policies and financial correspondence attended to thoroughly and promptly. Lapses and delays could be to the Fire Goat's disadvantage. He should also be wary of making too many spontaneous purchases. Costs could mount up and curtail other activities later on. Fire Goats, take note and be disciplined.

Overall, though, the Year of the Rooster is a fine one for the Fire Goat. There will be special times with loved ones to look forward to and pleasing headway at work. The Fire Goat will be greatly encouraged by those around him and their support can lead to other possibilities opening up. He has much in his favour this year but needs to put himself forward and make the most of his opportunities. If he does so, he can make this a constructive and satisfying year.

Tip for the Year
Value your relations with others. With their help, so much can become possible this year. Also, follow through your ideas. With purpose and good use of your skills, you can enjoy some good results and further your position.

The Earth Goat

As the Rooster year starts, the Earth Goat may well be giving some thought to the months ahead, specifically to the plans he would like to get underway. And with effort, a great many can be carried out. Rooster years reward planning and provide good opportunities for the earnest and willing.

For Earth Goats who are dissatisfied with their situation or have had a recent disappointment, this year can mark a turning point. However, to help the process, these Earth Goats would do well to concentrate on the present and near future rather than feel fettered by what has gone before. With resolve, they can change their outlook and make the most of the fresh opportunities that will enter their life this year. The significance of the Rooster year should *not* be underestimated.

Almost all areas of the Earth Goat's life will see key developments, and in view of the often considerable implications, it is important that he talks these over with his family and those with relevant knowledge. With good support, decisions can be made easier and uncertainties reduced. Throughout the year the Earth Goat should remember he is not alone and actively involve others in his thinking.

Over the year his work in particular could see considerable volatility. Changes in his industry, the updating of procedures and the implementation of new initiatives can all impact on his role. Some weeks could be particularly demanding, but by concentrating on what needs to be done and adapting to the changes (rather than resisting them), the Earth Goat could be offered further responsibilities and in the process enhance his prospects for the future. In some instances, what he is offered now could be a stepping stone to something greater.

While many Earth Goats will further their career with their current employer this year, for those who feel their prospects can be bettered by a move elsewhere, as well as those seeking work, the Rooster year can again be an important juncture. Obtaining a new position will require time, but by keeping alert for openings and considering other ways in which they could adapt their skills, many of these Earth Goats will secure the chance to establish themselves in a new role. Again, what occurs now can be successfully built on in the future. February, April, September and October could see encouraging developments.

All Earth Goats can also help their situation by being an active and visible presence in their workplace. This will do much to help their standing and prospects.

As a result of progress at work, many Earth Goats will improve their income this year, but money matters need careful handling. With large purchases and some repair costs likely, as well as possible deposits and all his regular activities, the Earth Goat's outgoings will be considerable. This is a year for discipline and good financial management. The Earth Goat should also be thorough when dealing with paperwork and keep documents safe and policies up-to-date. Lapses and losses could inconvenience him. Earth Goats, take note.

The Earth Goat is blessed with an enquiring mind and during the year he will be keen to develop certain interests. New ideas or equipment (or software) will inspire him and encourage him to do more. Creative pursuits are well aspected and other people could encourage the Earth Goat to make more of his talents. Some Earth Goats could find joining a course or local group opening up other possibilities too. Time spent furthering his own interests can bring the Earth Goat great pleasure this year as well as do him much personal good. With his often busy lifestyle, he can benefit from some 'me time'.

Travel, too, will appeal, with short breaks away being particularly appreciated. Some Earth Goats may also be tempted by events to do with their interests, including musical and sporting occasions. If they follow up their ideas, they can enjoy some lively times.

The Earth Goat's domestic life will also keep him busy. In addition to plans and improvements he is keen to carry out, he will do much to assist others. If he is a parent, his children could need help with their education as well as support during exam times. Earth Goats who have senior relations could also advise on certain decisions and undertakings. In all cases, the Earth Goat's thoughtfulness and input will be valued and he could play an influential part in the lives of those close to him over the year. In view of his many commitments, it is important that he sets aside time to spend with others and encourages shared activities. His ideas can lead to some special times. The summer could be particularly active and gratifying.

With the pressure on his time and resources, the Earth Goat will be more selective in his socializing this year, but while he may not actually meet certain friends as often as before, he will often be grateful for the advice they give on certain decisions (especially work-related) that he has to take. In turn, he will help someone close on what could be a delicate personal matter.

Unattached Earth Goats and those who have had recent personal difficulties will find that developments at work and the personal interests they pursue will often bring them into contact with new people, some of whom will become good friends. In some instances, significant romance will beckon. March, July, September and December could be interesting and rewarding months for meeting others.

The Earth Goat's qualities and personal strengths can reward him well in the Rooster year. In both his work and interests, he will have the chance to develop his knowledge and skills. These are constructive and instructive times. Much that is achieved now can also be the prelude to future success. On a personal level, the Earth Goat will find himself giving valued assistance to family members as well as enjoying times spent together. Overall, this will be an active and pleasing year for him, although to make the most of it he does need to seize his opportunities. With commitment and resolve, so much is possible.

Tip for the Year
Develop your skills and strengths. What you do now can not only help your present situation but also provide you with an important platform to build upon.

Famous Goats

Jane Austen, Lord Byron, Coco Chanel, Nat 'King' Cole, Jamie Cullum, Robert de Niro, Catherine Deneuve, Charles Dickens, Vin Diesel, Ken Dodd, Sir Arthur Conan Doyle, Douglas Fairbanks, Will Ferrell, Jamie Foxx, Bill Gates, Robert Gates, Mel Gibson, Whoopi Goldberg, Mikhail Gorbachev, John Grisham, Oscar Hammerstein, George Harrison, Billy Idol, Julio Iglesias, Sir Mick Jagger, Steve Jobs, Norah Jones, Nicole Kidman, Sir Ben Kingsley, Johanna Konta, Christine Lagarde, John le Carré, Matt LeBlanc, Franz Liszt, James McAvoy, Tim McGraw, Sir John Major, Michelangelo, Joni Mitchell, Rupert Murdoch, Randy Newman, Sinead O'Connor, Michael Palin, Aaron Paul, Eva Peron, Pink, Keith Richards, Flo Rida, Julia Roberts, William Shatner, Ed Sheeran, Queen Silvia of Sweden, Gary Sinise, Jerry Springer, Lana Turner, Mark Twain, Vangelis, John Wayne, Justin Welby, King Willem-Alexander of the Netherlands, Bruce Willis, Shailene Woodley.

20 February 1920 to 7 February 1921 — *Metal Monkey*

6 February 1932 to 25 January 1933 — *Water Monkey*

25 January 1944 to 12 February 1945 — *Wood Monkey*

12 February 1956 to 30 January 1957 — *Fire Monkey*

30 January 1968 to 16 February 1969 — *Earth Monkey*

16 February 1980 to 4 February 1981 — *Metal Monkey*

4 February 1992 to 22 January 1993 — *Water Monkey*

22 January 2004 to 8 February 2005 — *Wood Monkey*

8 February 2016 to 27 January 2017 — *Fire Monkey*

The Monkey

The Personality of the Monkey

The more open to possibility,
the more possibilities open.

The Monkey is born under the sign of fantasy. He is imaginative, inquisitive and loves to keep an eye on everything that is going on around him. He is never backward in offering an opinion or trying to sort out the problems of others. He likes to be helpful and his advice is invariably sensible and reliable.

The Monkey is intelligent, well read and always eager to learn. He has an extremely good memory and there are many Monkeys who have made particularly good linguists. The Monkey is also a convincing talker and enjoys taking part in discussions and debates. His friendly, self-assured manner can be very persuasive and he usually has little trouble in winning people round to his way of thinking. It is for this reason that he often excels in politics and public speaking. He is also particularly adept in PR work, teaching and any job that involves selling.

The Monkey can, however, be crafty, cunning and occasionally dishonest, and he will seize any opportunity to make a quick profit or outsmart his opponents. He has so much charm and guile that people often don't realize what he is up to until it is too late. But despite his resourceful nature, he does run the risk of outsmarting even himself. He has so much confidence in his abilities that he rarely listens to advice or is prepared to accept help from anyone. He likes to help others, but prefers to rely on his own judgement when dealing with his own affairs.

Another characteristic of the Monkey is that he is extremely good at solving problems and has a happy knack of extricating himself (and others) from the most hopeless of positions. He is the master of self-preservation.

With so many diverse talents, the Monkey is usually able to make considerable sums of money, but he does like to enjoy life and will think nothing of spending his money on some exotic holiday or luxury he has had his eye on. He can, however, become very envious if someone else has what he wants.

The Monkey is an original thinker and despite his love of company, he cherishes his independence. He has to have the freedom to act as he wants and any Monkey who feels hemmed in or bound by too many restrictions will soon become unhappy. Likewise, if anything becomes too boring or monotonous, the Monkey will soon lose interest and turn his attention to something else. He lacks persistence and this can often hamper his progress. He is also easily distracted, a tendency that he should try to overcome. By concentrating on one thing at a time, he will almost certainly achieve more in the long run.

The Monkey is a good organizer and even though he may behave slightly erratically at times, he will invariably have a plan at the back of his mind. On the odd occasion when his plans do not work out, he is usually quite happy to shrug his shoulders and put it down to experience. He will rarely make the same mistake twice and throughout his life he will try his hand at many different things.

The Monkey likes to impress and is rarely without followers or admirers. Many are attracted by his good looks, his sense of humour, or simply because he instils so much confidence in those around him.

Monkeys usually marry young and for it to be a success their partner must allow them time to pursue their many interests and indulge their love of travel. The Monkey has to have variety in his life and is especially well suited to those born under the sociable and outgoing signs of the Rat, Dragon, Pig and Goat. The Ox, Rabbit, Snake and Dog will also be enchanted by his resourceful and outgoing nature, but he is likely to exasperate the Rooster and Horse, and the Tiger will have little patience with his tricks. A relationship between two Monkeys will work well – they will understand each other and be able to assist each other in their various enterprises.

The female Monkey is intelligent, extremely observant and a shrewd judge of character. Her opinions are often highly valued and, having such a persuasive nature, she invariably gets her own way. She has many interests and involves herself in a wide variety of activities. She pays great attention to her appearance, is an elegant dresser and likes to take particular care over her hair. She can be a doting parent and will have many good and loyal friends.

Provided the Monkey can curb his desire to take part in everything that is going on around him and concentrate on one thing at a time, he can usually achieve what he wants in life. Should he suffer any disappointment, he is bound to bounce back. He is a survivor and his life is usually both colourful and eventful.

The Five Different Types of Monkey

In addition to the 12 signs of the Chinese zodiac there are five elements and these have a strengthening or moderating influence on the signs. The effects of the elements on the Monkey are described below, together with the years in which they were exercising their influence. Therefore Monkeys born in 1920 and 1980 are Metal Monkeys, Monkeys born in 1932 and 1992 are Water Monkeys, and so on.

Metal Monkey: 1920, 1980

The Metal Monkey is very strong-willed. He sets about everything he does with dogged determination and often prefers to work independently rather than with others. He is ambitious, wise and confident, and is certainly not afraid of hard work. He is very astute in financial matters and usually chooses his investments well. Despite his somewhat independent nature, he enjoys attending parties and social occasions and is particularly warm and caring towards his loved ones.

Water Monkey: 1932, 1992

The Water Monkey is versatile, determined and perceptive. He also has more discipline than some of the other Monkeys and is prepared to work towards a particular goal rather than be distracted by something else. He is not always open about his true intentions and when questioned can be particularly evasive. He can be sensitive to criticism but also very persuasive and usually has little trouble in getting others to fall in with his plans. He has a very good understanding of human nature and relates well to others.

Wood Monkey: 1944, 2004

This Monkey is efficient, methodical and extremely conscientious. He is also highly imaginative and is always trying to capitalize on new ideas or learn new skills. Occasionally his enthusiasm can get the better of him and he can get very agitated when things do not quite work out as he had hoped. He does, however, have a very adventurous streak and is not afraid of taking risks. He also loves travel. He is usually held in great esteem by his friends and colleagues.

Fire Monkey: 1956, 2016

The Fire Monkey is intelligent, full of vitality and has no trouble in commanding the respect of others. He is imaginative and has wide interests, although sometimes these can distract him from more useful and profitable work. He is very competitive and always likes to be involved in everything that is going on. He can be stubborn if he does not get his own way and he sometimes tries to indoctrinate those who are less strong-willed than himself. He is a lively character, attractive to others and loyal to his partner.

Earth Monkey: 1968

The Earth Monkey tends to be studious and well read, and can become quite distinguished in his chosen line of work. He is less outgoing than some of the other types of Monkey and prefers quieter and more solid pursuits. He has high principles, a very caring nature and can be most generous to those less fortunate than himself. He is usually successful in handling financial matters and can become very wealthy in old age. He has a calming influence on those around him and is respected and well liked. He is, however, especially careful about whom he lets into his confidence.

Prospects for the Monkey in 2017

The Monkey is likely to have made much of his own year (8 February 2016–27 January 2017) and fitted in a surprising amount. The closing months will continue to be active and he can enjoy some pleasing accomplishments. However, to make the most of this time, he should plan his activities early on, otherwise some weeks, especially towards the end of the year, will be rushed and unnecessarily pressured.

In his home life the Monkey can look forward to finishing off projects and implementing certain ideas. If he has been considering specific purchases, he could come across something ideal and often obtain it on advantageous terms. His canny eye will be on good form.

He will also appreciate the family and social occasions that take place and his social diary may fill up rapidly. This is another reason for remaining well organized.

At work the Monkey will have the chance to use his skills and judgement well, and while the pressures may be considerable, he can do his standing a lot of good. Monkey years favour their own sign's resourceful approach. They also encourage progress. For Monkeys seeking change or looking for work, chances can arise suddenly and even if what the Monkey is offered is initially on a temporary basis, he can often build on it in the future.

In general, the Monkey year is an encouraging one for the Monkey himself and by making the most of it, he can fare well and enjoy himself in the process.

The Year of the Rooster begins on 28 January and will be a reasonable one for the Monkey. While its structured nature may sometimes cramp his style, it will bring some pleasing personal times and good opportunities. It is also an excellent time for personal development.

At work, the aspects are encouraging for the Monkey, but he does need to remember that the Rooster year favours planning and *sticking to the rulebook*. This is no year for shortcuts or ad hoc arrangements. However, while the Rooster year may not allow the Monkey the latitude he favours, its discipline can work to his advantage. By focusing on his duties, he will not only have the chance to develop his skills but also to become more established in his line of work. This may not be a year for sweeping progress, but he can move forward steadily. He should look to take advantage of any training he is offered as well as keep himself informed of developments within his industry. By being involved and showing commitment, he can do his present *and future* situation great good.

Monkeys who feel there may be better opportunities elsewhere or who are seeking work will not find their quest easy. But if the Monkey shows initiative, highlights relevant strengths and is informed at interview, he may secure an opening. While some Monkeys rely a lot on their wits, the Rooster year favours preparation and discipline. When taking on a new position, if the Monkey concentrates on what needs to be done and works well with his new colleagues, he can quickly impress, and what he accomplishes now can pave the way for some of the more substantial advances that await in following years. April, June, October and November could see interesting developments.

Many Monkeys can look forward to a modest rise in income over the year, but they will still need to be vigilant in money matters. Not only could they be keen to replace certain expensive items (perhaps being attracted to a new phone or entertainment system), but they could also face additional costs relating to their home. In the Rooster year the Monkey needs to keep sensible control over the purse-strings. He should also be careful in his dealings with others, for there is a risk that he may fall victim to a scam, suffer from unscrupulous dealings or be let down by someone. If involved in any speculative venture or having reservations over a particular undertaking, it is important that the Monkey checks it out and seeks further advice. Monkeys, do be careful.

More positively, travel is favourably aspected and the Monkey should, if possible, try to make provision for a holiday over the year as well as take advantage of any chances of short breaks or weekends away. His enquiring nature can be well satisfied by his travels this year. Late summer and end of the year could see some additional (and sometimes surprising) travel opportunities.

With the Rooster year's emphasis on development, the Monkey can also derive much satisfaction from furthering his own interests. Not only can these offer a change from his more usual activities but sometimes give him the chance of additional exercise or social contact. Some Monkeys could become absorbed in projects and challenges they set themselves this year. Rooster years reward purpose.

With his outgoing nature, the Monkey enjoys company and there will certainly be plenty of social opportunities this year. His network of acquaintances is set to widen, and for Monkeys who have been feeling lonely, new friendships could add extra meaning to the year. However, in matters of the heart the Monkey should proceed steadily, enjoy the moment and let any romance strengthen over time rather than rush into a commitment. March, May, August and December could see the most social activity.

Throughout the year the Monkey will be kept busy and needs to be careful this does not impact on his home life. To be preoccupied or distracted could lead to difficulties. Also, while he and other family members will juggle many commitments, he should ensure time is set aside for shared undertakings. The Rooster year calls for good management of time.

Accommodation matters will require attention, especially as equipment could inconveniently break or the Monkey set about some home improvements with great enthusiasm. Although these can bring benefits (and possible savings), carrying them out could be time-consuming. Ideally, the Monkey should tackle one thing at a time rather than commit himself to too much. With thoughtfulness and good co-operation, however, his home life can go well, with April and the last quarter of the year proving especially satisfying.

Overall, the Year of the Rooster can be a fine one for the Monkey, but he does need to be watchful and disciplined. This is no year for taking risks. Extra care is particularly advised in money matters. However, by managing his time well, the Monkey can make useful headway as well as add considerably to his skills and knowledge. This is very much a year for personal and professional development. The Monkey has an enthusiastic nature and provided he channels his energies well, the Rooster year can reward him as well as prepare him for future progress.

The Metal Monkey

The Metal Monkey will have a busy year ahead and while he can look forward to some important gains, he does need to use his time effectively. To spread his energies too widely could lead to him engaging in many activities but not always obtaining the results he desires. This is a year for focus and acting on key objectives.

In his home life the Metal Monkey can see a great deal happen. Not only will he face some important choices this year, but others in his household will also have numerous demands. In view of these pressures, the Metal Monkey should encourage openness between all. Also, despite the general activity, he should ensure quality time together does not suffer. If he encourages shared undertakings and suggests occasions that everyone can enjoy, he can find his input making an appreciable difference.

With travel favourably aspected, he should, if possible, try to go away with his loved ones over the year. This can do everyone good. In addition, visits to local attractions and events can be very enjoyable. Travel can inject a pleasing element into the year.

The Metal Monkey will also be keen to carry out some home improvements, but he needs to plan these carefully and resist the temptation of committing himself to too much at any one time. Although the end results will be pleasing, the actual execution could be more disruptive and time-consuming than anticipated. Metal Monkeys, take note.

April and the last quarter of the year could be active times in the Metal Monkey household, with possible successes to celebrate.

In addition, the Metal Monkey will have good reason to value the contact he has with his friends, especially in view of some of his current decisions and dilemmas. Some of his friends will be able to speak with first-hand experience and their words will be worth heeding. The Metal Monkey will also appreciate the various social occasions of the year. March, May, August and December are likely to be particularly busy months. Over the year many Metal Monkeys will add to their social circle and, for the unattached, a significant romance could start in an unexpected way. Rooster years have the capacity to surprise and delight.

In view of his various commitments, it is important that the Metal Monkey preserves time for his own interests and recreational pursuits. Not only can these help him unwind but they may also be an outlet for his ideas and talents. Whether he prefers creative, practical or outdoor activities, they can be akin to a tonic for him. Some Metal Monkeys will enjoy attending events related to their interests and if anything special tempts the Metal Monkey this year, he should follow it up.

At work the Rooster year can see important developments. The many Metal Monkeys who are established in a career will now have excellent chances to further their position and professional knowledge. As advances occur in their industry, by keeping themselves informed and their skills up-to-date, many will be able to take on a more specialist role or become involved in new developments.

For Metal Monkeys who decide to change employer, and sometimes location, as well as those seeking work, the Rooster year can be significant. If they explore possibilities and talk to experts, there will be excellent chances for them to establish themselves in a new role.

For all Metal Monkeys, the Rooster year will be demanding work-wise, but what the Metal Monkey learns, and demonstrates to others, can be of value in following years.

Progress at work will often lead to an increase in income and some Metal Monkeys will also benefit from extra sums or bonus payments. However, with expensive purchases in mind, accommodation costs likely and repairs or replacements needed, the Metal Monkey's outgoings will be considerable and he should keep a close watch on his financial situation. If tempted by anything speculative or making an informal agreement with another person, he needs to exercise caution. Mistakes or misjudgements could cost him dearly. Metal Monkeys, take careful note.

Generally, however, the Year of the Rooster will be a full and interesting one for the Metal Monkey. Being keen and adaptable, he can make the most of the year's many possibilities and, by developing his knowledge, benefit his position both now *and* in the near future. He will value the support of those around him and his family and social life can be busy and pleasing. The Rooster year will provide a good mix of things to do and by being involved and seizing his opportunities, the Metal Monkey can gain a lot from what he experiences during it. A satisfying year.

Tip for the Year
Keep your lifestyle in balance and preserve time for your loved ones and for recreational pursuits. Also, take any chances to develop your skills and knowledge. What you do now is an investment in your future.

The Water Monkey

There is a Chinese proverb which reminds us, 'Diligence leads to riches,' and these words hold very true for the Water Monkey in the Rooster year. It is one offering great potential and the Water Monkey will have the opportunity to develop his skills and achieve some personal objectives. However, while encouraging, this is no year to be half-hearted, to trust to luck or to drift. Instead, it is one for focus and effort.

At work, many Water Monkeys will have experienced several changes of late, perhaps changing employers and/or taking on different duties. Although they will have made headway, some will feel they have not yet found their true niche or had the chance to develop in the way they want. For these Water Monkeys, as well as those on a particular career path, interesting times await. During the Rooster year some excellent opportunities can arise and many Water Monkeys will find themselves in just the right place at the right time.

The prospects are also encouraging for Water Monkeys seeking work. Although some may have grown disillusioned about their situation, they should have faith. By actively pursuing openings as well as contacting professional organisations, they can uncover some interesting possibilities this year. Some may decide to pursue a different type of work from what they have done before. Others may help their situation by taking advantage of training or refresher courses. Progress in the Rooster year requires determination, resolve and a willingness to learn, but the Water Monkey's efforts can be recognized and lead to a potentially important job offer. April, June, October and November could see encouraging developments.

Progress at work can lead to a welcome rise in income, but money matters do require careful handling this year. Without care, certain decisions and purchases could be regretted later and there is also the risk of some losses being incurred. The Water Monkey needs to consider his purchases carefully as well as exercise caution when entering into agreements. Informal arrangements or lending to another person could bring problems. Water Monkeys, take careful note, and be wary of risk, haste or proceeding without adequate checks.

Travel, however, is favourably aspected and if possible the Water Monkey should make provision for a holiday. And if events related to his interests appeal to him, he should find out more. They could be among the year's highlights.

In addition to his professional development, the Water Monkey can also derive much satisfaction from developing his personal interests. Whether inspired by ideas, joining others in shared activities or intrigued by something new, he will delight in what he does. Interests with an element of creativity could be particularly rewarding and if the Water Monkey can promote anything he produces or receive expert guidance, he could be encouraged further. The Rooster year rewards application and making the most of personal talents.

The Water Monkey will also value his contact with his friends and may seek their opinion over certain situations or dilemmas. By being forthcoming he can be helped and advised in many ways. And just as he may benefit from advice received, he can also reciprocate, especially as a close friend may face difficulties or have to contend with a stressful situation. Support this year will be mutual *and beneficial*.

The Water Monkey will also find his social circle widening and will have a good mix of occasions to attend. Some weeks could be especially busy, with a lot seeming to happen all at once. March, May, August and December could be particularly active.

For the unattached Water Monkey, a chance meeting can add great excitement to the year and potentially transform his situation.

For Water Monkeys with a partner, this too can be a special year. As the Water Monkey looks to further his situation, there will be anticipation to enjoy, excitement to share and choices to consider. The Water Monkey and his partner will have several plans in mind and by taking concerted action can accomplish a great deal. However, to get the best results, the Water Monkey will need to direct his energies towards specific outcomes rather than busy himself with too much all at once. Here again this is a year for planning and focus, but the love and support of another person can spur the Water Monkey on and help him reach new heights.

More senior family members can also provide useful help, and the Water Monkey should be forthcoming and speak openly about his current activities, plans and hopes. Over the year he will have many people rooting for him. However, he still needs to take action and proceed with care, determination and focus.

In general, the Year of the Rooster can be a rewarding one for the Water Monkey. It encourages personal and career development and what he learns now can lead to other opportunities in the near future. His personal and home life will be busy and pleasing, with many good times to share, and the Water Monkey will be considerably helped by the support of others. He has a lot in his favour this year and if he acts with resolve, he can build on his situation.

Tip for the Year

Develop your skills and knowledge. By investing in yourself, you can reap considerable rewards. 'Diligence leads to riches' and efforts made now can help your current *and* future prospects.

The Wood Monkey

With wide interests and a keen nature, the Wood Monkey has a talent for making the most of his situation. And in 2017 he can do well, although the year does require care, good planning and discipline.

As the year starts, Wood Monkeys born in 1944 will have plans they will be eager to get underway. As they have found, having objectives not only helps focus their energies but also leads to more being achieved. And the Wood Monkey is, after all, purposeful!

Some of his thinking will concern his home and he will be particularly keen to resolve some niggles. It could be that certain areas have become cluttered and need sorting out or that some equipment is failing or may no longer be adequate. Once the Wood Monkey starts to address these issues, other projects will often suggest themselves, and some undertakings may become more extensive than envisaged. But this is a year for action and the results can be satisfying.

Throughout the year the Wood Monkey will be grateful for the support of family members and will find the expertise of some particularly useful. As well as the transformations seen in many a Wood Monkey home, there will also be much to enjoy. Whether sharing interests, starting a new activity or taking advantage of what is available locally, the Wood Monkey will have a good mix of things to do.

He can also look forward to some special family occasions. He may see his family increase in numbers and will follow the progress of younger relations with considerable interest. While he may not want to interfere, the assistance he offers someone close could be more significant than he may realize. April and the last quarter of the year could see good news as well as be busy times domestically.

The Wood Monkey's social life can also be rewarding. Some of his interests can be enjoyed with other people and if he is part of an activity group or decides to join one over the year, he will appreciate what this opens up for him. He will also welcome opportunities to meet up with his friends, and the advice shared will often be mutually beneficial. Lonely Wood Monkeys should see what is happening locally and aim to get involved. Positive action can make a real difference this year. March, May, August and December could see the most social opportunities.

The Wood Monkey is blessed with an enquiring mind, and with personal interests well aspected this year, he should look to extend what he does in some way. This can be an inspiring time for him.

Travel, too, is well aspected and the Wood Monkey should aim to take a holiday this year as well as follow up any invitations he receives.

However, while many plans can be advanced, as with all years, problems can arise. In money matters in particular, great care is needed, and when making a major purchase or entering into an agreement, the Wood Monkey should check the terms and obligations and, if applicable, obtain further advice. He should be wary of making informal agreements or trusting someone on what could be flimsy information. Without extra vigilance, losses could occur. Wood Monkeys, take note.

These words apart, this can be a satisfying year for the senior Wood Monkey, with much to appreciate.

For the Wood Monkey born in 2004, the Rooster year will open up many possibilities. As he progresses in his education, he will be encouraged to explore and enjoy his talents and make greater use of the facilities available to him. By being involved, he can make great strides, building up his knowledge and sometimes his confidence levels too. This is a year to participate in what is going on around him.

The young Wood Monkey will develop some key interests this year, and by practising his skills and making the most of the encouragement given him, will appreciate what he gets to do.

There will be a good deal of camaraderie between him and his friends, and a lot of fun can be had this year, although if at any time the Wood Monkey has misgivings over a certain situation, he needs to exercise care and not go against his better judgement. There is a risk that he may be misled or let down and in this otherwise good year he needs to be circumspect.

There will be some good travel opportunities, however, and with his adventurous nature, the Wood Monkey will enjoy going away.

In addition, by involving himself in his home life and helping with various undertakings, he can benefit from greater rapport with those around him.

For all Wood Monkeys, whether born in 1944 or 2004, activity and involvement will bring results in the Rooster year. By following through their ideas, they can accomplish a great deal. The Wood Monkey will also be encouraged by the support of those around him and shared undertakings are favourably aspected. Personal interests and travel can also bring considerable pleasure, although the more senior Wood Monkey will need to be vigilant in money matters. However, with care and good use of his time, the Wood Monkey will be able to fit in a surprising amount this year and his efforts will reward him well.

Tip for the Year
Enjoy developing your interests and your strengths. If new activities or possibilities tempt you, explore them. Also, value your relations with those close to you. Their support can be of great help.

The Fire Monkey

This will be a satisfying year for the Fire Monkey, with circumstances helping many of his plans along. However, a key feature of Rooster years is that they favour planning and this is no time to drift or leave matters to chance. To get the best from the year, the Fire Monkey should give some thought to the things he would like to do and work towards them. Some objectives will not only give the year more structure but also make him more aware of the right chances to pursue.

Many of the Fire Monkeys in work will be content to remain in their role. However, for those who would welcome new challenges, the changes that take place over the year may offer the perfect opportunity to take on new responsibilities, including perhaps overseeing some of the changes. While new duties will mean additional demands, these Fire Monkeys can nevertheless enjoy a greater sense of fulfilment.

For Fire Monkeys who are keen to alter their working commitments and/or seeking work, the Rooster year can also open up interesting possibilities. By giving careful thought to what they would like to do, making enquiries and seeking the support of helpful contacts, many of these Fire Monkeys could secure the chance they have been hoping for. April, June, October and November could see important developments.

There will also be some Fire Monkeys who decide to retire this year. Again, by working towards the outcome they desire, they will be pleased with the decision they have made.

With often more time available, many Fire Monkeys will be keen to take their personal interests further this year. This is a great year to proceed with long-held goals and if the Fire Monkey has thoughts of writing a book or setting about another creative project, now is the time. Some Fire Monkeys could enrol on courses or be tempted by another pursuit. The Rooster year offers a wealth of possibilities.

Some Fire Monkeys will give some thought to their well-being, and fitness disciplines or certain diets may be appealing. By seeking advice on how to proceed, again many of these Fire Monkeys will be pleased with what they do.

The Rooster year also encourages travel and the Fire Monkey should aim to make provision for a holiday. By giving careful thought to his destination and what he would like to do while away, he will greatly enjoy himself. Shorter trips and local events could also feature prominently.

Although much can go well this year, one area which requires close attention is finance. When entering into agreements or taking decisions with important implications, the Fire Monkey should check the details and seek advice. He should also attend to forms and paperwork carefully. Lapses and delays could be to his disadvantage. Loans and informal agreements may also be problematic. In money matters, this is a year for caution and vigilance.

The Fire Monkey enjoys company and the Rooster year can provide a good mix of things to do. Whether attending parties, celebrating reunions or attending other events, he will find himself in demand. In addition, he will value the support of key friends this year, especially when taking decisions or under pressure. Many think highly of the Fire

Monkey and will be keen to assist. March, May, August and December could see the most social activity.

For Fire Monkeys who are lonely and would like to add something extra to their life, getting involved with community activities or joining a local group could be worth considering. This is a year favouring purposeful action.

The Fire Monkey's domestic life will also see a great deal happen this year. Some weeks could, though, be frenetic with activity, with everything seeming to happen at once. Some Fire Monkeys will become grandparents and there can be some exciting and joyous times, with the Fire Monkey eager to help.

In addition, he will be keen to proceed with plans for his home. He may have been thinking about some of these for some time. Although there could be unexpected snags, once everything is done, many Fire Monkeys will feel the effort and expense are justified.

Holidays with loved ones and shared interests can also bring great pleasure this year. This is a time for planning activities, sharing activities and appreciating time spent with loved ones. April and the last quarter of the year could be busy and often special times.

Overall, the Year of the Rooster can be a satisfying one for the Fire Monkey, but it does require determined action on his part. To realize his hopes, he needs to take the initiative, make enquiries, explore options and take decisions. However, as he will find, once he makes a start, others may offer support and circumstances assist too. The Rooster year will require effort, but the competent (and often lucky) Fire Monkey will turn much to both his present and future advantage and enjoy himself in the process.

Tip for the Year

Allow time for your personal interests. These can do you good. Also, manage your time well. With so much happening domestically, along with your other commitments, good organization will help you to do a surprising amount.

The Earth Monkey

The Earth Monkey has an enthusiastic nature and likes to get involved in a great many things. And his personality and drive help him make the most of situations. His prospects are encouraging this year. However, he will need to remain focused and channel his energies wisely. To over-commit himself, pay scant attention to potentially important matters or become distracted could undermine his efforts. This is a year for discipline.

At work there will be developments which impact on his role. Some workplaces could be affected by staff movements, particularly as long-established colleagues transfer or leave. As a result there will be oppor-tunities for many Earth Monkeys to advance their career, and their skills and in-house knowledge can be real assets.

With new responsibilities will come new pressures, though, and the early weeks of any new role can often be challenging. However, it is here that the Earth Monkey's strengths will come into their own. Not only does he enjoy good working relations with many of his colleagues, but his ability to master detail will impress those around him. Focus will be required, but many Earth Monkeys are set to do well.

The majority will remain with their present employer over the year, but a few may be headhunted. Some of these could find themselves in a dilemma. Before making a decision, they will need to check exactly what is on offer and what the implications might be.

For Earth Monkeys who are disenchanted by their present situation, as well as those seeking work, the year can again be significant. While secur-ing a new position will take time, by considering different ways of using their skills and widening their search, many will be successful. While their duties may be different from what they have done before, by showing commitment these Earth Monkeys can quickly establish themselves.

Work-wise, the Rooster year will ask a lot of the Earth Monkey, but in characteristic fashion he will rise to the challenge. April, June, October and November could see interesting opportunities.

The Earth Monkey is blessed with an enquiring nature and enjoys a variety of interests. And although he will be kept busy this year, it is important he does not let his interests drop. Not only can they help him relax but also be a satisfying outlet for his ideas and talents. Creative activities, including photography, could particularly appeal, and the Earth Monkey would do well to set time aside to further his skills. The accent this year is on developing strengths and talents.

For Earth Monkeys who lack regular exercise or rely a lot on convenience foods, more exercise or some dietary changes could make a difference to their energy levels. With guidance, these Earth Monkeys will be pleased with the positive changes they introduce. Some may even become inspired by a new fitness discipline.

Travel is favourably aspected and if possible the Earth Monkey should aim to go away during the year and visit places new. Planning his itinerary carefully will make his time away all the more meaningful.

One area where he will need to exercise particular care this year is finance. When entering into agreements, he should check the implications and, if necessary, obtain professional advice. He should also deal with important paperwork promptly and, if lending to another person, be careful over what is agreed. Mistakes, delays and misjudgements could be to his disadvantage. Earth Monkey, stay alert and vigilant.

Given his often busy lifestyle, the Earth Monkey will be more selective in his socializing this year but can still have a varied mix of occasions to enjoy. He will value his chances to spend time with others and some important connections can be made this year. For the unattached Earth Monkey, a chance meeting could in time become significant. March, May, August and December could be socially interesting months.

In his home life, the Earth Monkey will see considerable activity. With commitments and sometimes routines changing, good communication will be required. At busy times, the more family members can help one another, the easier it will be for all. But amid the high levels of activity, there will be many times to enjoy together, including holidays, trips and/ or special treats. Once again the Earth Monkey's ability to come up with ideas will be much appreciated. Also, when the inevitable problems occur (often caused by pressure), his thoughtfulness and ability to find solutions can be effective.

When he looks back on the Rooster year, he may be surprised by all the changes that have taken place. Often these will have occurred gradually but built up over the year. It is a time of steady but appreciable progress. To make the most of it, the Earth Monkey should focus on his goals and look to advance his position. What he achieves now can be to his present and future benefit, with the Rooster year having long-term implications. Throughout it he will be encouraged by the support of family and friends as well as enjoy a variety of activities. Overall, a full and satisfying year.

Tip for the Year
You will have many demands on your time this year, but make sure these do not make incursions into your home life or prevent you from enjoying the rewards of your efforts. Allow quality time for others and for your own interests.

Famous Monkeys

Gillian Anderson, Jennifer Aniston, Christina Aguilera, Patricia Arquette, J. M. Barrie, Kenny Chesney, Colette, John Constable, Patricia Cornwell, Daniel Craig, Joan Crawford, Miley Cyrus, Leonardo da Vinci, Timothy Dalton, Bette Davis, Danny De Vito, Celine Dion, Michael Douglas, Mia Farrow, Carrie Fisher, F. Scott Fitzgerald, Ian Fleming, Paul Gauguin, Ryan Gosling, Eva Green, Jake Gyllenhaal, Jerry Hall, Tom Hanks, Harry Houdini, Charlie Hunnam, Hugh Jackman, Katherine Jenkins, Julius Caesar, Buster Keaton, Alicia Keys, Gladys Knight, Taylor Lautner, George Lucas, Bob Marley, Kylie Minogue, V. S. Naipaul, Lisa Marie Presley, Debbie Reynolds, Little Richard, Diana Ross, Tom Selleck, Wilbur Smith, Rod Stewart, Elizabeth Taylor, Dame Kiri Te Kanawa, Justin Timberlake, Harry Truman, Ben Whishaw, Venus Williams.

8 February 1921 to 27 January 1922 — *Metal Rooster*

26 January 1933 to 13 February 1934 — *Water Rooster*

13 February 1945 to 1 February 1946 — *Wood Rooster*

31 January 1957 to 17 February 1958 — *Fire Rooster*

17 February 1969 to 5 February 1970 — *Earth Rooster*

5 February 1981 to 24 January 1982 — *Metal Rooster*

23 January 1993 to 9 February 1994 — *Water Rooster*

9 February 2005 to 28 January 2006 — *Wood Rooster*

28 January 2017 to 15 February 2018 — *Fire Rooster*

The Rooster

The Personality of the Rooster

With a clear destination
and firm will,
I raise my sails
to the winds of fortune.

The Rooster is born under the sign of candour. He has a flamboyant and colourful personality and is meticulous in all that he does. He is an excellent organizer and wherever possible likes to plan his various activities well in advance.

The Rooster is usually highly intelligent and very well read. He has a good sense of humour and is an effective and persuasive speaker. He loves discussion and enjoys taking part in any sort of debate. He has no hesitation in speaking his mind and is forthright in his views. He does, however, lack tact and can easily damage his reputation or cause offence by some thoughtless remark or action. He has a very volatile nature and should always try to avoid acting on the spur of the moment.

He is usually very dignified in his manner and conducts himself with an air of confidence and authority. He is adept at handling financial matters and organizes his financial affairs with considerable skill. He chooses his investments well and is capable of achieving great wealth. Most Roosters use their money wisely, but there are a few who are the reverse and are notorious spendthrifts. Fortunately, the Rooster has great earning capacity and is rarely without sufficient funds to tide himself over.

Another characteristic of the Rooster is that he invariably carries a phone, notebook or scraps of paper around with him. He is constantly writing himself reminders or noting down important facts lest he forgets – the Rooster cannot abide inefficiency and conducts all his activities in an orderly, precise and methodical manner.

The Rooster is usually very ambitious, but can be unrealistic in some of what he hopes to achieve. He occasionally lets his imagination run away with him and while he does not like any interference from others, it would be in his own interests to listen to their views a little more often. He also does not like criticism, and if he feels anybody is doubting his judgement or prying too closely into his affairs, he is certain to let his feelings be known. He can also be rather self-centred and stubborn over relatively trivial matters, but to compensate for this he is reliable, honest and trustworthy, and this is appreciated by all who come into contact with him.

Roosters born between the hours of five and seven, both at dawn and sundown, tend to be the most extrovert of their sign, but all Roosters like to lead an active social life and enjoy attending parties and big functions. The Rooster usually has a wide circle of friends and is able to build up influential contacts with remarkable ease. He often belongs to several clubs and societies and involves himself in a variety of different activities. He is particularly interested in the environment, humanitarian affairs and anything affecting the welfare of others. He has a very caring nature and will do much to help those less fortunate than himself.

He also gets much pleasure from gardening, and while he may not spend as much time in the garden as he would like, his garden is invariably well kept and productive.

The Rooster is generally very distinguished in his appearance and if his job permits, he will wear an official uniform with great pride and dignity. He is not averse to publicity and takes great delight in being the centre of attention. He often does well at PR work or any job which brings him into contact with the media. He also makes a very good teacher.

The female Rooster leads a varied and interesting life. She involves herself in many different activities and there are some who wonder how she can achieve so much. She often holds very strong views and, like her male counterpart, has no hesitation in speaking her mind or telling others how she thinks things should be done. She is supremely efficient and well organized and her home is usually very neat and tidy. She has good taste in clothes and usually wears smart but very practical outfits.

The Rooster usually has a large family and takes a particularly active interest in the education of his children. He is very loyal to his partner and will find that he is especially well suited to those born under the signs of the Snake, Horse, Ox and Dragon. Provided they do not interfere too much in his various activities, the Rat, Tiger, Goat and Pig can also establish a good relationship with him, but two Roosters together are likely to squabble and irritate each other. The rather sensitive Rabbit will find the Rooster a bit too blunt for his liking, and the Rooster will quickly become exasperated by the ever-inquisitive and artful Monkey. He will also find it difficult to get on with the anxious Dog.

If the Rooster can overcome his volatile nature and exercise tact, he will go far in life. He is capable and talented and will make a lasting – and usually favourable – impression almost everywhere he goes.

The Five Different Types of Rooster

In addition to the 12 signs of the Chinese zodiac there are five elements and these have a strengthening or moderating influence on the signs. The effects of the elements on the Rooster are described below, together with the years in which they were exercising their influence. Therefore Roosters born in 1921 and 1981 are Metal Roosters, Roosters born in 1933 and 1993 are Water Roosters, and so on.

Metal Rooster: 1921, 1981

The Metal Rooster is a hard and conscientious worker. He knows exactly what he wants in life and sets about everything in a positive and determined manner. He can at times appear abrasive and he would almost certainly do better if he were willing to reach a compromise with others rather than hold so rigidly to his beliefs. He is very articulate and most astute when dealing with financial matters. He is loyal to his friends and often devotes much energy to working for the common good.

Water Rooster: 1933, 1993

This Rooster has a very persuasive manner and can easily gain the co-operation of others. He is intelligent, well read and enjoys taking part in discussions and debates. He has a seemingly inexhaustible amount of energy and is prepared to work long hours in order to secure what he wants. He can, however, waste a lot of valuable time worrying over minor and inconsequential details. He is approachable, has a good sense of humour and is highly regarded by others.

Wood Rooster: 1945, 2005

The Wood Rooster is honest, reliable and often sets himself high standards. He is ambitious, but also more prepared to work in a team than some of the other types of Rooster. He usually succeeds in life but does have a tendency to get caught up in bureaucratic matters and attempt too many things at the same time. He has wide interests, likes to travel and is very caring and considerate towards his family and friends.

Fire Rooster: 1957, 2017

This Rooster is extremely strong-willed. He has many leadership qualities, is an excellent organizer and is most efficient in his work. Through sheer force of character he often secures his objectives, but he does have a tendency to be very forthright and not always consider the feelings of others. If he can learn to be more tactful he can often succeed beyond his wildest dreams.

Earth Rooster: 1969

This Rooster has a deep and penetrating mind. He is efficient, perceptive and particularly astute in business and financial matters. He is also persistent and once he has set himself an objective, he will rarely allow himself to be deflected from achieving his aim. He works hard and is held in great esteem by his friends and colleagues. He usually enjoys the arts and takes a keen interest in the activities of the various members of his family.

Prospects for the Rooster in 2017

The Year of the Monkey (8 February 2016–27 January 2017) will not have been the easiest for the Rooster. Being methodical and liking to plan his activities, he could have found situations in the Monkey year exasperating and sometimes been in a uncharacteristic quandary over certain decisions. The pressures are not set to ease in the closing quarter of the year and he will continue to face numerous demands.

At work many Roosters would prefer to concentrate on their existing duties but could have additional tasks to deal with, perhaps through staff shortages or new objectives being set. Quite a few Roosters will despair over what is happening. However, what occurs can give the Rooster the chance to add to his skills, learn more about his industry and come into contact with other colleagues, and his performance in often difficult situations can enhance his reputation. September and December could see potentially important developments.

With the closing months of the year being a traditionally expensive time, the Rooster should keep a close watch on his spending and make early provision for large purchases and any gifts he has planned.

His home life will see much activity at this time and there may need to be compromises over certain arrangements. The more that can be agreed upon in advance, the better. Equipment breakages or delays in the delivery of certain items may be inconvenient and the Rooster may have to sort out several problems. However, amid all the activity there will be some lively and agreeable occasions and travel opportunities to look forward to, especially as 2016 draws to a close.

The Rooster will be keen to celebrate the start of his own year and with good reason. With his own sign ruling, he will feel more in charge of his own destiny and better able to proceed in the way *he* wants. And with a disciplined approach, he can make significant gains.

For any Rooster who has felt held back in recent years and disappointed with his progress, this is a time to focus on the present and regard this year as the start of a new chapter in his life. If he has plans and objectives in mind, now is the time to set them in motion. As Virgil noted, 'Fortune favours the bold.' In the Rooster's own year, which begins on 28 January, fortune will favour the bold and enterprising.

In his work this can be a time of decision-making. For Roosters who are discontented in their present role or have been in the same position for some time and are feeling staid, this is an excellent time to consider other options. As they realize, it rests with them to bring the changes they want, and by exploring possibilities they may succeed in finding an ideal challenge. For some, this could involve a change of commute or location, but they will often be buoyed up by being in a new working environment and having the opportunity for professional growth.

Similarly, Roosters seeking work should put past frustrations behind them and actively follow up any openings that interest them. They know they have much to offer and many will be given an opportunity they can build on. Often what they are offered will be different from what they have done before and will require some adjustment, but it will give them the chance to develop in new ways.

For Roosters following a particular career, again this is a year for progress. Having proved themselves in some often demanding situations, many will now secure promotion and advance their career. Again new duties can be daunting, but by immersing themselves in their role and being their conscientious selves, these Roosters will quickly establish themselves.

February, April, July and November could see significant work developments for the Rooster. However, such are the aspects that possibilities can open up at almost any time.

Another feature of the year will be the way the Rooster extends his knowledge and skills. Often this will come through his work, but if he feels an additional qualification would help or is keen to become more proficient in a certain skill, he should follow it up. By broadening his skills, he will not only gain professionally, but open up other possibilities in the process.

This also applies to his personal interests. If there are activities the Rooster would like to pursue or projects he wants to carry out, he should act. 'There is no time like the present' and the inspired Rooster can get great pleasure from what he starts in his own year.

Progress made at work will increase the income of many Roosters, but care is still needed in financial matters. During the year the Rooster may well be tempted by large purchases, including equipment and appliances. Rather than rushing these, he needs to allow time to determine what best meets his needs *and his budget*. Some Roosters are spendthrift and discipline is advised. Also, with the Rooster being one who likes to look ahead, if he is able to start a savings plan or add to a pension policy, this could be something he is grateful for in years to come. Rooster years reward good financial management.

With his busy lifestyle the Rooster should aim to take a holiday this year, and if a certain destination appeals to him, he should make enquiries. Trips booked early on in the year can be something to look forward to later on.

As someone who enjoys conversation and company, the Rooster will also enjoy the social aspects of the year. There will be excellent chances for him to widen his circle of friends and contacts and he may well be on impressive form. Any Roosters who start the year lonely or despondent should make the most of any chances to go out and immerse themselves what is going on around them. Positive action can bring sparkle and new meaning to their year. March, May, August and October could see the most social activity.

Roosters who find love could, however, find it helpful to let their romance blossom over time rather than rush. This way each will get to know the other better. The Rooster's own year is capable of bringing him much personal happiness.

His home life can also be rewarding, with the Rooster himself often playing a central role. He will have ideas concerning improvements and domestic arrangements, and by planning these out, will ensure that a lot happens over the year. And when those in his household are facing work changes or other pressures, his attentiveness and matter-of-fact ways (he speaks openly and honestly) will assist in many a situation. He will also be instrumental in arranging some family occasions over the year and some good times can be had. May, August and September could be particularly active months.

The Year of the Rooster is one of great possibility for the Rooster himself. It is a time to make plans and set them in motion. Whether advancing his work position or his interests or taking up something new, the Rooster should make the most of his year. With self-belief and determination, he can achieve (and enjoy) a great deal. He will be encouraged by the support of others and although this is a year to keep careful control over the purse-strings, in so many respects the Rooster can help make his own year a very special one.

The Metal Rooster

The Metal Rooster is ambitious and has high hopes for his future. And with this being a Rooster year, he will feel impelled to move his situation forward. His actions can yield important results. However, he will need to be flexible, make the most of situations *as they arise* and adjust his approach accordingly. As the proverb reminds us, 'There are many routes to the top.'

As the Rooster year starts, the Metal Rooster will have several clear aims in mind and furthering his career is likely to be one of them. During the year, several developments will assist him. There may be internal reorganization, vacancies caused by staff movement and alterations in workload, and quite a few Metal Roosters will be well positioned to benefit.

For Metal Roosters who feel their prospects could be bettered by a move elsewhere, as well as those seeking a position, the Rooster year can again have significant developments in store. By widening the scope of their search, seeking advice and, if eligible, taking advantage of training courses, these Metal Roosters could be alerted to positions which use their skills in different ways. Again, a certain flexibility will be required, but the positions these Roosters take on now can help re-energize their career. February, April, July and November could see significant developments, but chances could occur at almost any time and need to be seized.

The Metal Rooster can also help his situation by working closely with his colleagues and being active in the workplace. With his competence and personal presence, he will impress many this year and gain support and valuable contacts.

Progress made at work may also increase his income, but with his existing commitments and a busy lifestyle, he needs to watch his spending and make early provision for larger plans and outgoings. He also needs to be wary about succumbing to too many impulse buys. The cost of these can mount up. In addition, if he has doubts over any transaction, he should seek clarification. Financially, this is a year for care.

The Metal Rooster often has wide-ranging interests and can be knowledgeable (and passionate) about a certain subject or recreational pursuit. In this Rooster year he should put this to good use, perhaps by setting himself a new challenge or sharing his knowledge with others. With the year's emphasis on progress, he can derive much personal value from what he does.

With this being the Year of the Rooster, the Metal Rooster may also decide to make some personal resolutions for the year, including exercising more and improving his diet. By remaining disciplined, he can benefit from these lifestyle changes.

With his inquisitive nature, he enjoys travel and should not only aim to take a holiday over the year but also to visit attractions or events that appeal to him. Some of these could occur in his locality and by taking advantage of them he can enjoy some entertaining and absorbing times.

His domestic life can be especially pleasing this year, with many plans going forward. Shared activities can result in a special synergy being created and a lot happening. Also, once plans are started, the early momentum can quickly get things underway.

The Metal Rooster will also value the special times he shares with his loved ones and the support they can offer. He in turn will encourage those around him, and if a parent, the love, input and time he gives to his children may have more significance than he realizes. May, August and September will be active and gratifying months both domestically and for travel.

With his busy lifestyle, the Metal Rooster has many contacts and the Rooster year will provide some good social opportunities. Not only will the Metal Rooster enjoy talking to his friends and getting their thoughts on current plans and activities, but he will give valued assistance to several close friends, including on what could be a delicate issue. Here his discretion and wise counsel will be much appreciated. March, May, August and October could see the most social activity.

For Metal Roosters who may have experienced recent problems in their personal life and/or would welcome romance, the Rooster year can mark a turning point. By making the most of the present, including their chances to go out, these Metal Roosters can form a friendship which could quickly become significant. Rooster years are keen to assist their own, but to fully benefit the Metal Rooster needs to remain active and involved.

The element of metal reinforces the resolve of a sign, and this is certainly true of the Metal Rooster. Keen to further himself, he will seize the chance to make important headway this year and achieve many of his objectives. And when he takes action, powerful forces can be set in motion and he can benefit from helpful circumstances. He will also be assisted by the support of others, and joint action can also help advance plans and open up possibilities. In money matters, discipline and care are needed, but overall the Year of the Rooster holds good prospects for the Metal Rooster.

Tip for the Year
Manage your time well and share some with your loved ones. Also, look to develop your skills, both professionally and in your personal interests. With your talents and thoroughness, you can gain a lot this year. Use it well, for your actions can help you in substantial ways.

The Water Rooster

The fact that this is the Year of the Rooster will give impetus to the Water Rooster's activities. He will feel this is a special time and in many ways it will be. It is a time for forging ahead with plans, enjoying some pleasing (and often memorable) experiences and laying the foundations for future growth. However, to make the most of it, the Water Rooster needs to have self-belief and act with determination. Some of his actions may put him outside his comfort zone, but to realize his potential, act he must.

His personal life is especially well aspected. Many Water Roosters enjoying newfound romance will find their love blossoming over the year and some will celebrate their engagement or marriage or settle down together. Water Roosters who start the year alone or who have had a romance recently flounder could find someone new entering their life and bringing fresh joy and hope. The Rooster year can be personally significant for many Water Roosters.

Water Roosters who already have a partner will also find this an exciting time, as they take their plans and hopes forward. Some under-takings will be ambitious and require working towards over the year, but with effort, a remarkable amount can happen. Once action is taken, luck can play a part too. The Water Rooster will have a lot in his favour this year. In addition, when making what could be major decisions, he could find it helpful to draw on the assistance of senior relations. He should not feel – or act – alone.

Although there will be a lot of practical activity over the year, there will also be many other activities to enjoy. The Rooster year will bring a lively mix of things to do. The Water Rooster's personal interests can often have a strong social element and Water Roosters who move to a new area will have the chance to establish a new social circle. While some may initially feel lonely, by venturing out and joining a local inter-est group, they can quickly make new friends. On a personal level, the Rooster year can bring good times but the Water Rooster needs to reach out and make the most of what is available.

Socially, March, May, August and October to early November could be active months, although at most times of the year there will be events to look forward to.

With his busy lifestyle and ambitious personal plans, the Water Rooster's spending will be high this year and he needs to be disciplined in money matters. Ideally he should set limits on how much he spends when he goes out as well as set funds aside for specific purposes and be wary of impulse buys. This is a year for vigilance and careful financial management. Water Roosters, take note.

The Water Rooster should, however, aim to save up for a holiday (though he could benefit from a last-minute offer and so save considerable outlay). Eager to experience new places, he will enjoy his time away. In addition, some Water Roosters will take advantage of short breaks.

The aspects are encouraging for work matters. With their capacity to learn and desire to advance, Water Roosters already in a position will make the most of the chances that come their way, perhaps taking advantage of training, providing cover for an absent colleague or applying for a greater role. Often this will be with their existing employer and senior colleagues will be supportive.

For Water Roosters who decide to look elsewhere, as well as those seeking work, the Rooster year can again have significant developments in store. By keeping alert for openings and not being too restrictive in their search, many could now obtain the chance to establish themselves in a new role. In some instances, this could come about in a curious way or in the wake of disappointment, but seem as if it was meant to be. February, April, July and November could see key developments.

Some Water Roosters will be in education this year, and often completing courses. With a lot resting on their results, these Water Roosters should focus on what needs to be done and work consistently. The qualifications many now gain can be a springboard to opportunities that await in the future.

Whatever his situation, the Water Rooster will derive much pleasure from his personal interests over the year, especially any that provide him with an outlet for his talents. Some projects could develop in exciting fashion. The Rooster year is rich in possibility and the inspired and keen Water Rooster can benefit from some luck along the way.

In general, the Year of the Rooster will be a busy and favourable one for the Water Rooster. However, it will require effort. If the Water Rooster is half-hearted or wavering, chances could be missed and his outcomes less satisfactory. If he adds to his knowledge and seizes his opportunities, however, he can help his current situation *and* future prospects. And on a personal level, affairs of the heart will often be special and there will be plans to share and much to enjoy.

Tip for the Year
Believe in yourself. To realize your potential you need to put yourself forward, embrace new challenges and make the most of your opportunities. Also, value the love and support of those who are special to you.

The Wood Rooster

When the Wood Rooster sets himself a task, he does it well. Resolute, conscientious and practical, he is a doer, and in the Year of the Rooster he will do a great deal.

For the Wood Rooster born in 1945, there will be ideas he will be keen to get underway, and by planning these out and going through them with those around him, he can achieve a lot this year. His ideas could be wide-ranging and in some cases could be aspirations he has been nurturing for some time. They may include travelling to places he has long wanted to see as well as visiting attractions nearer to where he lives, perhaps museums, places of interest or cultural centres. By setting time aside for their plans, many Wood Roosters can satisfy some long-held desires.

The Wood Rooster will also delight in his interests. With the Rooster year's emphasis on development, he could become intrigued by a new pursuit and aim to learn more about it. The Wood Rooster likes a challenge. A further advantage will be that some of his interests (including courses he may start) can have a strong social element and he can enjoy a lot of additional fun. Wood Roosters who are alone would find joining an activity group well worth considering. In addition some Wood Roosters could derive considerable pleasure from helping in their community in some way or supporting a worthwhile cause. The Wood Rooster has a talent for using his time well. March, May, August and October could see particularly good social opportunities.

The Wood Rooster will also enjoy tackling practical projects on his home, although once started, they can have a tendency to mushroom, with one idea leading on to another. However, whether decluttering certain areas, altering the arrangements of some rooms or updating equipment, many a Wood Rooster will be on inspired form. Amid all the practical activity, there will be important family occasions to share, perhaps the personal or academic success of a younger relation, a job promotion or a birth. May and late July to the end of September could be busy times.

Although a lot is set to go well this year, one area which requires close attention is finance. In view of the Wood Rooster's plans, his outgoings will be considerable and will need to be budgeted for. The Wood Rooster needs to remain disciplined and guard against too many impulse buys. He should also attend to paperwork promptly and properly. Oversights could be to his disadvantage. Wood Roosters, take note.

For the Wood Rooster born in 2005, the Rooster year can also open up good possibilities. As he advances in his education, he will gain access to new equipment, and this, together with his advancing knowledge, will allow him to do more and help reveal new aptitudes. These can be illuminating and exciting times.

On a personal level, many young Wood Roosters will grow in confidence, and for those who may be shyer, new friends and shared activities can help bring out their qualities.

Some Wood Roosters will be involved in a change of school this year, and while this can be daunting, they will quickly come to appreciate the opportunities it brings. Again it is a case of being receptive and embracing current situations.

For all Wood Roosters, whether born in 1945 or 2005, the Rooster year offers great possibility. It is a year to act on ideas as well as develop skills. A lot can be undertaken and many personal benefits gained. The Wood Rooster will value the support he receives as well as the special relationships he has with those around him. Rooster years look after the Rooster sign and this can be a fulfilling and personally pleasing year for the Wood Rooster.

Tip for the Year
Make plans. And then act. With purpose, you can make a lot happen this year. Also, enjoy and develop your interests. New projects and activities can be inspiring and lead on to other possibilities.

The Fire Rooster

This is the Year of the Fire Rooster and it promises to be a special one for him. Though he may have been frustrated with developments in recent years, he will now feel able to achieve the results he wants. In many ways, this can be a successful *and* fulfilling year for him.

His domestic life will be particularly gratifying. Not only will loved ones be keen to mark his sixtieth year but they may have some special surprises lined up. The love and affection shown him may touch the Fire Rooster deeply.

With travel favourably aspected, many Fire Roosters will treat themselves to a special holiday to celebrate their birthday. Additional travel opportunities could arise late in 2017 or early 2018. There will also be chances to enjoy several short breaks away. For Fire Roosters who enjoy seeing places new, the Rooster year offers many possibilities.

In addition to commemorating his birthday, the Fire Rooster can look forward to some family news which will especially delight him, perhaps the career success of a loved one or the birth of a grandchild. Family developments can be a source of joy to many a Fire Rooster this year. The summer in particular could be lively and special.

With this being his own year, the Fire Rooster will be keen to go ahead with ideas he has been nurturing for some time. Some will relate to home improvements, and whether improving comforts or buying new equipment (sometimes related to entertainment), the Fire Rooster will be pleased with the choices he makes. Positive changes will be seen in many a Fire Rooster home this year.

The Fire Rooster will also derive much pleasure from his interests and may decide to try something different or set himself a new personal challenge. For some this will have a keep-fit element. Other Fire Roosters may resolve to improve their diet. By seeking medical advice on the best way to proceed, they may be delighted with the results. By taking action, the Fire Rooster can really benefit from his own year.

A lot he undertakes can have a good social element too, and for Fire Roosters who have had recent personal difficulty or who have moved to a new area and are feeling lonely, this is a year to reach out and explore what is available. By making the most of their new situation, these Fire Roosters can make some good friends and re-energize their social life. For the unattached, romantic possibilities may add sparkle to their year. March, May, August and October will see some good social opportunities.

The Fire Rooster's year also holds interesting prospects as far as his work position is concerned. For Fire Roosters who are established where they are and skilled in their role, it can bring unexpected developments. Colleagues could suddenly leave, creating promotion possibilities, and there could be special projects requiring the Fire Rooster's expertise. As a result, he could find his position greatly enhanced. He often prides himself on his discipline, thoroughness and organizational abilities, and these, together with his reputation, can be a winning combination this year.

Fire Roosters who would welcome more substantial change or who are seeking a position will find the year can offer fresh starts. By not being too restrictive in their quest and highlighting their skills and achievements to prospective employers, many will secure a position which will allow them to use their strengths in new ways. The Fire Rooster can make important headway in his own year but he needs to seize his chances. February, April, July and November could be significant months work-wise.

Financially, this is a year for discipline and good management. With some sizeable purchases likely, as well as travel expenses, the Fire Rooster's outgoings will be considerable. To help, he should make early provision for key plans as well as keep within his allotted budget. Overspending or succumbing to too many indulgences could lead to economizing later. When entering into agreements, he also needs to check the paperwork and the implications. Oversights could be to his disadvantage. Fire Roosters, take note.

In most respects, though, this will be a splendid year for the Fire Rooster. It is one for making plans and exploring ideas. Determined to make the most of it, the Fire Rooster will enjoy developing new interests, setting himself personal challenges and sharing quality time with his loved ones. His own year can reward him well – very well.

Tip for the Year
Set your plans in motion in your own year and enjoy what you do. Also, value your relations with those who are close to you.

The Earth Rooster

Forward-thinking and keen to make the most of his situation, the Earth Rooster likes to keep himself active and informed. And his qualities will serve him particularly well in what can be a successful and personally rewarding year.

As the year starts, the Earth Rooster should decide on some objectives. Having aims not only sits comfortably with his psyche but will also give him something to strive towards over the next 12 months. Any Earth Rooster who may start the year dissatisfied with recent progress, having battled with concerns during the previous Monkey year, should turn his attention to the present rather than what has gone before. This is his sign's own year and can usher in exciting opportunities and sometimes new starts.

At work the aspects are especially encouraging. Earth Roosters who are well established in a career and who may have been with their current employer for some time will often find their commitment rewarded with the offer of promotion. In some cases, the Earth Rooster will have been working towards this for some time and it will mark an important stage in his ongoing development.

The majority of Earth Roosters will make deserved progress with their current employer, but those who have become despondent due to lack of opportunity should actively make enquiries elsewhere. A few could find their specialist knowledge attractive to other employers and be prime candidates when positions fall vacant. Others may find themselves on a new career path and be re-energized by what they now take on.

For Earth Roosters seeking work, again the Rooster year can bring some attractive propositions. By making enquiries, talking to experts and keeping alert for vacancies in their area, they can secure the chance to re-establish themselves. February, April, July and November could see encouraging developments, but throughout the year the Earth Rooster should keep alert for possibilities.

All Earth Roosters should not only work closely with their colleagues but also build up their connections. If applicable, joining a professional organization or attending work-related events could do the Earth Rooster's prospects a lot of good.

Although the Earth Rooster will find himself contending with many time pressures this year, he should not allow his personal interests to fall away. These can be a valuable outlet for certain talents as well as sometimes offer the chance of additional exercise. Some can have a good social element as well and in this busy year the Earth Rooster does need to allow himself to have a respite now and then. With his enquiring nature, he could find new activities intriguing him. If so, he will get much personal value from following them up. Rooster years encourage venturing forward and finding out more.

Travel is favourably aspected, and if he is able, the Earth Rooster should aim to go away at some time during the year. By planning this in advance, he can fit in a surprising amount, including visits to some impressive attractions. Some Earth Roosters could find there are unexpected windows of opportunity to go away, and by taking advantage of them they will enjoy much that takes place, including some surprises.

The Earth Rooster's domestic life is set to be busy this year. With some purchases for the home to consider, along with the improvements he is keen to carry out, the Rooster year could see him immersed in much deliberation and practical activity. As choices seem to multiply and/or projects hit snags, certain undertakings could be more disruptive and time-consuming than envisaged. However, while this may be exasperating for the Earth Rooster (and his household), the advantages gained will more than compensate.

With the Earth Rooster and/or his partner likely to be affected by work changes in the Rooster year, there will also be alterations to routine to consider and domestic changes to make. Here the Earth Rooster's organizational abilities will be greatly valued, as will his support when others are faced with decisions or pressures. Also, while he and those around him will juggle many commitments, by setting aside time for shared interests, the Earth Rooster can enjoy many domestic highlights over the year. May and late July to the end of September could be active and gratifying months.

On a social level, the Earth Rooster will find himself in demand and will enjoy receiving invitations to gatherings and spending time with his friends. Any Earth Rooster who has had some recent personal difficulty should consider joining in with activities in their area or attending an interest group. With a willingness to move forward, he can meet like-minded people and make some significant friendships. And for a few of these Earth Roosters, a chance encounter can lead to love.

The Rooster year can surprise and encourage the Earth Rooster, but to get the best out of it, he needs to be proactive. March, May, August and October could see the most social activity.

In view of his busy lifestyle and possibly extensive home improvements, the Earth Rooster will need to keep watch on his spending and financial situation this year. Without care, his outgoings could exceed what he has budgeted for. Ideally, this is a year for keeping tight control over the purse-strings and making advance provision for plans and known expenses. Also, while usually thorough, the Earth Rooster should not be lax over paperwork. Mistakes could cost him dearly. Earth Roosters, take note and be thorough.

Overall, though, this is an encouraging year for the Earth Rooster. It is a time to seize the initiative, seek out opportunities and move forward. This year the Earth Rooster is in the driving seat and able to steer the course he wants. Re-energized by this, he will also be helped by favourable circumstances and benefit from the support he receives from those around him. He has a lot in his favour this year, although to get the most from it he needs to act with determination. As Virgil noted, 'Fortune favours the bold,' and it will certainly favour the bold and enterprising Earth Rooster this year.

Tip for the Year
You have great skills and capabilities. Believe in yourself and take them further. You have much to offer and can now do so. Good luck. Your successes will be richly deserved.

Famous Roosters

Fernando Alonso, Beyoncé, Cate Blanchett, Barbara Taylor Bradford, Gerard Butler, Sir Michael Caine, the Duchess of Cambridge, Enrico Caruso, Eric Clapton, Joan Collins, Rita Coolidge, Daniel Day-Lewis, Minnie Driver, the Duke of Edinburgh, Gloria Estefan, George Ezra, Paloma Faith, Roger Federer, Errol Flynn, Benjamin Franklin, Dawn French, Stephen Fry, Joseph Gordon-Levitt, Melanie Griffith, Josh Groban, Goldie Hawn, Katharine Hepburn, Paris Hilton, Jay-Z, Catherine Zeta Jones, Quincy Jones, Diane Keaton, Søren Kierkegaard, D. H. Lawrence, David Livingstone, Matthew McConaughey, Jayne Mansfield, Steve Martin, Paul Merton, Bette Midler, Ed Miliband, Van Morrison, Willie Nelson, Kim Novak, Yoko Ono, Dolly Parton, Matthew Perry, Michelle Pfeiffer, Natalie Portman, Priscilla Presley, Kelly Rowland, Paul Ryan, Jenny Seagrove, Carly Simon, Britney Spears, Justin Spieth, Johann Strauss, Verdi, Richard Wagner, Serena Williams, Neil Young, Renée Zellweger.

28 January 1922 to 15 February 1923 — *Water Dog*

14 February 1934 to 3 February 1935 — *Wood Dog*

2 February 1946 to 21 January 1947 — *Fire Dog*

18 February 1958 to 7 February 1959 — *Earth Dog*

6 February 1970 to 26 January 1971 — *Metal Dog*

25 January 1982 to 12 February 1983 — *Water Dog*

10 February 1994 to 30 January 1995 — *Wood Dog*

29 January 2006 to 17 February 2007 — *Fire Dog*

The Dog

The Personality of the Dog

I have my values
and beliefs.
These are my beacon
in an ever-changing world.

The Dog is born under the signs of loyalty and anxiety. He usually holds very firm views and beliefs and is the champion of good causes. He hates any sort of injustice or unfair treatment and will do all in his power to help those less fortunate than himself. He has a strong sense of fair play and will be honourable and open in all his dealings.

The Dog is very direct and straightforward. He is never one to skirt round issues and speaks frankly and to the point. He can be stubborn, but he is prepared to listen to the views of others and will try to be as fair as possible in coming to his decisions. He will readily give advice where it is needed and will be the first to offer assistance when things go wrong.

The Dog instils confidence wherever he goes and there are many who admire him for his integrity and resolute manner. He is a very good judge of character and can often form an accurate impression of someone very shortly after meeting them. He is also very intuitive and can frequently sense how things are going to work out long in advance.

Despite his friendly and amiable manner, the Dog is not a big socializer. He dislikes having to attend large functions or parties and much prefers a quiet meal with friends or a chat by the fire. He is an excellent conversationalist and is often a marvellous raconteur of amusing stories and anecdotes.

The Dog is also quick-witted and his mind is always alert. He can keep calm in a crisis and although he does have a temper, his outbursts tend to be short-lived. He is loyal and trustworthy, but if he ever feels badly let down or rejected by someone, he will rarely forgive or forget.

The Dog usually has very set interests. He prefers to specialize and become an expert in a chosen area rather than dabble in a variety of different activities. He usually does well in jobs where he feels that he is being of service to others and is often suited to careers in the social services, the medical and legal professions and teaching. He does, however, need to feel motivated in his work. He has to have a sense of purpose and if ever this is lacking he can quite often drift through life without ever achieving very much. Once he has the motivation, however, very little can prevent him from securing his objective.

Another characteristic of the Dog is his tendency to worry and to view things rather pessimistically. Quite often his worries are totally unnecessary and are of his own making. Although it may be difficult, worrying is a habit that all Dogs should try to overcome.

The Dog is not materialistic or particularly bothered about accumulating great wealth. As long as he has the money necessary to support his family and to spend on the occasional luxury, he is more than happy. However, when he does have any spare money he tends to be rather a spendthrift and does not always put it to its best use. He is also not a very good speculator and would be advised to get professional advice before entering into any major long-term investment.

The Dog will rarely be short of admirers, but he is not an easy person to live with. His moods are changeable and his standards high, but he will be loyal and protective to his partner and will do all in his power to provide a comfortable home. He can get on extremely well with those born under the signs of the Horse, Pig, Tiger and Monkey, and can also establish a sound and stable relationship with the Rat, Ox, Rabbit, Snake and another Dog, but will find the Dragon a bit too flamboyant for his liking. He will also find it difficult to understand the imaginative Goat and is likely to be highly irritated by the candid Rooster.

The female Dog is renowned for her beauty. She has a warm and caring nature, although until she knows someone well she can be both secretive and very guarded. She is highly intelligent and despite her calm and tranquil appearance can be extremely ambitious. She enjoys sport and other outdoor activities and has a happy knack of finding bargains in the most unlikely of places. She can also get rather impatient when things do not work out as she would like.

The Dog usually has a very good way with children and can be a doting parent. He will rarely be happier than when he is helping someone or doing something that will benefit others. Providing he can cure himself of his tendency to worry, he will lead a very full and active life, and in that life he will make many friends and do a tremendous amount of good.

The Five Different Types of Dog

In addition to the 12 signs of the Chinese zodiac there are five elements and these have a strengthening or moderating influence on the signs. The effects of the elements on the Dog are described below, together with the years in which they were exercising their influence. Therefore Dogs born in 1970 are Metal Dogs, Dogs born in 1922 and 1982 are Water Dogs, and so on.

Metal Dog: 1970

The Metal Dog is bold, confident and forthright and sets about everything he does in a resolute and determined manner. He has a great belief in his abilities and no hesitation about speaking his mind or devoting himself to some just cause. He can be rather serious at times and can become anxious and irritable when things are not going according to plan. He tends to have very specific interests and it would certainly help him if he were to broaden his outlook and become more involved in group activities. He is extremely loyal and faithful to his friends.

Water Dog: 1922, 1982

The Water Dog has a very direct and outgoing personality. He is an excellent communicator and has little trouble in persuading others to fall in with his plans. He does, however, have a somewhat carefree nature and is not as disciplined or as thorough as he should be in certain matters. Neither does he keep as much control over his finances as he should, but he can be most generous to his family and friends and will make sure that they want for nothing. He is usually very good with children and has a wide circle of friends.

Wood Dog: 1934, 1994

This Dog is a hard and conscientious worker and will usually make a favourable impression wherever he goes. He is less independent than some of the other types of Dog and prefers to work in a group rather than on his own. He is popular, has a good sense of humour and takes a keen interest in the activities of the various members of his family. He is often attracted to the finer things in life and can obtain much pleasure from collecting stamps, coins, pictures or antiques. He prefers to live in the country rather than the town.

Fire Dog: 1946, 2006

This Dog has a lively, outgoing personality and is able to establish friendships with remarkable ease. He is an honest and conscientious worker and likes to take an active part in all that is going on around him. He also likes to explore new ideas and providing he can get the necessary support and advice, he can often succeed where others have failed. He does, however, have a tendency to be stubborn. Providing he can overcome this, he can often achieve considerable fame and fortune.

Earth Dog: 1958

The Earth Dog is very talented and astute. He is methodical and efficient and is capable of going far in his chosen profession. He tends to be rather quiet and reserved, but has a very persuasive manner and usually secures his objectives without too much opposition. He is generous and kind and always ready to lend a helping hand when it is needed. He is also held in very high esteem by his friends and colleagues and is usually most dignified in his appearance.

Prospects for the Dog in 2017

A lot happens quickly in the Monkey year (8 February 2016–27 January 2017) and the Dog may be involved in many activities, sometimes with success but sometimes not, as he may be drawn into matters not of his choosing. However, while the Monkey year will bring its pressures, it will bring opportunities too.

In the closing months the Dog will need to use his time well and concentrate on key priorities. To spread his attention too widely could limit his effectiveness. In his home life in particular, arrangements should be agreed upon early on and activities spread out. With more substantial purchases too, time needs to be allowed to consider options and make choices without pressure.

The Dog will see an increase in social activity at this time and some unexpected invitations may delight him. The end of the year could be capped with some pleasing personal news or a much-heralded occasion.

At work many Dogs will find their skills in demand and there may be scope for some to increase their role. September and November could see possible openings but, as with so much in the Monkey year, this is a time for the Dog to focus, to put himself forward and make the most of what arises.

The Rooster year begins on 28 January and will be a mixed one for the Dog. He may be uneasy about some developments but can also look forward to some personal triumphs. The Rooster year will certainly test him, but next year is the Dog's own year and what happens now (both good and bad) can prepare him for the opportunities that lie ahead.

During the year, the Dog should bear in mind that Rooster years favour convention and proceeding along established lines. This means that the Dog's more idealistic notions may not always get the reception he would like. At times this year, discretion would not come amiss. Dogs, especially more vociferous ones, take note.

At work, parts of the year will be demanding. Complex tasks, the slow workings of bureaucracy and problems caused by change could all result in the Dog facing frustrations. And, being conscientious, he will not want to fall behind or let others down. However, while the pressures can sometimes be intense, as Benjamin Franklin suggested, problems can be opportunities in disguise. If the Dog concentrates on what needs to be done and uses his skills and judgement well, he can highlight (as well as discover) certain aptitudes and enhance his reputation. While the Rooster year may be demanding, it will show the stuff the Dog is made of.

Many Dogs will remain with their present employer over the year, though with altered and more extensive duties. However, for those seeking change, as well as those looking for work, the Rooster year can have significant developments in store. Obtaining a new position will require great effort, but the Dog is by nature tenacious and can be successful in his quest. Also, if he takes on a position which is different from what he has done before, by showing commitment, he can quickly establish himself in his new role and have the chance to acquire what can be valuable new skills. March, June, September and November could see considerable activity.

Although the Dog will have many demands on his time, to drive himself relentlessly or give scant thought to his own well-being could leave him lacking his usual sparkle. In the Rooster year all Dogs should strive for a balanced lifestyle and, if lacking regular exercise, try to incorporate some into their schedule. If reliant on fast food, healthier alternatives could also be to their advantage, including in raising energy levels.

Personal interests can also play an important part this year, especially as many Dogs will have ideas they will be keen to follow through or events they would like to attend. Rooster years can be inspiring but require good management of time. Looking ahead, if there are skills the Dog thinks could be useful or an interest he would like to learn more about, he should find out more. Positive action can be to his present *and* future advantage.

With his busy lifestyle, the Dog's outgoings will be considerable, however, and throughout the year he should watch his spending levels.

Without care, outgoings could creep up. Also, if involved in any large transaction, he should compare prices, terms and implications. Extra attention could prevent mistakes as well as lead to better decisions.

As a sign the Dog is renowned for his loyalty and many people value his dependable nature. Unfortunately, though, a certain friendship could come into question this year when another person is not as reliable or supportive as the Dog expected them to be. Some Dogs may also find their trust has been broken. However, while the Rooster year can bring its disappointments, these will pass. Where one friendship may flounder, another could quickly take its place. The Dog relates well to others and there will be much socializing for him to appreciate this year. March, April, July and September could be active months.

The Dog's home life will also see great activity, especially as he will be keen to make improvements, including rectifying niggling problems or updating equipment. However, practical undertakings can be problematic, and throughout the year the Dog should discuss his thoughts and possible solutions with others, including professionals where necessary. This is no time to proceed regardless. Also, some activities could be more disruptive than initially envisaged and the Dog should factor this into his plans. Dogs, take note – prepare well and do involve everyone concerned in your undertakings.

Work pressures and other commitments which leave the Dog (or other family members) tired or preoccupied also need to be taken into account, but with understanding and good communication, tensions can be eased and pressures lightened. All years have their difficulties and this one will be no exception. However, Rooster years do provide a good mix of highs and lows, and personal successes enjoyed by the Dog and other family members can be a source of much joy, as can shared occasions, some of which will just happen and be all the more appreciated for their spontaneity. June, July and December could be special months, with travel also possible.

Overall, the Year of the Rooster will be a demanding one for the Dog and during it he will need to proceed steadily. Haste does not suit his psyche in any event. Ideally, he should plan out his undertakings and give careful thought to how best he can manage his time and situation.

Next year is his own year and if he can add to his knowledge now it can be to his advantage then. In his work and personal interests in particular, this is a year to build. He also needs to manage his resources carefully as well as liaise well with others. Rooster years can bring their difficult moments, but with attentiveness, these can often be minimized and will not detract from the many achievements enjoyed. This will be an action-filled year, not always smooth, but rewarding and with far-reaching significance.

The Metal Dog

A notable feature of the Metal Dog is his commitment. When he takes on an obligation or sets himself an objective, he strives hard to do what is required. However, he is also realistic, and rather than rush, he likes to proceed steadily. And this sums up the Rooster year for him: it will be a time of steady but satisfying progress. Some developments may cause him to re-evaluate his situation, but next year is his own year and what happens now will prepare him for the opportunities that lie ahead.

At work, although many Metal Dogs would be content to focus on their current duties, developments could impact on their role. In some workplaces there could be considerable staff movement and changes in key personnel. In addition, new systems could prove disruptive. Some of what happens will affect the Metal Dog's ability to carry out his duties and, being conscientious, this is something which will concern him. At almost any time of the year he could find himself with altered duties, an increased workload or having to deputize for another person. However, despite the pressures, these can be times of opportunity. As changes occur, staff will be required to take on greater roles and the Metal Dog may be well placed to benefit. Some of the year's developments may not be what he was envisaging, but will nevertheless enable him to move his career forward.

For Metal Dogs who feel they can better their prospects by a move elsewhere, as well as those seeking work, the Rooster year can also hold significant developments. Although vacancies in the type of work they favour may be limited, by considering other ways of using their skills and keeping alert for openings, they can succeed in their quest. This will take time and the Metal Dog may sometimes be daunted by the responsibilities he eventually takes on, but the accent this year is on steady growth. March to mid-April, June, September and November could see important opportunities.

Progress made at work will increase the income of many Metal Dogs, but this will be an expensive year. With some home repairs likely, as well as major purchases and other outgoings, the Metal Dog will need to keep a close watch on spending and make early provision for key plans. He also needs to be careful when dealing with financial correspondence or taking on new commitments and should, if appropriate, obtain professional advice. This is not a year to be lax or take risks. Metal Dogs, take note.

Domestically, this will be a busy year with some exciting developments to celebrate. A younger relation could get engaged or married or enjoy a much-deserved academic or work-related success, and this will mean a great deal to the Metal Dog. As always, he will be there to support and advise as necessary.

Additional pleasure this year can come from travel. A planned (and much-anticipated) holiday can be particularly appreciated. June to early August and December could be fine and active months in the Metal Dog's household.

However, while there will be much to enjoy, there will also be difficulties. Equipment could fail, unanticipated expenses arise and complex decisions need to be made. Discussion and flexibility will help. With problems of a practical nature, contacting those with the knowledge to assist could save the Dog (and others) additional anxiety. Dogs, take note, and do be prepared to draw on the help that is available to you.

While the Metal Dog will have many commitments this year, he should also preserve some time for his personal interests. These can not only give him the chance to unwind but also inspire him. Especially for Metal Dogs who are feeling staid, this is a year to be alert for new activities. They can be rewarding both now and in the future.

While the Metal Dog often likes to keep his social life relatively low key, developments this year can lead to him meeting others and making some useful connections, both personally and professionally. His person-able nature will delight quite a few people this year, with March, April, July and September particularly favourable and interesting months socially. However, while there will be good times, as is the way with the Rooster year, a disagreement could occur and this will need to be addressed lest it escalates. Rooster years can have their tricky moments.

As the Chinese proverb reminds us, 'Slow and steady wins the race.' This fits in well with the Metal Dog's psyche. Slowly and steadily he can acquire knowledge, strengthen his skills and enhance his reputation, and these can all be significant in the near future. Domestically, this will be a busy year with good news to share but decisions and problems to talk through as well. To help his lifestyle balance, the Metal Dog should allow time for personal interests and consider taking up new ones. These can bring him pleasure as well as a respite from all the activity. Overall, a demanding but significant year.

Tip for the Year
Add to your skills and knowledge in both your work and your personal interests. That way you will be strengthening your prospects for the future. Also, enjoy your relations with those who are special to you. Their support will encourage you.

The Water Dog

This will be an action-packed year for the Water Dog and while there will be times when he will despair of all he has to do, he will nevertheless accomplish an enormous amount. Significantly, what he succeeds in doing now can often be built upon in the Dog year that follows.

To make the most of the Rooster year the Water Dog does, though, need to keep alert to developments and adapt accordingly. By being flexible and making the most of situations as they arise, he may not only benefit now but also find that one step forward can lead to others.

One area which is especially well aspected is personal and professional development, and throughout the year the Water Dog should seize any chances to extend his skills and knowledge. If there is a qualification he feels could be useful or a skill that would enable him to do more, he should investigate how he could obtain it. In some instances, training will be available through his work, but if not, or he is keen to develop a more recreational skill, he should check out the courses available, including online. By investing in himself he will be adding to his capabilities and widening his options for later.

At work this can be a demanding year, with the Water Dog's workload complicated by additional pressures and niggling problems. Some parts of the year will be exasperating and may prevent the Water Dog from giving as much attention to certain aspects of his work as he would like. However, the situations that arise can highlight his strengths and help his reputation.

The majority of Water Dogs will remain with their present employer over the year and have the chance to extend their role and gain further insight into their industry. For those who decide to move elsewhere, as well as those seeking work, the Rooster year will be challenging. Obtaining a new position will require time, and with competition likely to be fierce, showing initiative by finding out more about the duties involved can make an important difference. Water Dogs who do take on a different role will find that by showing commitment and working well with their colleagues, they can prepare themselves for further advances. March, June, September and November could see considerable activity and some chances arising.

Financially, although many Water Dogs will enjoy a rise in income, this will be an expensive year. The Water Dog could face additional outgoings and also have plans of his own in mind, possibly family activities or a holiday. To do all he wants will require discipline and good control over spending. He could find it helpful to keep a set of accounts to keep better track of his position. Money matters do require careful attention this year and if the Water Dog enters into any agreements, he should check the terms carefully.

The Water Dog has an enquiring nature and over the year he could become intrigued by new activities or inspired by new ideas. By following these up, he can not only derive much personal satisfaction from what he does but also come into contact with like-minded people.

Indeed, during the year many Water Dogs can look forward to some particularly interesting and convivial occasions. Any Water Dog who is feeling lonely or has had recent personal problems will find that joining a community or interest group could restore some sparkle to their life. For the unattached, a chance meeting could become more meaningful as the year progresses. March, April, July and September could see the most social activity, although, in view of the prevailing aspects, if a friendship issue concerns the Water Dog at any time, he should try to resolve it rather than ignore it. Minor matters could escalate if he is not careful.

The Water Dog's home life will see great activity. Both the Water Dog and his partner (and sometimes children) could find themselves affected by changing routines and domestic adjustments will be needed. There will be much to consider, but with support, flexibility and good dialogue, changes can be successfully introduced and some unexpected advantages follow on. If a parent, the Water Dog will also be keen to guide and encourage his children as well as share in their delight as new skills are mastered. More senior relations will also be glad of his input on certain undertakings. Many a Water Dog will be at the heart of family activities this year. June, July and December could be special months, although whenever possible, activities should be spread out throughout the year.

Overall, the Year of the Rooster will be a busy one for the Water Dog, with many pressures and some problems to contend with. His work situation could be particularly demanding but also instructive and good preparation for the opportunities that await next year. Personal interests can also develop well and the Water Dog should add to his skills and consider setting himself new challenges. He will, though, need to be careful in money matters and keep a close watch on spending. On a personal level, he will find himself in demand, while domestically he will be a great support to those around him. This will be a demanding year, but there will be a lot to be gained and some hard-earned successes to enjoy.

Tip for the Year
Have self-belief. There will be challenges to face but you have it within you to learn, prove yourself and ultimately succeed. This year can be significant in highlighting your personal strengths.

The Wood Dog

There is a Chinese proverb which reminds us, 'Walk slowly and you won't fall down; act carefully and you won't make mistakes.' This advice holds very true for the Wood Dog in the Rooster year. It will be a year of significant opportunities and, by proceeding carefully and in tune with what he feels is right, he can learn a lot from it.

The Wood Dog's personal life will be especially busy. For those with a partner, there will be hopes to realize and plans to tackle, including perhaps marrying or settling down together. While enthusiastic, the Wood Dog will also need to be disciplined and avoid committing himself to too many undertakings at any one time. With more ambitious plans, he needs to give careful thought to costs and implications. Rooster years favour planning and a 'one step at a time' approach will ensure better outcomes.

Although the Rooster year will have its pressures it will also contain many highlights. The Wood Dog (and partner) could enjoy some pleasing personal news and will have a good mix of things to do, including travel. While the Wood Dog likes to make his own decisions, if he would welcome another opinion, or advice, consulting senior relations may lead to help in unexpected ways.

For the unattached, affairs of the heart could become significant, with Cupid's arrow striking suddenly and dramatically. Wood Dogs who have experienced recent personal upset could find changing circumstances bringing them into contact with others and their prospects, and often love life, becoming much more positive. Mid-February to early May, July and September could see interesting developments.

The Wood Dog will also value the social opportunities of the year and parties, events and, for the music enthusiast, concerts can give rise to some exciting occasions. The Rooster year will certainly contain a good mix of things to do and Wood Dogs who are feeling lonely or who move over the year should take note of what is happening in their area. Getting involved can brighten their situation.

However, while there will be good times to enjoy, the Rooster year will have its troubling moments and the situation of a friend could worry the Wood Dog. His levelheadedness and empathy can help.

In money matters, with purchases, costly undertakings and some deposits likely, the Wood Dog will need to be disciplined. If required to borrow, he should check the terms and seek professional advice when necessary. The resources of many Wood Dogs will be stretched this year. However, the Wood Dog can look forward to some luck, perhaps in the form of a special offer, a gift or a shrewd purchase.

At work the Wood Dog can look forward to making important headway, but again, effort will be required. For those already established in a position, developments in their workplace are likely to impact on their role. When personnel change or are absent, they may be faced with additional responsibilities and pressures. Situations may not be helped by new objectives, deadlines or problems over supply or equipment. The Wood Dog's role will not always be easy this year, but by doing his best and showing initiative, he can enhance his reputation. The problems of the year may also lead to him working more closely with senior colleagues and this will give him an added chance to impress.

For Wood Dogs who desire change, as well as those seeking work, the Rooster year will be challenging. Many of these Wood Dogs will face disappointments, but the Rooster year is famed for its moments of luck. An opening found and followed up by chance (or word of mouth) could lead to a position being offered. And while this could involve a steep learning curve, it could give the Wood Dog the chance to establish himself in a new role. Such are the workings of the year that some Wood Dogs will chance upon a career they will make their future. March, June, September and November could see helpful developments.

For Wood Dogs in education, effort will once again be required, but with focus and self-belief they can gain significant results. And again, these can be something they can build upon.

The Year of the Rooster will ask a lot of the Wood Dog and progress will be hard-won, but the Wood Dog is tenacious and by making the most of his situation he will learn a lot and help his prospects in the process. He will value the love and friendship of those who are close to him and there will be special times to enjoy. More senior relations can give important assistance. Spending needs to be watched, but overall, slowly and steadily, this is a year of laying the foundations for the exciting times ahead.

Tip for the Year

This is an excellent year to show your potential. Seize any chances to gain experience and build connections. You have a lot to offer and can ultimately benefit from the effort you make now. Also, enjoy the special times you will share with your loved ones.

The Fire Dog

This will be a full and satisfying year for the Fire Dog and despite some challenges he can benefit from many of its developments. With a willing approach and flexibility on his part, he is set to do well.

Fire Dogs born in 1946 will, in particular, see considerable activity in their domestic life. During the year younger relations could enjoy some keynote occasions as well as face important decisions concerning work, relocation or personal matters. Here the Fire Dog's understanding may be especially valued and he may play an influential part on several occasions. In the summer there could be some especially gratifying family news as well as the chance to meet relations (or very close friends) not seen for some time.

The Fire Dog will also be keen to carry out some practical undertakings, including replacing outdated equipment. Although he may start these tasks in earnest, practical projects could turn out more complicated and costly than expected. Also, where technical matters are concerned, original ideas may need to be revised as other considerations come into play. Some flexibility – and expert guidance – could be needed.

The Fire Dog keeps himself well informed about what is going on in his locality and several activities and events could tempt him over the year. If he follows these up, some enjoyable (and occasionally unusual) times can be had. In addition, he could be attracted by some locally run courses or recreational pursuits that take place over the year. Participating could add something extra to his lifestyle. For the lonely Fire Dog, local activities and recreational groups could offer new friendships and be well worth considering. March, April, July and September could see the most social activity.

One area which will require particular attention this year is finance. With family expenses, costly purchases and other outgoings, the Fire Dog will need to watch his spending and overall situation. Too many outgoings all at once could lead to shortfalls and to adjustments having to be made. The Fire Dog should also attend to bureaucratic matters with care. Although this may be irksome, delays or oversights could be to his disadvantage. If he has any doubts, he should seek clarification.

The Fire Dog will also enjoy his travels this year and whether visiting attractions some distance away or enjoying those closer to home, he can look forward to seeing some interesting sights as well as trying some new experiences. Some spur of the moment trips could be particularly appreciated, with the unexpectedness adding to the fun. Early summer could be an active and interesting time for travel possibilities.

Overall, this can be a full and interesting year for the Fire Dog born in 1946, although to make the most of it, he does need to be flexible. However, with awareness, support and willingness to seize his opportunities, he will be pleased with how his activities develop.

For the Fire Dog born in 2006, the Rooster year will also see important events. For some of these Fire Dogs there will be a change of school and a plethora of new subjects to learn. There will be daunting and demanding times, but by showing commitment and putting in the effort, many of these young Fire Dogs will make important progress as well as show their potential in certain areas.

These Fire Dogs will also enjoy developing their recreational interests, and by taking advantage of the resources available to them, can make encouraging progress and will be supported by those around them. With friends, too, there will be good camaraderie and some lively times to share, although mixed in with these there could be a problem with another person. If worried, the Fire Dog should seek advice rather than keep his anxieties to himself. 'A worry shared *is* a worry halved.'

The young Fire Dog can also look forward to some interesting trips, including visits to special attractions, and could develop an interest in certain activities as a result. Rooster years can be illuminating and have long-term benefits.

As with all years, this one will have its ups and downs. During it, the Fire Dog, whether born in 1946 or 2006, will take great satisfaction in many of his activities and enjoy some pleasing results. But the year will also bring its challenges. It is important that the Fire Dog remembers that support is there for him should he need it. However, the Rooster year will allow him to engage in many activities and enjoy some good results. His domestic life and personal interests can be especially reward-ing and shared activities can bring him great pleasure.

Tip for the Year
Enjoy your personal interests and develop your skills. Keep alert to opportunities and make the most of the facilities available to you. With a willing attitude, you can do – and enjoy – a lot this year.

The Earth Dog

The Earth Dog has many fine gifts and among them is his ability to read situations and sense the right time to act. And his awareness and timing will prove very useful this year.

Rooster years favour planning and as this one starts the Earth Dog should consider what he would like to see happen. By setting himself some aims, he can make this a constructive and significant time. And with next year being his own year, he will have an excellent chance to build on this year's accomplishments.

His work situation will see some volatility. Working practices may be altered over the year and new initiatives launched. However, as changes are considered and implemented, many Earth Dogs will find themselves having greater input in their workplace as well as making better use of their specializations. Work-wise, the Rooster year will be a challenging one but may give the Earth Dog an increased sense of fulfilment. And his ability to respond well to situations can lead to important progress being made.

The majority of Earth Dogs will remain with their current employer over the year, albeit in a considerably enhanced position, but some will be tempted by opportunities elsewhere. By keeping alert and making enquiries (here their network of contacts could prove helpful), many will successfully make the move they want. Rooster years favour determined action and the Earth Dog's strengths and timing will often be to his advantage in this one.

For Earth Dogs seeking work, there may also be interesting developments in store. Although their quest will be difficult and at times disheartening, their persistence and initiative can lead to positions being found. In some cases these can be a considerable change from previous roles but offer an ideal challenge. March, June, September and November could see encouraging developments.

Another area which can bring potential reward this year is the Earth Dog's personal interests. Again, by setting himself objectives for the year (which will often include starting something new), he will enjoy the way these develop. The Earth Dog likes to have purpose and could be on inspired form this year. Creative activities are particularly well aspected and could meet with an encouraging response.

With his full lifestyle, commitments and travel opportunities (especially in early summer), the Earth Dog's outgoings will be considerable and he will need to keep a close watch on his level of spending. If he can make early provision for some purchases, this will not only help his budgeting but in some instances allow him to improve on his original idea. Rooster years favour planning and discipline. The Earth Dog also needs to be especially careful when attending to financial correspondence. He is usually meticulous, but should he have any questions or uncertainties, he should get these addressed lest mistakes are made. Earth Dogs, take note.

Socially, while the Earth Dog may not like particularly large gatherings, he will enjoy meeting up with his friends and some of the more informal and celebratory occasions he goes to. He will enjoy a good rapport with some of the people he meets this year, often through mutual acquaintances, and shared interests can be a helpful link. However, should a tricky social situation arise, he needs to be his guarded and discreet self. Rooster years require care. Here the Earth Dog's perceptive nature will again be a valuable asset. March, April, July and September could be pleasing and convivial months.

Domestically, the Earth Dog will often be keen to proceed with plans, purchases and improvements. However, while enthusiastic, he needs to be realistic in what he can embark on at any one time and to talk his plans over with his loved ones, taking into account their views and the likely disruption involved. Once underway, some undertakings could run into snags and delays, and the increased pressure and inconvenience could lead to awkward moments. Earth Dogs, take note and be forewarned.

Despite this, the Earth Dog and his loved ones will enjoy some very special moments, perhaps celebrating a personal or shared milestone or individual success. Also, by being aware of what is happening in his locality, the Earth Dog will often learn of events and activities that he and other family members could enjoy together. June, July and December could be particularly active months.

Much is set to happen in this Rooster year and the Earth Dog's enthusiasm and commitment will often deliver good results. He does need to manage his finances carefully and be forthcoming about his plans and intentions, but with support, care and his usual awareness, he can make this a fulfilling year and build on his achievements in his own splendid year which follows.

Tip for the Year

Set yourself some objectives for the year and work towards them. With your strengths and strong sense of purpose, you can accomplish a great deal. However, do liaise well with those around you and be mindful of their views.

Famous Dogs

Brigitte Bardot, Gary Barlow, Candice Bergen, Justin Bieber, Andrea Bocelli, David Bowie, Jimmy Buffett, George W. Bush, Kate Bush, the Duke of Cambridge, Naomi Campbell, Peter Capaldi, Mariah Carey, King Carl XVI Gustaf of Sweden, José Carreras, Paul Cézanne, Cher, Sir Winston Churchill, Bill Clinton, Leonard Cohen, Abbie Cornish, Matt Damon, Charles Dance, Dame Judi Dench, Jamie Dornan, Kirsten Dunst, Dakota Fanning, Joseph Fiennes, Robert Frost, Judy Garland, George Gershwin, Anne Hathaway, Barry Humphries, Holly Hunter, Michael Jackson, Jennifer Lopez, Sophia Loren, Andie MacDowell, Shirley MacLaine, Melissa McCarthy, Madonna, Norman Mailer, Barry Manilow, Freddie Mercury, Nicki Minaj, Liza Minnelli, Simon Pegg, Elvis Presley, Tim Robbins, Susan Sarandon, Claudia Schiffer, Dr Albert Schweitzer, Sylvester Stallone, Robert Louis Stevenson, Sharon Stone, Nicola Sturgeon, Mother Teresa, Uma Thurman, Donald Trump, Voltaire, Lil Wayne, Shelley Winters.

16 February 1923 to 4 February 1924 — *Water Pig*

4 February 1935 to 23 January 1936 — *Wood Pig*

22 January 1947 to 9 February 1948 — *Fire Pig*

8 February 1959 to 27 January 1960 — *Earth Pig*

27 January 1971 to 14 February 1972 — *Metal Pig*

13 February 1983 to 1 February 1984 — *Water Pig*

31 January 1995 to 18 February 1996 — *Wood Pig*

18 February 2007 to 6 February 2008 — *Fire Pig*

The Pig

The Personality of the Pig

It's the doing,
the giving,
the playing the part,
that makes life what it is.
And what it can be.

The Pig is born under the sign of honesty. He has a kind and understanding nature and is well known for his abilities as a peacemaker. He hates any sort of discord or unpleasantness and will do everything in his power to sort out differences of opinion or bring opposing factions together.

He is also an excellent conversationalist and speaks truthfully and to the point. He dislikes any form of falsehood or hypocrisy and is a firm believer in justice and the maintenance of law and order. In spite of these beliefs, however, he is reasonably tolerant and often prepared to forgive others for their wrongdoings. He rarely harbours grudges and is never vindictive.

The Pig is usually very popular. He enjoys other people's company and likes to be involved in joint or group activities. He will be a loyal member of any club or society and can be relied upon to lend a helping hand at functions. He is also an excellent fundraiser for charities and is often a great supporter of humanitarian causes.

The Pig is a hard and conscientious worker and is particularly respected for his reliability and integrity. In his early years he will try his hand at several different jobs, but he is usually happiest where he feels that he is being of service to others. He will unselfishly give up his time for the common good and is highly valued by his colleagues and employers.

The Pig has a good sense of humour and invariably has a smile, joke or some whimsical remark at the ready. He loves to entertain and to please others, and there are many Pigs who have been attracted to careers in show business or who enjoy following the careers of famous stars and personalities.

There are, unfortunately, some who take advantage of the Pig's good nature and impose upon his generosity. The Pig has great difficulty in saying 'no', and although he may dislike being firm, it would be in his own interests to say occasionally, 'Enough is enough.' He can also be rather naïve and gullible; however, if at any stage in his life he feels that he has been badly let down, he will try to become self-reliant. There are many Pigs who have become entrepreneurs or forged a successful career on their own after some early disappointment in life. Although the Pig tends to spend his money quite freely, he is usually very astute in financial matters and there are many Pigs who have become wealthy.

Another characteristic of the Pig is his ability to recover from setbacks reasonably quickly. His faith and his strength of character keep him going. If he thinks that there is a job he can do or there is something that he wants to achieve, he will pursue it with dogged determination. He can also be stubborn and no matter how many may plead with him, once he has made his mind up he will rarely change his views.

Although the Pig may work hard, he also knows how to enjoy himself. He is a great pleasure-seeker and will quite happily spend his hard-earned money on a lavish holiday or an expensive meal – for the Pig is a connoisseur of good food and wine – or a variety of recreational activities. He also enjoys small social gatherings and if he is in company he likes he can very easily become the life and soul of the party. He does, however, tend to become rather withdrawn at larger functions or when among strangers.

The Pig is a creature of comfort and his home will usually be fitted with the latest in luxury appliances. Where possible, he will prefer to live in the country rather than the town and will opt to have a big garden, for the Pig is usually a keen and successful gardener.

The Pig is very popular with others and will often have numerous romances before he settles down. Once settled, however, he will be loyal to his partner and he will find that he is especially well suited to those born under the signs of the Goat, Rabbit, Dog and Tiger and also to another Pig. Due to his affable and easy-going nature he can also establish a satisfactory relationship with all the remaining signs of the Chinese zodiac, with the exception of the Snake. The Snake tends to be wily, secretive and very guarded, and this can be intensely irritating to the honest and open-hearted Pig.

The female Pig will devote much time and energy to the needs of her partner and children. She will try to ensure that they want for nothing and their pleasure is very much her pleasure. Her home will either be very clean and orderly or hopelessly untidy. Strangely, there seems to be no in-between with Pigs – they either love housework or detest it! The female Pig does, however, have considerable talents as an organizer and this, combined with her friendly and open manner, enables her to secure many of her objectives. She also has very good taste in clothes.

The Pig is usually lucky in life and will rarely want for anything. Provided he does not let others take advantage of his good nature and is not afraid of asserting himself, he will go through life making friends, helping others and winning the admiration of many.

The Five Different Types of Pig

In addition to the 12 signs of the Chinese zodiac there are five elements and these have a strengthening or moderating influence on the signs. The effects of the elements on the Pig are described below, together with the years in which they were exercising their influence. Therefore Pigs born in 1971 are Metal Pigs, Pigs born in 1923 and 1983 are Water Pigs, and so on.

Metal Pig: 1971

The Metal Pig is more ambitious and determined than some of the other types of Pig. He is strong, energetic and likes to be involved in a wide variety of different activities. He is very open and forthright in his views, although he can be a little too trusting at times and has a tendency to accept things at face value. He has a good sense of humour and loves to attend parties and other social gatherings. He has a warm, outgoing nature and usually has a large circle of friends.

Water Pig: 1923, 1983

The Water Pig has a heart of gold. He is generous and loyal and tries to remain on good terms with everyone. He will do his utmost to help others, but sadly there are some who will take advantage of his kind nature and he should, in his own interests, be a little more discriminating and be prepared to stand firm against anything that he does not like. Although he prefers the quieter things in life, he has a wide range of interests. He particularly enjoys outdoor pursuits and attending parties and social occasions. He is a hard and conscientious worker and invariably does well in his chosen profession. He is also gifted in the art of communication.

Wood Pig: 1935, 1995

This Pig has a friendly, persuasive manner and is easily able to gain the confidence of others. He likes to be involved in all that is going on around him but can sometimes take on more responsibility than he can properly handle. He is loyal to his family and friends and derives much pleasure from helping those less fortunate than himself. He is usually an optimist and leads a very full, enjoyable and satisfying life. He also has a good sense of humour.

Fire Pig: 1947, 2007

The Fire Pig is both energetic and adventurous and sets about everything he does in a confident and resolute manner. He is very forthright in his views and does not mind taking risks in order to achieve his objectives. He can, however, get carried away by the excitement of the moment and ought to exercise more caution in some of the enterprises in which he gets involved. He is usually lucky in money matters and is well known for his generosity. He is also very caring towards the members of his family.

Earth Pig: 1959

This Pig has a kindly nature. He is sensible and realistic and will go to great lengths in order to please his employers and to secure his aims and ambitions. He is an excellent organizer and is particularly astute in business and financial matters. He has a good sense of humour and a wide circle of friends. He also likes to lead an active social life, although he does sometimes have a tendency to eat and drink more than is good for him.

Prospects for the Pig in 2017

The Year of the Monkey (8 February 2016–27 January 2017) will have been a varied one for the Pig. While progress will have been made, it will have come as a result of much effort. Monkey years have their opportunities but require commitment and for the Pig to make the most of developing situations. This will continue to be the case in the remaining Monkey months.

At work many Pigs will experience a flurry of activity as workloads change and staff movements (including absences) occur. For some, this will be an opportunity to take on new responsibilities. November could be a key month and January 2017 could also see possibilities to pursue.

The Pig can also look forward to an increase in social activity at this time, with some lively occasions to enjoy. For the unattached, there could be romantic possibilities towards the end of the year, while for those newly in love, the closing months could be very special.

The Pig will also be keen to fit a lot into his domestic life, but with many calls on his time, he will need to be well-organized and spread his commitments out. Also, rather than conduct his life at a frenetic pace, he could appreciate time spent simply relaxing with his loved ones.

His outgoings will be greater than normal at this time and while pleased with the gifts and other items he purchases, he could find it helpful to set a budget for end-of-year spending.

*   *   *

The Year of the Rooster starts on 28 January and will be an encouraging one for the Pig. In particular it will give him the chance to make more of his special talents. And once he takes action, circumstances will often assist.

Self-improvement is well aspected and as the Rooster year starts the Pig should consider ways of improving himself and his lifestyle. Some Pigs may decide to exercise more, start a fitness discipline or improve their diet. Others may choose to develop a skill, enrol on a course or gain a further qualification. Whatever he does, the Pig's positive actions will reinforce the positive nature of the year.

The favourable aspects also apply to his work situation. With the experience he has built up, he may well find himself being offered greater responsibilities or taking on new assignments. Senior colleagues in particular could be encouraging. As a result, many Pigs will make good headway in their current place of work, with their prospects growing as their involvement increases.

For Pigs who decide to move on or who are seeking work, the Rooster year can again have significant developments in store. These Pigs should not be too restrictive in the type of work they are considering. By being open-minded, many could find a position offering a new challenge. Although this may involve considerable adjustment, by showing commitment the Pig can quickly make his mark. February, April, July and October could see good possibilities.

Although work aspects are encouraging, at some time the Pig may be troubled by the attitude of a colleague or petty office politics. If so, he should focus on the tasks to be done rather than allow himself to be distracted. By remaining professional he will again be demonstrating his qualities and will successfully overcome many an issue. However, he does need to be aware of the sensitivities (and touchiness) of some of his colleagues.

Progress at work will increase the income of many Pigs, but spending will still need to be watched. Without care, outgoings could be greater than intended and economies have to be made later. The Pig should also be wary of risk and, if tempted by anything speculative, be aware of the implications. Money can be made this year, but it can very easily be lost. Pigs, take note.

The Pig's home life will see some interesting times. Although the Pig and his loved ones will have many commitments, the Rooster year favours coming together and sharing activities. Such times will not only be good for relationships and rapport but appreciated by all. The Pig's sense of fun can also add a lot to family life this year. April, July and September could see the most activity.

However, while a lot will go well, sometimes tiredness will cause tension or a disagreement arise over a domestic issue. In such cases, discussion will be helpful, as will a willingness to rally round during times of stress. That way, the more awkward moments of the year can be quickly defused and not overshadow the many shared pleasures.

The Pig enjoys his social life and the Rooster year will again be rich in possibility. Any Pig who is feeling lonely, perhaps as a result of a recent change in circumstances or location, will find that by taking an interest in activities in his area, he can make new friends. March, July, August and October could be lively and interesting months, and for the unattached, serious romance can beckon, with some Pigs (especially those who met someone last year or early in 2017) settling down together and/or marrying. On a personal level, these are potentially special times.

The Pig likes to keep himself busy and he will find the Rooster year a rewarding one. In his work there will be opportunities to make important progress, while in terms of self-improvement, whether he is looking to improve his fitness levels, alter his diet or learn a skill, he can benefit from what he does. Domestically and socially, there will be much to appreciate, although, when problems arise (as they do in any year), the Pig does need to address them rather than hope they will go away. He may not like unpleasantness, but good communication (and frankness) will often help. He also needs to be disciplined in money matters, but overall his energy, interests and skills can make this a productive year for him.

The Metal Pig

There is a Chinese proverb which it could be helpful for the Metal Pig to bear in mind this year: 'You must invest a little to gain a lot.' By investing in himself this year, the Metal Pig can prepare the way for some substantial gains in the future.

With many Metal Pigs now well established in their line of work, there will be good opportunities for them to take on a greater role. Often this will be with their present employer and their in-house experience will be a valuable asset. As staff move on and changes are made (and the Rooster year could see quite a few), the Metal Pig will often be ideally positioned to benefit. He can help his prospects by taking advantage of any training he is offered and keeping himself informed of developments in his industry. If applicable, joining a professional organization, attending events and networking could also help. By embracing his chances and raising his profile, he will be investing in himself *and* his future.

There will, though, be some Metal Pigs who feel they have accomplished all they can in their present line of work or with their current employer. For these Metal Pigs, and those seeking work, the Rooster year can again have significant developments in store. Although the job-seeking process can be wearying, by not being too restrictive in their quest, they could uncover some interesting possibilities. While these may entail a lot of adjustment, by showing commitment, many of these Pigs will quickly mark themselves out for future progress. For quite a few, this Rooster year will re-energize their career. February, April, July and October could see positive developments.

With his enquiring mind and hopes for the future, the Metal Pig may choose to do some reading or studying this year or enrol on a course. Whether for professional reasons or personal interest, by investing in himself in this way, he can get much value from it. Some Metal Pigs will be keen to try out a different interest or take an existing one in a new direction.

Also, if the Metal Pig is sedentary for much of the day and feels lacking in regular exercise, he would do well to address it. By seeking medical advice on appropriate forms of exercise *and taking action*, he can make a real difference, and find some activities fun to do as well.

Travel too will feature on the agenda of many Metal Pigs. Some will decide to visit destinations which have long appealed to them. Again, when opportunities arise, they need to be followed up. 'There is no time like the present.'

Financially, many Metal Pigs will enjoy a rise in income, but spending needs to be watched and early provision made for large outgoings. This is no year for the Metal Pig to be lax or take risks. He should also look after his valuables, including his personal possessions. A loss could be upsetting. Metal Pigs, be vigilant.

The Metal Pig's domestic life will see considerable activity, with some special occasions taking place. The Metal Pig will frequently be giving advice as well as making arrangements. April, July and September are likely to be particularly busy times.

However, while a lot is set to go well, changes could lead to pressures and practical projects prove protracted. Over the year, patience will be needed and any areas of difficulty will need to be talked through. Domestically this can be a satisfying year, but all years have their awkward moments and this one will be no exception.

With its cultural overtones, the Rooster year will, however, offer the Metal Pig many chances to attend events or visit attractions. There will be much to do and to share with family and friends. Any Metal Pigs who are lonely can inject new pleasures into their lifestyle by involving them-selves in what is happening around them. March, July, August, October and the end of the year could see the most social activity.

However, while the Metal Pig will enjoy excellent relations with most people over the year, should he find himself in a disagreement or trou-bled by another person's attitude, he needs to proceed carefully. If not watched, minor issues could escalate and undermine an otherwise good year. Metal Pigs, take note.

The Metal Pig has great determination and his current efforts are capable of bringing him significant rewards. By building on his skills and knowledge he can not only make good headway now but also help his subsequent progress. Timely developments can assist him, especially at work. He will need to be vigilant in money matters and be sure to liaise with others over important decisions or any concerns. However, the Rooster year is one of great possibility and by building on his present position, the Metal Pig can succeed both personally and professionally.

Tip for the Year
Embrace the present and its opportunities. Build on your skills, consider new activities and enjoy what opens up. With a keen approach, you can benefit now *and* help your future position.

The Water Pig

The Water Pig will have seen important changes in recent years and while some will have gone in his favour, there will have been disappointments and regrets too. The Rooster year will give him an excellent opportunity to move forward as well as tackle some areas of concern. It can be a constructive *and* satisfying time for him.

His home life will see considerable activity. Water Pigs who are parents will be keen to guide their children and the time they give can strengthen the bonds they share. The Water Pig often has an imaginative streak which young minds respond well to. Some senior relations, too, although not wanting to trouble the Water Pig, will be grateful for his assistance and thoughtful counsel.

The Water Pig will also have various objectives of his own this year, perhaps home improvements, taking certain interests further or advancing his career. April, July and September could be especially active months. However, the Water Pig does need to focus and prioritize. To spread his energies too widely will not only increase pressures but also lead to possible oversights. Rooster years favour planning and structure.

In addition, the Water Pig will need to be careful in money matters. With expensive plans and new commitments likely, he should keep control over his budget. He also needs to be wary of rushing decisions, and should he have doubts over any financial matter, he should seek professional advice.

Being disciplined with his spending will leave more funds available for pleasurable activities, and the Water Pig may particularly enjoy taking a holiday during the year as well as visiting local attractions and attending a variety of social occasions. He has a sociable nature and his social circle is set to grow considerably this year. Some of the people he meets could be helpful to him in the near future. March, July, August and October could see the most social activity, and for the unattached Water Pig, romantic prospects are promising. However, new romances should be allowed to develop in their own time rather than be rushed.

Also, although the Water Pig's relations with many of those around him will be positive, he does have a sensitive side and there could be times when the words of another person upset him. This could be in a professional situation or be a comment by a friend or even someone close. Although hurt, the Water Pig should, in his usual inimitable way, address any areas of disagreement and heal any rift, as well as accept that all relationships have their ups and downs. Fortunately, such instances will be the exception, but the Rooster year could have a few troubling moments and the Water Pig needs to keep them in perspective.

At work the aspects are encouraging. With many Water Pigs now established in a career, there will be excellent chances for them to advance to a higher level and add to their knowledge and experience. Senior colleagues could be helpful in arranging training and supporting their progress. By showing themselves willing to embrace new procedures, many could find themselves being offered more specialist tasks and playing an increasingly influential role in their workplace.

Many Water Pigs will further their position with their present employer, but for those who favour a change or are seeking work, the Rooster year can be significant. One of its key aspects is self-development, and by looking at different ways of using their strengths, these Water Pigs may set their career on an interesting and sometimes very different path. February, April, July and October could see potentially significant developments.

Although the Water Pig will be busy this year, he should ensure his personal interests do not get sidelined. With the emphasis on self-development, activities started this year can open up new possibilities.

With his hopes and ambitions, the Water Pig realizes he needs to put himself forward and take action. And by making the most of the opportunities this Rooster year will bring, he can learn a lot. This is a time for personal and career development. He does need to be wary of rush and avoid financial risks, but will enjoy a lively domestic and social life and can make much headway in this positive year.

Tip for the Year

Decide on your priorities. With your skills, support and personal talents, you can succeed in many areas this year but you need to channel your efforts and time and focus on your key objectives. Also, enjoy your relations with those who are special to you. Their love and support can add sparkle to your year.

The Wood Pig

Two of the key features of the Rooster year are that it favours planning and self-development and both are very applicable to the Wood Pig this year.

For the many Wood Pigs studying for qualifications, there will be many pressures as they prepare for approaching exams, have coursework to complete and seek to master new complexities. This can be an exacting time, but by focusing and keeping in mind the rewards that can ultimately be gained, many of these Wood Pigs will be pleased with what they accomplish this year. By investing time and energy in their development, they will also be investing in their future.

As a result of their studying, many will find new possibilities opening up. For some, research or work experience they carry out can bring them into contact with employers and lead to possible openings or ways forward being suggested. The accent this year is on preparing for the next stages in life and the Wood Pig's commitment can prove of far-reaching value.

Some Wood Pigs will start the year uncertain of the direction they wish to follow, but as the year proceeds, ideas and openings will occur which will give them new incentive. With his abilities and personal qualities, the Wood Pig has an exciting future ahead of him and this Rooster year can be influential in what lies ahead. If needing guidance or information, it is important that the Wood Pig avails himself of the expertise available to him. As the Chinese proverb suggests, 'If you ask for directions, you won't get lost.'

For Wood Pigs in work or seeking it, again there will be important developments in store. Many of the Wood Pigs already in employment will feel ready to move on from what they are currently doing. If there are openings in their place of work, they should put themselves forward as well as take advantage of any training that is available. By indicating their desire to move forward, many will be rewarded with increased responsibilities. The Wood Pig can also help his prospects by raising his profile and attending work-related events. His qualities can impress others and highlight his potential.

This also applies to Wood Pigs seeking work. While the job-seeking process can be disheartening, by showing initiative in their application and at interview, many of these Wood Pigs will be given a chance and, once established, quickly be able to make further progress. For quite a few, that initial foothold can lead to what can be a very successful future. February, April, July and October could see encouraging developments, but possibilities could arise at almost any time and need to be followed up quickly.

With the encouraging aspects, this is also an excellent time for the Wood Pig to consider developing his personal interests or trying something new. As is the way this year, new ideas can occur suddenly and some will develop in exciting fashion.

Travel, too, can be highly enjoyable, with the Wood Pig delighting in the places he sees and the lively times he has while away. Late summer can see some good possibilities.

With his busy lifestyle, his finances will, however, be stretched this year and he will need to be disciplined in his spending. To overindulge or spend on a whim could lead to shortfalls and later economies. The Wood Pig should also be wary of anything speculative. This is not a year for risk. Without care, mistakes and losses could occur. Wood Pigs, be warned.

The Wood Pig enjoys company and can look forward to a lively mix of social occasions this year, including parties and enjoyable times with friends. His personal interests can also have a social element to them and his studies or work may bring him into contact with some people with whom he will enjoy a good rapport. The social circle of many a Wood Pig is set to increase this year.

Affairs of the heart can add excitement too. However, while many new romances will develop well this year, with some Wood Pigs settling down with another person, for a few, there will be some difficult choices to make. What occurs can be part of life's rich learning experience, and for the minority of Wood Pigs who do find relationships (or friendships) floundering, there will be the chance to move on, older but wiser. Demanding though parts of this year may be (academically, profession-ally or personally), what happens can pave the way to better times ahead.

For Wood Pigs with a partner, there will be important matters to address. The Wood Pig may have high hopes and many ideas, but also an often limited budget. Plans will need to be considered carefully this year, and often undertaken in stages. However, this is an excellent year for enjoying shared interests and looking to develop these together.

Overall, the Rooster year will allow the Wood Pig to build on his skills and ready himself for present and future opportunities. This is a year when many Wood Pigs can establish themselves and show their true potential. However, the Rooster year also requires discipline. If the Wood Pig holds back, allows chances to slip through his grasp or takes risks, he can come to regret it. As an individual, he has much potential and should look to make the most of it. He will benefit from the support and goodwill of many people this year and his lifestyle can be lively and often fun. But with this Rooster year being an important stage in his subsequent success, the importance of the opportunities it brings should not be underestimated. Wood Pig, seize those opportunities.

Tip for the Year
Be alert to what is going on around you. A lot happens for a reason and being aware of what is happening will help you decide which direction to follow and which choices are right for you. This is an important year. Use it well, put in the effort and enjoy the rewards.

The Fire Pig

This will be a constructive year for the Fire Pig. It marks the start of a new decade in his life and he will be determined to make something of it. However, to get his plans underway, he does need to discuss them with others and decide on the best course of action. By carefully considering what needs to be done and when, he will see more happening. Rooster years favour planning and the Fire Pig's methodical nature will be an asset in this one.

For the Fire Pig born in 1947, his objectives will often be related to his interests, and whether completing a project or learning a skill (perhaps one he has long considered), by putting his thoughts into action, he will be satisfied with what he does.

With a lot often happening locally, the Fire Pig should also keep alert for activities he could take part in and social groups he could perhaps join. The Rooster year encourages participation. The Fire Pig will also be encouraged by the support of those around him and sharing activities with others will add meaning and impetus to certain undertakings.

With this being his seventieth year, the Fire Pig may also decide to take a special holiday. By planning this in advance, he could find he is able to include additional places of interest while away. There will also be several other travel opportunities throughout the year, including, for some Fire Pigs, the chance to visit family or friends living some distance away.

The Fire Pig will also find his loved ones keen to commemorate his seventieth year in style. Some of their ideas and thoughts could particularly delight him as well as underline their affection for him. In addition to enjoying any occasions arranged for him, the Fire Pig may have good reason to be proud of the success of a younger relation. What they achieve, often as a result of great effort, may be a highlight of his year.

Some Fire Pigs may decide to mark their seventieth year by starting an exercise discipline (including perhaps walking more) and giving some consideration to their diet. By seeking medical advice, many will soon feel the benefit. If any other health issue concerns the Fire Pig during the year, again he should seek medical advice. This is a year favouring constructive action.

The Fire Pig has a strongly practical nature and will also be keen to go ahead with various ideas for his home, including updating equipment and smartening certain areas. By involving other family members, he could enjoy some noticeable benefits. However, he does need to keep his zealous nature in check and focus on specific tasks rather than tackling too much at any one time. Some projects could be more extensive than initially thought!

He also needs to pay close attention to financial correspondence. Although this may be irksome, a delay or oversight could be to his disadvantage. Fire Pigs, take note. Similarly, when considering major purchases, the Fire Pig should check his options and the terms of any agreement. Financial matters need care this year.

Throughout the year the Fire Pig will appreciate contact with his friends and be glad of their opinions when taking certain decisions. He will have the chance to reciprocate when a friend experiences some anguish, and his empathy and thoughtfulness will be appreciated. However, while usually so masterful in his relations with others, he could find himself in an awkward situation this year. If so, he should do his best to defuse the tension and resolve the issue rather than ignore it or leave it to fester. Fortunately this warning only applies to a minority of Fire Pigs and talking things over will often considerably ease their worries. March, mid-June to the end of August and October will see the most social activity.

For the Fire Pig born in 2007, again this is a year rich in possibility. In their education, many of these Fire Pigs will enjoy the resources they are now permitted to use and their new knowledge will allow them to do more. Naturally curious, the young Fire Pig can make this an illuminating year.

With his outgoing nature, he will also enjoy some good times with his close friends. However, a friendship issue could be upsetting. If troubled at any time, the Fire Pig should tell others and seek support. No year is free of difficult moments and this one is no exception.

Overall, though, the young Fire Pig can make good progress this year and enjoy many new experiences. By making the most of his situation, he can do a great deal as well as discover some talents and start some recreational activities he can take further in the future.

Whether born in 1947 or 2007, the Fire Pig will find this a satisfying year. It is a time to forge ahead with plans and follow through ideas. The Fire Pig will benefit from the support of those around him and a joint approach will lead to more happening. With this being the start of a new decade in their life, many Fire Pigs will want to make this year special and will set themselves new goals or projects or take up new interests. And they can take pleasure in the many benefits that will often follow on.

Tip for the Year
Make plans for the year and act upon them. Inspired and keen, you can do – and ultimately gain – a great deal. Also, enjoy your relations with those who are close to you. They will be important to your year and their support and affection will be encouraging.

The Earth Pig

The element of earth helps to give a sign focus and during the Rooster year the Earth Pig can look forward to making steady progress. Rooster years are encouraging and if the Earth Pig has been nurturing certain hopes or had it in mind to try a new activity or visit a particular destination, this is a year to act. As many Earth Pigs will find, when plans are set in motion, helpful developments will often follow on.

One area which is especially well aspected is personal development. The Earth Pig may be tempted by local or online courses or set time aside for study and research or take up a new activity, but whatever he chooses, by furthering his skills and knowledge he can reinforce the constructive nature of the year.

In addition, with the expertise many Earth Pigs now have in certain areas, they may choose to share their knowledge with others or take their interest to a new level.

This can be an immensely satisfying time for personal interests and for Earth Pigs who enjoy writing or some other aspect of the creative arts, ideas they have this year could fill them with enthusiasm.

The Rooster year can also bring good travel possibilities and some Earth Pigs will be keen to attend special events. If they follow up their ideas, these can be among the year's highlights. May and August will see good travel opportunities, as will the closing weeks of the year.

The Earth Pig will enjoy sharing many of his activities with his loved ones, and if plans are agreed on together, more can be set in motion. Synergy will be an important factor during the year.

The Earth Pig will be keen to make home improvements too, including updating equipment and smartening certain areas. Active and inspired, he will enjoy carrying out his plans, although with some projects likely to be time-consuming, he should concentrate on one task at a time.

There will also be some family matters to address, perhaps relating to changing work patterns or the situation of younger or more senior relations. Discussion will help resolve many dilemmas satisfactorily, and amid the pressures there will also be family occasions and news to enjoy. April, July, September and the end of the year could be active and rewarding times.

With his engaging manner, the Earth Pig enjoys company and his circle of friends and acquaintances is set to grow this year. For those who are alone and may have had recent personal problems, a person they meet or activity group they join can considerably brighten their situation. March, July, August and October could see some good social opportunities.

Although the aspects are generally encouraging this year, there are two areas that require especial care. In money matters, the Earth Pig should keep a close watch on spending and check the terms when entering into any new agreement. He should attend to financial paperwork carefully as well as keep documents safe. Losses or lapses could be to his disadvantage. This is also no year for rush or risk, and if the Earth Pig is tempted by anything speculative, care is advised.

The other troubling area could concern a rift with another person. Ideally, the Earth Pig affected should talk the issue through and resolve it before it escalates. Here his personable nature and ability to work towards consensus can help, but he does need to be alert to these potentially awkward aspects.

Work prospects are encouraging, though, and in keeping with the constructive nature of the year many Earth Pigs will continue to make satisfying headway. With their expertise, they may not only be increasingly involved in certain projects and initiatives but also guide more junior colleagues.

The majority of Earth Pigs will remain with their present employer this year, but some will be tempted by a position elsewhere or be keen to make a change. For these Earth Pigs, as well as those seeking work, their efforts can bring the opportunity they seek, but there may be a steep learning curve too. However, as he has so often shown, when challenged, the Earth Pig often produces his best. February, April, July and October could see key developments.

The Earth Pig has a talent for making the most of his situation and the Rooster year will give him the chance to do just that. This is a time for carrying out plans and working towards aspirations. Personal interests can be pleasing, and new skills and knowledge of benefit. The Earth Pig will also appreciate how much can be shared. Domestic projects and travel are favourably aspected, although spending needs to be watched and an issue with another person could need resolving. However, in many respects, this Rooster year is an encouraging one and the Earth Pig's abilities will help him to improve himself, his position and his future.

Tip for the Year
Allow time for personal development and build on your strengths. You have an enquiring mind and purposeful nature. Look to learn and move forward.

Famous Pigs

Bryan Adams, Woody Allen, Julie Andrews, Marie Antoinette, Fred Astaire, Pam Ayres, Emily Blunt, Humphrey Bogart, Samantha Cameron, Henry Cavill, Hillary Rodham Clinton, Glenn Close, Sacha Baron Cohen, the Duchess of Cornwall, Noël Coward, Simon Cowell, Oliver Cromwell, Billy Crystal, the Dalai Lama, Ted Danson, Richard Dreyfuss, Ralph Waldo Emerson, Mo Farah, Henry Ford, Gillian Flynn, Emmylou Harris, Ernest Hemingway, Chris Hemsworth, Henry VIII, Conrad Hilton, Alfred Hitchcock, Roy Hodgson, Sir Elton John, Tommy Lee Jones, Carl Gustav Jung, Stephen King, Kevin Kline, Miranda Lambert, Hugh Laurie, Jerry Lee Lewis, Meat Loaf, Ewan McGregor, Ricky Martin, Johnny Mathis, Queen Máxima of the Netherlands, Pippa Middleton, Morrissey, Wolfgang Amadeus Mozart, George Osborne, James Patterson, Maurice Ravel, Ronald Reagan, Winona Ryder, Carlos Santana, Arnold Schwarzenegger, Steven Spielberg, Lord Sugar, David Tennant, Emma Thompson, Justin Trudeau, Carrie Underwood, David Walliams, the Duchess of York.

Appendix

The relationships between the 12 animal signs, both on a personal level and a business level, are an important aspect of Chinese horoscopes and in this appendix the compatibility between the signs is shown in the two tables that follow.

Also included are the names of the signs ruling the hours of the day and from this it is possible to find your ascendant and discover yet another aspect of your personality.

Finally, to supplement the earlier chapters on the personality and horoscope of the signs, I have included a guide on how you can get the best out of your sign and the year.

Relationships between the Signs

Personal Relationships

Key

1. Excellent. Great rapport.
2. A successful relationship. Many interests in common.
3. Mutual respect and understanding. A good relationship.
4. Fair. Needs care and some willingness to compromise in order for the relationship to work.
5. Awkward. Possible difficulties in communication and few interests in common.
6. A clash of personalities. Very difficult.

	Rat	Ox	Tiger	Rabbit	Dragon	Snake	Horse	Goat	Monkey	Rooster	Dog	Pig
Rat	1											
Ox	1	3										
Tiger	4	6	5									
Rabbit	5	2	3	2								
Dragon	1	5	4	3	2							
Snake	3	1	6	2	1	5						
Horse	6	5	1	5	3	4	2					
Goat	5	5	3	1	4	3	2	2				
Monkey	1	3	6	3	1	3	5	3	1			
Rooster	5	1	5	6	2	1	2	5	5	5		
Dog	3	4	1	2	6	3	1	5	3	5	2	
Pig	2	3	2	2	2	6	3	2	2	3	1	2

Business Relationships

Key

1. Excellent. Marvellous understanding and rapport.
2. Very good. Complement each other well.
3. A good working relationship and understanding can be developed.
4. Fair, but compromise and a common objective are often needed to make this relationship work.
5. Awkward. Unlikely to work, either through lack of trust or understanding or the competitiveness of the signs.
6. Mistrust. Difficult. To be avoided.

	Rat	Ox	Tiger	Rabbit	Dragon	Snake	Horse	Goat	Monkey	Rooster	Dog	Pig
Rat	2											
Ox	1	3										
Tiger	3	6	5									
Rabbit	4	3	3	3								
Dragon	1	4	3	3	3							
Snake	3	2	6	4	1	5						
Horse	6	5	1	5	3	4	4					
Goat	5	5	3	1	4	3	3	2				
Monkey	2	3	4	5	1	5	4	4	3			
Rooster	5	1	5	5	2	1	2	5	5	6		
Dog	4	5	2	3	6	4	2	5	3	5	4	
Pig	3	3	3	2	3	5	4	2	3	4	3	1

Your Ascendant

The ascendant has a very strong influence on your personality and will help you gain an even greater insight into your true personality according to Chinese horoscopes.

The hours of the day are named after the 12 animal signs and the sign governing the time you were born is your ascendant. To find your ascendant, look up the time of your birth in the table below, bearing in mind any local time differences in the place you were born.

11 p.m.	to	1 a.m.	The hours of the Rat
1 a.m.	to	3 a.m.	The hours of the Ox
3 a.m.	to	5 a.m.	The hours of the Tiger
5 a.m.	to	7 a.m.	The hours of the Rabbit
7 a.m.	to	9 a.m.	The hours of the Dragon
9 a.m.	to	11 a.m.	The hours of the Snake
11 a.m.	to	1 p.m.	The hours of the Horse
1 p.m.	to	3 p.m.	The hours of the Goat
3 p.m.	to	5 p.m.	The hours of the Monkey
5 p.m.	to	7 p.m.	The hours of the Rooster
7 p.m.	to	9 p.m.	The hours of the Dog
9 p.m.	to	11 p.m.	The hours of the Pig

Rat

The Rat ascendant is likely to make the sign more outgoing, sociable and careful with money. A particularly beneficial influence for those born under the signs of the Rabbit, Horse, Monkey and Pig.

Ox

The Ox ascendant has a restraining, cautionary and steadying influence that many signs will benefit from. This ascendant also promotes self-confidence and willpower and is especially good for those born under the signs of the Tiger, Rabbit and Goat.

Tiger

The Tiger ascendant is a dynamic and stirring influence that makes the sign more outgoing, action-orientated and impulsive. A generally favourable ascendant for the Ox, Tiger, Snake and Horse.

Rabbit

The Rabbit ascendant has a moderating influence, making the sign more reflective, serene and discreet. A particularly beneficial influence for the Rat, Dragon, Monkey and Rooster.

Dragon

The Dragon ascendant gives strength, determination and ambition to the sign. A favourable influence for those born under the signs of the Rabbit, Goat, Monkey and Dog.

Snake

The Snake ascendant can make the sign more reflective, intuitive and self-reliant. A good influence for the Tiger, Goat and Pig.

Horse

The Horse ascendant will make the sign more adventurous, daring and on some occasions fickle. Generally a beneficial influence for the Rabbit, Snake, Dog and Pig.

Goat

The Goat ascendant will make the sign more tolerant, easy-going and receptive. It could also impart some creative and artistic qualities. An especially good influence for the Ox, Dragon, Snake and Rooster.

Monkey

The Monkey ascendant is likely to impart a delicious sense of humour and fun to the sign. It will make the sign more enterprising and outgoing – a particularly good influence for the Rat, Ox, Snake and Goat.

Rooster

The Rooster ascendant helps to give the sign a lively, outgoing and very methodical manner. Its influence will increase efficiency and is good for the Ox, Tiger, Rabbit and Horse.

Dog

The Dog ascendant makes the sign more reasonable and fair-minded and gives an added sense of loyalty. A very good ascendant for the Tiger, Dragon and Goat.

Pig

The Pig ascendant can make the sign more sociable and self-indulgent. It is also a caring influence and one that can make the sign want to help others. A good ascendant for the Dragon and Monkey.

How to Get the Best from your Chinese Sign and the Year

Each of the 12 Chinese signs possesses its own unique strengths and by identifying them you can use them to your advantage. Similarly, by becoming aware of possible weaknesses you can do much to rectify them and in this respect I hope the following sections will be useful. Also included are some tips on how you can get the best from the year.

The Rat

The Rat is blessed with many fine talents, but his undoubted strength lies in his ability to get on with people. He is sociable, charming and a good judge of character. He also possesses a shrewd mind and is good at spotting opportunities.

However, to make the most of his abilities, he does need to impose some discipline upon himself. He should resist the (sometimes very great) temptation of getting involved in too many activities all at the same time and should decide upon his priorities and objectives. By concentrating his energies on specific matters he will fare much better. Also, given his personable manner, he should seek out positions where he can use his personal relations skills to good effect. For a career, sales and marketing could prove ideal.

The Rat is astute in dealing with finance, but while often thrifty, he can sometimes give way to moments of indulgence. Although he deserves to enjoy the money he has so carefully earned, it would sometimes be in his interests to exercise restraint when tempted to satisfy too many expensive whims!

The Rat's family and friends are important to him and while he is loyal and protective towards them, he does tend to keep his worries and concerns to himself and would be helped if he were more willing to discuss his anxieties. Others think highly of him and are prepared to do a lot to help him, but for them to do so the Rat does need to be less guarded.

With his sharp mind, keen imagination and sociable manner, he does, however, have much in his favour. When he has commitment, he can be irrepressible and, given his considerable charm, often irresistible as well! Provided he channels his energies wisely, he can make much of his life.

ADVICE FOR THE RAT'S YEAR AHEAD

General Prospects
This is an active year encouraging participation and making the most of ideas and opportunities, and by nature the Rat is resourceful, but he does need to take the initiative and make the most of his situation.

Career Prospects
Changes in the workplace can bring promotion opportunities or the chance of different duties. It is an excellent year for the Rat to extend his skills or even take his career in a new direction.

Finance
An expensive year. Spending needs to be watched and risks and hasty decisions avoided. Important paperwork needs close attention.

Relations with Others
The Rat will do a lot for others this year and should avail himself of their help too. Shared activities are favourably aspected and the Rat's domestic and social life will be busy and often special. New friendships and romance can brighten the prospects of many Rats who start the year unattached.

The Ox

Strong-willed and resolute, the Ox certainly has a mind of his own! He is persistent and sets about achieving his objectives with dogged determination. In addition he is reliable and tenacious and is often a source of inspiration to others. He is an achiever, and he often achieves a great deal. However, to really excel, he would do well to try and correct some of his weaknesses.

Being so resolute and having such a strong sense of purpose, the Ox can be inflexible and narrow-minded. He can be resistant to change and prefers to set about his activities in his own way rather than be dependent on others. His dislike of change can sometimes be to his detriment and if he were prepared to be more adaptable and adventurous he would find his progress easier.

The Ox would also be helped if he were to broaden his range of interests and become more relaxed in his approach. At times he can be so preoccupied with his own activities that he is not always as mindful of others as he should be, and his demeanour can sometimes be studious and serious. There are times when he would benefit from a lighter touch.

However, the Ox is true to his word and loyal to his family and friends. He is admired and respected by others and his tremendous willpower usually enables him to achieve a great deal in life.

ADVICE FOR THE OX'S YEAR AHEAD

General Prospects
An encouraging year. If the Ox acts with determination (not usually a problem), he can accomplish a great deal. This is also a good year for personal and career development. If the Ox furthers his knowledge, important opportunities can come his way.

Career Prospects
The Ox likes to proceed step by step and this year will encourage him. By seeking out and seizing opportunities, he can make headway, including, in some cases, securing a new position with good future potential. A year for building strengths, although colleague relations will need to be watched.

Finance
A year to be vigilant and thorough. Informal agreements and loans could be problematic and the terms of all transactions need to be

checked. The Ox also needs to be wary of scams and dubious speculative ventures.

Relations with Others

The active nature of the Rooster year will lead to a lot happening in the Ox's domestic and social life. This is a year to join with others. Romantic prospects are favourable, and if alone, the Ox should aim to go out more and meet new people. Positive action can bring rewards.

The Tiger

Lively, innovative and enterprising, the Tiger enjoys an active lifestyle. He has a wide range of interests, an alert mind and a genuine liking of other people. He loves to live life to the full. However, despite his enthusiastic and well-meaning ways, he does not always make the most of his considerable potential.

Being so versatile, the Tiger does have a tendency to jump from one activity to another or dissipate his energies by trying to do too much at the same time. To make the most of himself, he should try to exercise a certain amount of self-discipline. Ideally, he should decide how best he can use his abilities, give himself some objectives and then stick to them. If he can overcome his restless tendencies, he will find he will accomplish far more.

Also, in spite of his sociable manner, the Tiger likes to retain a certain independence in his actions, and while few begrudge him this, he would sometimes find life easier if he were more prepared to work in conjunction with others. His reliance on his own judgement does sometimes mean that he excludes the views and advice of those around him, and this can be to his detriment. He may possess an independent spirit, but he must not let it go too far!

The Tiger does, however, have much in his favour. He is bold, original and quick-witted. If he can keep his restless nature in check, he can enjoy considerable success. In addition, with his engaging personality, he is well liked and much admired.

ADVICE FOR THE TIGER'S YEAR AHEAD

General Prospects

A promising year, but it does require commitment and making the most of situations *as they are*. By participating and using his ideas and strengths to advantage, the Tiger can gain a great deal.

Career Prospects

Excellent and sometimes unanticipated chances can arise. By being involved and responding to developments, the Tiger may be well placed to advance. It is also a good year for adding to skills. Commitment will be encouraged and rewarded.

Finance

An improved year but spending needs to be carefully controlled and haste and impulsiveness watched.

Relations with Others

A year for the Tiger to participate in a variety of occasions and to network and raise his profile. His personal talents can reward him well, but he does need to stay mindful of others and watch his independent (and sometimes rebellious) streak. The more he joins and shares with others, the better.

The Rabbit

The Rabbit is certainly one who appreciates the finer things in life. With his good taste, companionable nature and wide range of interests, he knows how to live well – and usually does!

However, for all his *finesse* and style, the Rabbit does possess traits he would do well to watch. His desire for a settled lifestyle makes him err on the side of caution. He dislikes change and as a consequence can miss out on opportunities. Also, there are many Rabbits who will go to great lengths to avoid difficult and fraught situations, and again, while few may relish these, sometimes in life it is necessary to take risks or stand your ground. At times it would certainly be in the Rabbit's interests to be bolder and more assertive in going after what he desires.

The Rabbit also attaches great importance to his relations with others and while he has a happy knack of getting on with most people, he can be sensitive to criticism. Difficult though it may be, he should really try to develop a thicker skin and recognize that criticism can provide valuable learning opportunities, as can some of the problems he strives so hard to avoid.

However, with his agreeable manner, keen intellect and shrewd judgement, the Rabbit does have a lot in his favour and invariably makes much of his life – and enjoys it too!

ADVICE FOR THE RABBIT'S YEAR AHEAD

General Prospects
The Rabbit may not be comfortable with the pressures and developments of the year, but by making the most of emerging opportunities, he can fare well and, importantly, prepare himself for future success.

Career Prospects
The changes of the year, while sometimes placing the Rabbit outside his comfort zone, will open up good opportunities and he should take full advantage of any chances to add to his skills and further his career.

Finance
The Rabbit should be his careful and cautious self. When conducting important transactions and attending to official correspondence, he should check the details and be aware of the implications. This is a year to be attentive and thorough.

Relations with Others
The Rabbit is a people person and will delight in the many shared activities and occasions the Rooster year will bring. In his home life he will often instigate a great deal and his personal interests can help extend his social circle.

The Dragon

Enthusiastic, enterprising and honourable, the Dragon possesses many admirable qualities and his life is often full and varied. He always gives his best and even though not all his endeavours meet with success, he is nonetheless resilient and hardy, and is much admired and respected.

However, for all his qualities, the Dragon can be blunt and forthright and, through sheer strength of character, sometimes domineering. It would certainly be in his interests to listen more closely to others rather than be so self-reliant. Also, his enthusiasm can sometimes get the better of him and he can be impulsive. To make the most of his abilities, he should give himself priorities and set about his activities in a disciplined and systematic way. More tact and diplomacy might not come amiss either!

However, with his lively and outgoing manner, the Dragon is popular and well liked. With good fortune on his side (and the Dragon is often lucky), his life is almost certain to be eventful and fulfilling. He has many talents, and if he uses them wisely he will enjoy much success.

ADVICE FOR THE DRAGON'S YEAR AHEAD

General Prospects
The Dragon has great energy and this is a year for focus and resolve and showing others just what he is capable of.

Career Prospects
There will be excellent chances for the Dragon to further his career. The Rooster year rewards effort and initiative and he should actively pursue openings and keep informed of developments. Gains made now can open up further possibilities.

Finance
A financially improved year with carefully thought through plans and purchases bringing pleasure and benefit. If the Dragon has funds that are not immediately needed, saving can benefit him in the future.

Relations with Others

Professionally, the Dragon can gain a lot from the support of his colleagues and this is a good year to raise his profile. In his home life shared plans and individual successes can be much appreciated. While there will be many social occasions to enjoy, affairs of the heart need care and attention.

The Snake

The Snake is blessed with a keen intellect. He has wide interests, an enquiring mind and good judgement. He tends to be quiet and thoughtful and plan his activities with considerable care. With his fine abilities, he often does well in life, but he does possess traits which can undermine his progress.

The Snake is often guarded in his actions and sometimes loses out to those who are more action-oriented and assertive. He also likes to retain a certain independence in his actions and this too can hamper his progress. It would be in his interests to be more forthcoming and involve others more readily in his plans. The Snake has many talents and possesses a warm and rich personality, but there is a danger that this can remain concealed behind his often quiet and reserved manner. He would fare better if he were more outgoing and showed others his true worth.

However, the Snake is very much his own master. He invariably knows what he wants in life and is often prepared to journey long and hard to achieve his objectives. He does, though, have it in his power to make that journey easier. Lose some of that reticence, Snake, be more open and assertive, and do not be afraid of the occasional risk!

ADVICE FOR THE SNAKE'S YEAR AHEAD

General Prospects

An excellent year for the Snake, but to benefit he needs to be proactive. With resolve, he can make important headway and enjoy favourable outcomes, but this is no time to let chances drift.

Career Prospects

A year to move ahead, to keep alert for opportunity and to take on new challenges. For the ambitious and aspiring, these are important times.

Finance

The Snake's efforts and enterprise can reward him well. With plans and purchases, extra time and attention can lead to shrewd decisions.

Relations with Others

With this year being so encouraging, the Snake should join forces with others rather than just rely on his own efforts. With support and good-will, he will succeed in far more. His home and social life can bring him much pleasure and a variety of occasions to share and enjoy, while new friendships and romance can be significant.

The Horse

Versatile, hardworking and sociable, the Horse makes his mark wherever he goes. He has an eloquent and engaging manner and makes friends with ease. He is quick-witted, has an alert mind and is certainly not averse to taking risks or experimenting with new ideas.

He possesses a strong and likeable personality, but he does also have his weaknesses. With his wide interests he does not always finish everything he starts and he would do well to be more persevering. He has it within him to achieve considerable success, but to make the most of his talents he does need to overcome his restless tendencies. When he has made plans, he should stick with them.

The Horse loves company and values both his family and friends. However, there will have been many a time when he will have lost his temper or spoken in haste and regretted his words later. Throughout his life he needs to keep his temper in check and be diplomatic in tense situations, otherwise he could jeopardize the respect and good relations he so values.

However, the Horse has a multitude of talents and a lively and outgoing personality. If he can overcome his restless and volatile nature, he can lead a rich and highly fulfilling life.

ADVICE FOR THE HORSE'S YEAR AHEAD

General Prospects
The Horse will need to proceed carefully this year. In particular he should avoid intransigence and adapt to the year's changes. With flexibility, he will find what opens up for him can be all the more substantial.

Career Prospects
The Horse will have the opportunity to build on his skills and acquire new ones. However, he will need to adapt and be a part of his workplace. A too independent or inflexible approach could undermine his prospects, whereas if he makes the most of his current situation, he can do well.

Finance
A costly year with the Horse needing to watch his spending and take his time over important purchasing decisions.

Relations with Others
Domestically, a year to share interests and activities. The Horse's social life will be active, with new friendships and romance particularly appreciated, but he needs to be attentive to others and alert to awkward undercurrents. Increased awareness is so very important this year.

The Goat

The Goat has a warm, friendly and understanding manner and gets on well with most people. He is generally easy-going, has a fond appreciation of the finer things in life and possesses a rich imagination. He is often artistic and enjoys the creative arts and outdoor activities.

However, despite his engaging manner, there lurks beneath his skin a sometimes tense and pessimistic nature. The Goat can be a worrier and without the support and encouragement of others can feel insecure and be hesitant in his actions.

To make the most of himself he should aim to become more assertive and decisive as well as more at ease with himself. He has much in his favour, but he really does need to be bolder and promote himself more. He would also be helped if he were to sort out his priorities and set about his activities in an organized and disciplined manner. There are some Goats who tend to be haphazard in the way they go about things and this can hamper their progress.

Although the Goat will always value the support of others, it would also be in his interest to become more independent and not be so reticent about striking out on his own. He does, after all, possess many talents, as well as a sincere and likeable personality, and by giving his best he can make his life rich, rewarding and enjoyable.

Advice for the Goat's Year Ahead

General Prospects
A year for application. The Goat can do well and benefit from many emerging opportunities but he needs to act with determination. If he makes the effort, he can reap the rewards.

Career Prospects
The Rooster year can highlight the Goat's strengths and encourage him to make more of his creative talents, but he needs to put in the effort and rise to the challenge. This is no time to be slack or idle. For the hard-working, the rewards can be substantial.

Finance
Lifestyle improvements, including a possible move, can make this a year of considerable spending. Outgoings need to be watched and plans carefully considered and costed.

Relations with Others
The busy Goat will need to draw on the support of those around him but in turn will assist others. Domestically and socially, a lively year, with shared activities doing the Goat good. Romance, new friendships and business contacts can all be potentially important.

The Monkey

Lively, enterprising and innovative, the Monkey certainly knows how to impress. He has wide interests, a good sense of fun and relates well to others. He also possesses a shrewd mind and often has a happy knack of turning events to his advantage.

However, despite his versatility and considerable gifts, he does have his weaknesses. He often lacks persistence, can get distracted easily and also places tremendous reliance upon his own judgement. While his belief in himself is a commendable asset, it would certainly be in his interests to be more mindful of the views of others. Also, while he likes to keep tabs on all that is going on around him, he can be evasive and secretive with regard to his own feelings and activities, and again a more forthcoming attitude would be to his advantage.

In his desire to succeed, the Monkey can also be tempted to cut corners or be crafty and he should recognize that such actions can rebound on him!

However, he is resourceful and his sheer strength of character will ensure that he has an interesting and varied life. If he can channel his considerable energies wisely and overcome his sometimes restless tendencies, his life can be crowned with success. And with his amiable personality, he will have many friends.

ADVICE FOR THE MONKEY'S YEAR AHEAD

General Prospects
A satisfying year although the Monkey will need to be disciplined and use his time well. Rooster years require application, and the more

focused the Monkey is, the better his results will be. This is no time to be half-hearted or give less than his best.

Career Prospects

While steady progress can be made, one of the most valuable aspects of the year will be the chance to gain skills and experience. By making the most of this, the Monkey can impress others and do his prospects great good.

Finance

The Monkey needs to be vigilant. Spending levels need to be watched, the terms of agreements checked and the Monkey should be particularly careful if lending to another person.

Relations with Others

In this busy year, the Monkey needs to set aside time for his friends and loved ones. He will be encouraged by the support he is given over the year. Important new friends and sometimes new romances can prove significant.

The Rooster

With his considerable bearing and incisive and resolute manner, the Rooster cuts an impressive figure. He has a sharp mind, is well informed on many matters and expresses himself clearly and convincingly. He is meticulous and efficient in his undertakings and commands a great deal of respect. He also has a genuine and caring interest in others.

The Rooster has much in his favour, but there are some aspects of his character that can tell against him. He can be candid in his views and over-zealous in his actions, and sometimes he can say or do things he later regrets. His high standards also make him fussy, even pedantic, and he can get diverted into relatively minor matters when in truth he could be occupying his time more profitably. This is something all Roosters would do well to watch. Also, while the Rooster is a great planner, he can sometimes be unrealistic in his expectations. In making plans –

indeed, in most of his activities – he would do well to consult others. He would benefit greatly from their input.

The Rooster has many talents as well as commendable drive and commitment, but to make the most of himself he does need to channel his energies wisely and watch his candid and sometimes volatile nature. With care, however, he can make a success of his life, and with his wide interests and outgoing personality, he will enjoy the friendship and respect of many.

Advice for the Rooster's Year Ahead

General Prospects
The Rooster knows in himself he is capable of a great deal – now is the time to shine. It is his year and it is a time to plan, to participate and to act with determination. Used well, it can also leave a powerful legacy for him to build on.

Career Prospects
Whether furthering his existing role or seeking something new, this is a year for the Rooster to move forward. Good opportunities await but the Rooster does need to seize the moment.

Finance
All the planning and activity of the year will lead to much outlay and the Rooster will need to keep track of his spending and be wary of too many hasty purchases. A year for careful control and discipline.

Relations with Others
By liaising well with others and drawing on their support, the Rooster can see a great deal happen. Whether domestically, socially or romantically, the Rooster year favours the Rooster himself and helps bring out his finer qualities. This is a year for him to make more of himself and to engage with others.

The Dog

Loyal, dependable and with a good understanding of human nature, the Dog is well placed to win respect and admiration. He is a no-nonsense sort of person and hates any sort of hypocrisy and falsehood. With the Dog you know where you stand and, given his direct manner, where he stands on any issue. He also has a strong humanitarian nature and often champions good causes.

The Dog has many fine attributes, although there are certain traits that can prevent him from either enjoying or making the most of his life. He is a great worrier and can get anxious over all manner of things. Although it may not always be easy, he should try to rid himself of the 'worry habit'. Whenever he is tense or concerned, he should be prepared to speak to others rather than shoulder his worries all by himself. In some cases, they could even be of his own making! Also, he has a tendency to look on the pessimistic side and he would certainly be helped if he were to view his undertakings more optimistically. He does, after all, possess many skills and should have faith in his abilities. Another weakness is his tendency to be stubborn over certain issues. If he is not careful, at times this could undermine his position.

If the Dog can reduce the pessimistic side of his nature, he will not only enjoy life more but also find he is achieving more. He possesses a truly admirable character and his loyalty, reliability and sincerity are appreciated by all he meets. In his life he will do much good and befriend many people – and he owes it to himself to enjoy life too. Sometimes it might help him to recall the words of another Dog, Sir Winston Churchill: 'When I look back on all these worries, I remember the story of the old man who said on his deathbed that he had had a lot of trouble in his life, most of which never happened.'

ADVICE FOR THE DOG'S YEAR AHEAD

General Prospects
This can be a useful year, especially in furthering the Dog's experience and laying the foundations of future growth (something potentially

important with next year being the Dog's own year). However, he needs to be alert to what is going on around him and act accordingly.

Career Prospects
An often demanding year, but one that can highlight the Dog's strengths. By showing commitment and extending his skills and experience, he will be helping his present situation and preparing himself for future opportunities.

Finance
With expensive plans in mind, the Dog should be disciplined in his spending and take the time to reflect over his larger outlays. A year for control and good management.

Relations with Others
This is a year to join others and by pursuing his interests, the Dog can widen his social circle. While a friendship issue may concern him, the connections he builds now can be to his benefit. Shared undertakings are favourably aspected.

The Pig

Genial, sincere and trusting, the Pig gets on well with most people. He has a kind and caring nature, a dislike of discord and often a good sense of humour. In addition, he has a fondness for socializing and enjoying the good life!

The Pig possesses a shrewd mind, is particularly adept at dealing with business and financial matters and has a robust and resilient nature. Although not all his plans may work out as he would like, he is tenacious and will often rise up and succeed after experiencing setbacks and difficulties. In his often active and varied life he can accomplish a great deal, although there are certain aspects of his character that can tell against him. If he can modify these or keep them in check then his life will certainly be easier and possibly even more successful.

In his activities the Pig can sometimes overcommit himself and while he does not want to disappoint, he would certainly be helped if he were to set about his activities in an organized and systematic manner and give himself priorities at busy times. He should also not allow others to take advantage of his good nature and it would be in his interests to be more discerning. There will have been times when he has been gullible and naïve; fortunately, he quickly learns from his mistakes. However, he possesses a stubborn streak and if new situations do not fit in with his line of thinking, he can be inflexible. Such an attitude may not always be to his advantage.

The Pig is a great pleasure-seeker and while he should enjoy the fruits of his labours, he can sometimes be self-indulgent and extravagant. This is also something he would do well to watch.

However, though the Pig may possess some faults, those who come into contact with him are invariably impressed by his integrity, amiable manner and intelligence. If he uses his talents wisely, his life can be crowned with considerable achievement and he will also be loved and respected by many.

ADVICE FOR THE PIG'S YEAR AHEAD

General Prospects
The enterprising Pig can fare well this year although he needs to pay attention to developments going on around him. If he takes note of situations and acts accordingly, he can benefit in many ways. A year of possibility.

Career Prospects
An excellent year to build on skills and move ahead. By remaining active and raising his profile the Pig will see his efforts noticed and often rewarded.

Finance

A year for care and control over the purse-strings. The Pig should be wary of risk or speculation and, if entering into agreements, check the details carefully.

Relations with Others

A busy year with many good times. Romance and new friendships can bring much joy, although a disagreement or some pettiness may be of concern. If affected, the Pig should address the issue and aim to defuse it.

A Closing Thought

I hope that having read *Your Chinese Horoscope 2017* you have found it of value and interest.

The Rooster year favours planning and good organization, and by focusing on what you want, you can help make it happen. Take action – this is no year to stand still. Within you, you have great ability. Use it well, for in some way the Rooster year can *and will* reward you.

I wish you good fortune.

Neil Somerville